Stanley Lane-Poole

Studies in a Mosque

Stanley Lane-Poole

Studies in a Mosque

ISBN/EAN: 9783743368460

Manufactured in Europe, USA, Canada, Australia, Japa

Cover: Foto ©Lupo / pixelio.de

Manufactured and distributed by brebook publishing software (www.brebook.com)

Stanley Lane-Poole

Studies in a Mosque

STUDIES IN A MOSQUE

BY

STANLEY LANE-POOLE,
LAURÉAT DE L'INSTITUT DE FRANCE.

LONDON:
W. H. ALLEN & CO., 13 WATERLOO PLACE.
PUBLISHERS TO THE INDIA OFFICE.
———
1883.

PREFACE.

A common subject binds these essays together; they all treat of Islām in its manifold phases, from its birth at Mekka to its apotheosis in the Persian Miracle Play.; even the Sabians may be called, in a sense, a Korānic sect. It is true the treatment is slight, and many important developments of the Mohammadan religion are scarcely touched upon; but the essays were written not for the learned but for the general reader, and I believe he will pardon the lack of elaboration. If my words bring a few more workers to the great field here sketched out, and induce a wider interest in the religion which still keeps its hold upon so vast a number of our fellow subjects, the republication of these essays will be abundantly justified.

The chapters on the Korān, the Persian Miracle Play, and the Sabians, are reprinted by permission from the *Edinburgh Review;* that on an Eastern Reformation from the *Saturday Review;* while the first three appeared in my introduction to Lane's " Selections from the Kur-án," and are republished with Messrs. Trübner's kind consent. The chapter on the Brotherhood of Purity appears for the first time.

S. L.-P.

Cairo, *Feb.* 1883.

CONTENTS.

STUDIES IN A MOSQUE.

CHAPTER I.

THE ARABS BEFORE ISLAM.

Oh, our manhood's prime vigour!   No spirit feels waste,
Not a muscle is stopped in its playing nor sinew unbraced.
Oh, the wild joys of living! the leaping from rock up to rock,
The strong rending of boughs from the fir-tree, the cool silver
    shock
Of the plunge in the pool's living water, the hunt of the bear,
And the sultriness showing the lion is couched in his lair.
And the meal, the rich dates yellowed over with gold-dust divine,
And the locust flesh steeped in the pitcher, the full draught of
    wine,
And the sleep in the dried river-channel where bulrushes tell
That the water was wont to go warbling so softly and well.
How good is man's life, the mere living! how fit to employ
All the heart and the soul and the senses for ever in joy!
                                                —Saul.

BETWEEN Egypt and Assyria, jostled by each but yielding to neither, lay a strange country, unknown save at its marches even to its neighbours, dwelt-in by a people that held itself aloof from all the earth—a people whom the great empires of the ancient world in vain essayed to conquer, against whom the power of Persia,

Egypt, Rome, Byzantium was proven impotence, and at whose hands even the superb Alexander, had he lived to test his dream, might for once have learnt the lesson of defeat. Witnessing the struggle and fall of one and another of the great tyrannies of antiquity, yet never entering the arena of the fight;—swept on its northern frontier by the conflicting armies of Khusru and Cæsar, but lifting never a hand in either cause;—Arabia was at length to issue forth from its silent mystery, and, after baffling for a thousand years the curious gaze of strangers, was at last to draw to itself the fearful eyes of all men. The people of whom almost nothing before could certainly be asserted but its existence was finally of its own free will to throw aside the veil, to come forth from its fastnesses, and imperiously to bring to its feet the kingdoms of the world......

It is not all Arabia of which I speak. The story to tell has nothing as yet to say to the " happy " tilled lands of the south, or the outlying princedoms of Hīra and Ghassān bordering the territories and admitting the suzerainty of Persia and Rome. These lands were not wrapped in mystery : the Himyerite's kingdom in the Yemen, the rule of Zenobia at Palmyra, were familiar to the nations around. But the cradle of Islām was not here.

Along the eastern coast of the Red Sea, sometimes thrusting its spurs of red sandstone and porphyry into the waves, sometimes drawing away and leaving a wide stretch of lowland, runs a rugged range of mountain. One above another, the hills rise from the coast, leaving here and there between them a green valley, where you may see an Arab settlement or a group of Bedawīs watering their flocks. Rivers there are none; and the streams that gather from the rainfall are scarcely formed but they sink into the parched earth. Yet at times beneath the dried-up torrent-beds a rivulet trickles through, and straightway there spreads a rich oasis dearly prized by the wanderers of the desert. All else is bare and desolate. Climb hill after hill, and the same sight meets the eye—barren mountain-side, dry gravelly plain, and the rare green valleys. At length you have reached the topmost ridge ; and you see, not a steep descent, no expected return to the plain, but a vast desert plateau, blank, inhospitable, to all but Arabs uninhabitable. You have climbed the Hijāz—the " barrier "—and are come to the steppes of the Nejd—the " highland." In the valleys of this barrier-land are the Holy Cities, Mekka and Medīna. Here is the birthplace of Islām : the Arab tribes of the Hijāz and the Nejd were the first disciples of Mohammad.

One may tell much of a people's character from its home. Truism as it seems, there is yet a meaning in the saying that the Arabs are peculiarly the people of Arabia. Those who have travelled in this wonderful land tell us of the quickening influence of the air and scene of the desert. The fresh breath of the plain, the glorious sky, the stillness of the wide expanse, trod by no step but your own, looked upon only by yourself and perhaps yonder solitary eagle or the wild goat leaping the cliffs you have left behind,—the absolute silence and aloneness, bring about a strange sense of delight and exultation, a bounding-up of spirits held in long restraint, an unknown nimbleness of wit and limb. The Arabs felt all this and more in their bright imaginative souls. A few would settle in villages, and engage in the trade which came through from India to the West; but such were held in poor repute by the true Bedawīs, who preferred above all things else the free life of the desert. It is a relief to turn from the hurry and unrest of modern civilisation, from the never-ending strife for wealth, for position, for pleasure, even for knowledge, and look for a moment on the careless life of the Bedawy. He lived the aimless, satisfied life of some child; he sought no change; he was supremely content with the exquisite sense of simple existence; he was happy because he lived. He dreaded the dark After-death; he thrust it from his thoughts as often as it would seek to force itself upon him. Utterly fearless of man and fortune, he took no thought for the morrow : whatever it brought forth, he felt confidently his strength to enjoy or endure; only let him seize the happiness of to-day while it shall last, and drain to the dregs the overbrimming cup of his life. He was ambitious of glory and victory, but it was not an ambition that clouded his joy. Throughout a life that was full of energy, of passion, of strong endeavour after his ideal of desert perfectness, there was yet a restful sense of satisfied enjoyment, a feeling that life was of a surety well worth living.

For the Arab had his ideal of life. The true son of

the desert must in the old times do more than stretch his limbs contentedly under the shade of the overhanging rock. He must be brave and chivalrous, generous, hospitable; ready to sacrifice himself and his substance for his clan; prompt to help the needy and the traveller; true to his word, and, not least, eloquent in his speech.

Devotion to the clan was the strongest tie the Arab possessed. Though tracing their descent from a common traditional ancestor, the great northern family of Bedawīs was split up into numerous clans, owning no central authority, but led, scarcely governed, each by its own chief, who was its most valiant and best-born man. The whole clan acted as one being; an injury done to one member was revenged by all, and even a crime committed by a clansman was upheld by the whole brotherhood. Though a small spark would easily light-up war between even friendly clans, it was rarely that those of kin met as enemies. It is told how a clan suffered long and oft-repeated injuries from a kindred clan without one deed of revenge. "They are our brothers," they said; "perhaps they will return to better feelings; perhaps we shall see them again as they once were." To be brought to poverty or even to die for the clan, the Arab deemed his duty—his privilege. To add by his prowess or his hospitality or his eloquence to the glory of the clan was his ambition.

A mountain* we have where dwells he whom we shelter there,
    lofty, before whose height the eye falls back blunted:

---

* *I.e.*, the glory of the clan.

Deep-based is its root below ground, and overhead there soars
    its peak to the stars of heaven whereto no man reaches.
A folk are we who deem it no shame to be slain in fight,
    though that be the deeming thereof of Salūl and 'Amir;
Our love of death brings near to us our days of doom,
    but their dooms shrink from death and stand far distant.
There dies among us no lord a quiet death in his bed,
    and never is blood of us poured forth without vengeance.
Our souls stream forth in a flood from the edge of the whetted
      swords :
    no otherwise than so does our spirit leave its mansion.
Pure is our stock, unsullied; fair is it kept and bright
    by mothers whose bed bears well, and fathers mighty.
To the best of the uplands we wend, and when the season comes
    we travel adown to the best of fruitful valleys.
Like rain of the heaven are we : there is not in all our line
    one blunt of heart, nor among us is counted a niggard.
We say nay when so we will to the words of other men,
    but no man to us says nay when we give sentence.
When passes a lord of our line, in his stead there rises straight
    a lord to say the say and do the deeds of the noble.
Our beacon is never quenched to the wanderer of the night,
    nor has ever a guest blamed us where men meet together.
Our Days* are famous among our foemen, of fair report,
    branded and blazed with glory like noble horses.
Our swords have swept throughout all lands both west and east
    and gathered many a notch from the steel of hauberk-
      wearers ;
Not used are they when drawn to be laid back in their sheaths
    before that the folk they meet are spoiled and scattered.
If thou knowest not, ask men what they think of us and them
    —not alike are he that knows and he that knows not.
The children of Ed-Dayyān are the shaft of their people's mill,
    —around them it turns and whirls, while they stand
      midmost.*

---

* Battles.

† This and the other verses quoted in this chapter are taken
from the translations of old Arab poetry contributed by Mr. C.
J. Lyall, Secretary to the Chief Commissioner, Assam, to the

The renown of the clan was closely wrapped up with the Arab chieftain's personal renown. He was very sensitive on the point of honour, and to that notion he attached a breadth of meaning which can scarcely be understood in these days. Honour included all the different virtues that went to make up the ideal Bedawy. To be proved wanting in any of these was to be dishonoured. Above all things, the man who would " keep his honour and defile it not " must be brave and hospitable—

> A rushing rain-flood when he gave guerdons :
> when he sprang to the onset, a mighty lion.

The Arab warrior was a mighty man of valour. He would spend whole days in the saddle, burdened with heavy armour, in the pursuit of a foe, seeking the life of the slayer of his kin, or sweeping down upon the caravan of rich merchandise which his more peaceful countrymen of the towns were carrying through the deserts. The Arab lived mainly by plunder. His land did not yield him food—unless it were dates, the Bedawy's bread—and he relied on the success of his foraging expeditions for his support. These he conducted with perfect good-breeding ; he used no violence when it could be avoided ; he merely

---

" Journal of the Royal Asiatic Society of Bengal" (Translations from the Hamāseh and the Aghānī ; The Mo'allaqah of Zuheyr ; Translations from the Hamāseh). They imitate the metres of the original Arabic verse, but are nevertheless as literal as need be. The transliteration of proper names in the verses (and in other quotations) has been assimilated to the system adopted in this work.

relieved the caravan from the trouble of carrying any further the goods of which he was himself willing to take charge, urging, if necessary, the unfair treatment of his forefather Ishmael as an excellent reason for pillaging the sons of Isaac. "When a woman is the victim, no Bedouin brigand, however rude, will be ill-mannered enough to lay hands upon her. He begs her to take off the garment on which he has set his heart, and he then retires to a distance and stands with eyes averted, lest he should do violence to her modesty."

The poems of the early Arabs are full of the deeds of their warriors, the excitement of the pitched battle, the delight of the pursuit, the raid on the sleeping camp, the trial of skill between rival chiefs, and the other pictures of a warrior's triumph. Here we find little of the generosity of war: mercy was rarely exercised and hatred was carried to its extreme limits; quarter was neither asked nor given; to despatch a wounded man was no disgrace; the families of the vanquished were enslaved. Notwithstanding his frank genial nature, the Arab was of a dangerously quick temper, derived, he boasted, from eating the flesh of the camel, the surliest and most ill-conditioned of beasts. If he conceived himself insulted, he was bound to revenge himself to the full, or he would have been deemed dishonoured for ever. And since his fiery temper easily took offence, the history of the early Arabs is full of the traditions of slight quarrels and their horrible results—secret assassination and the long-lasting blood-feud.

Many the warriors, noon-journeying, who, when
    night fell, journeyed on and halted at dawning—
Keen each one of them, girt with a keen blade
    that when one drew it flashed forth like the lightning—
They were tasting of sleep by sips, when, as
    they nodded, thou didst fright them, and they were
      scattered.
Vengeance we did on them: there escaped us
    of the two houses none but the fewest.
And if Hudheyl* broke the edge of his† sword-blade—
    many the notch that Hudheyl gained from him!
Many the time that he made them kneel down on
    jagged rocks where the hoof is worn with running!
Many the morning he fell on their shelter,
    and after slaughter came plunder and spoiling!
Hudheyl has been burned by me, one valiant
    whom Evil tires not though they be wearied—
Whose spear drinks deep the first draught, and thereon
    drinks deep again of the blood of foemen.
Forbidden was wine, but now is it lawful:
    hard was the toil that made it lawful!
Reach me the cup, O Sawād son of 'Amr!
    my body is spent with gaining my vengeance.
To Hudheyl we gave to drink Death's goblet,
    whose dregs are disgrace and shame and dishonour.
The hyena laughs over the slain of Hudheyl, and
    the wolf—see thou—grins by their corpses,
And the vultures flap their wings, full-bellied
    treading their dead, too gorged to leave them.

The contempt which the Arab, with a few noble
exceptions, felt for the gentler virtues is seen in these
lines :—

Had I been a son of Māzin, there had not plundered my herds
    the sons of the Child of the Dust, Dhuhl son of Sheybān!

---

* A tribe.

† The subject of the poem, mentioned in the second hemistich
of the third verse as "thou," whose death the supposed author
("one valiant") avenged.

There had straightway arisen to help me a heavy-handed kin,
    good smiters when help is needed, though the feeble bend to
      the blow :
Men who, when Evil bares before them his hindmost teeth,
    fly gaily to meet him, in companies or alone.
They ask not their brother, when he lays before them his wrong
    in his trouble, to give them proof of the truth of what
      he says.
But as for my people, though their number be not small,
    they are good for nought against evil, however light it be ;
They requite with forgiveness the wrong of those that do them
    wrong,
    and the evil deeds of the evil they meet with kindness and
      love;
As though thy Lord had created among the tribes of men
    themselves alone to fear Him, and never one man more !
Would that I had in their stead a folk who, when they ride forth,
    strike swiftly and hard, on horse or on camel borne !

A point on which the temper of the Bedawy was easily touched was his family pride. The Arab prized good blood as much in men as in his horses and camels. In these he saw the importance of breed, and in men he firmly believed the same principle held good. With the tenacious memory of his race, he had no difficulty in recalling the whole of a complicated pedigree, and he would often proudly dwell on the purity of his blood and the gallant deeds of his forefathers. He would challenge another chief to show a more noble descent, and hot disputes and bitter rivalries often came of these comparisons.

But if noble birth brought rivalry and hatred, it brought withal excellent virtues. The Arab nobleman was not a man who was richer, idler, and more luxurious than his inferiors; his position, founded upon descent, depended for its maintenance on personal qualities. Rank brought with it onerous obligations. The chief, if he would retain and carry on the repute of his line, must not only be fearless and ready to fight all the world; he must be given to hospitality, generous to kith and kin, and to all who cry unto him. His tent must be so pitched in the camp that it shall not only be the first that the enemy attacks, but also the first the wayworn stranger approaches; and at night fires must be kindled hard by to guide wanderers in the desert to his hospitable entertainment. If a man came to an Arab noble's tent and said, " I throw myself on your honour," he was safe from his enemies until they had trampled on the dead body of his host. Nothing was baser than to give up a guest; the treachery was rare, and brought endless dishonour upon the clan in which the shame had taken place. The poet extols the tents—

Where dwells a kin great of heart, whose word is enough to shield
    whom they shelter when peril comes in a night of fierce strife
        and storm;
Yea, noble are they; the seeker of vengeance gains not from them
    the blood of his foe, nor is he that wrongs them left without
        help.

The feeling lasted even under the debased rule of Muslim despots; for it is related that a governor was once ordering some prisoners to execution, when one of them asked for a drink of water, which was immediately given him. He then turned to the governor and said, " Wilt thou slay thy guest?"—and was forthwith set free. A pledge of protection was inferred in the giving of hospitality, and to break his word was a thing not to be thought upon by an Arab.

He did not care to give an oath; his simple word was enough, for it was known to be inviolable. Hence the priceless worth of the Arab chief's voice of welcome: it meant protection, unswerving fidelity, help, and succour.

There was no bound to this hospitality. It was the pride of the Arab to place everything he possessed at the service of the guest. The last milch-camel must be killed sooner than the duties of hospitality be neglected. The story is told of Hātim, a gallant poet-warrior of the tribe of Tayyi, which well illustrates the Arab ideal of hostship. Hātim was at one time brought to the brink of starvation by the dearth of a rainless season. For a whole day he and his family had eaten nothing, and at night, after soothing the children to sleep by telling them some of those stories in which the Arabs have few rivals, he was trying by his cheerful conversation to make his wife forget her hunger. Just then they heard steps without, and a corner of the tent was raised. "Who is there?" said Hātim. A woman's voice replied, "I am such a one, thy neighbour. My children have nothing to eat, and are howling like young wolves, and I have come to beg help of thee." "Bring them here," said Hātim. His wife asked him what he would do; if he could not feed his own children, how should he find food for this woman's? "Do not disturb thyself," he answered. Now Hātim had a horse, renowned far and wide for the purity of his stock and the fleetness and beauty of his paces. He would not kill his favourite for himself or even for his own children; but now he went out and slew him, and prepared him with fire for the strangers' need. And when he saw them eating with his wife and children, he exclaimed, " It were a shame that you alone should eat whilst all the camp is perishing with hunger "; and he went and called the neighbours to the meal, and in the morning there remained of the horse nothing but his bones. But the master, wrapped in his mantle, sat apart in a corner of the tent.

This Hātim is a type of the Arab nature at its noblest. Though renowned for his courage and skill in war, he never suffered his enmity to overcome his generosity. He had sworn an oath never to take a man's life, and he strictly observed it, and always withheld the fatal blow. In spite of his clemency, he was ever successful in the wars of his clan, and brought back from his raids many a rich spoil, only to spend it at once in his princely fashion. His generosity and faithful observance of his word at times placed him in positions of great danger; but the alternative of denying his principles seems never to have occurred to his mind. For instance, he had imposed upon himself as a law never to refuse a gift to him that asked it of him. Once, engaged in single combat, he had disarmed and routed his opponent, who then turned and said, " Hātim, give me thy spear." At once he threw it to him, leaving himself defenceless; and had he not met an adversary worthy of himself, this had been the last of his deeds. Happily Hātim was not the only generous warrior of the Arabs, and his foe did not avail himself of his advantage. When Hātim's friends remonstrated with him on the rashness of an act which, in the spirit of shopkeepers, they held quixotic, Hātim said, "What would you have me to do? He asked of me a gift!"

It was Hātim's practice to buy the liberty of all captives who sought his aid: it was but another application of the Arab virtue of hospitality. Once a captive called to him when he was on a journey and had not with him the means of paying the ransom. But he was not wont to allow any difficulties to baulk him of the exercise of his duty: he had the prisoner released, stepping meanwhile into his chains until his own clan should send the ransom.

Brave, chivalrous, faithful, and generous beyond the needful of Arab ideal—so that his niggardly wife, using the privilege of high dames, divorced him because he was ever ruining himself and her by his open hand—Hātim filled up the measure of Arab virtue by his eloquence, and such of his poems as have come down to us reflect the nobility of his life. As a youth he had shown a strong passion for poetry, and would spare no means of doing honour to poets. His grandfather, in despair of the boy's extravagance, sent him away from the camp to guard the camels, which were pastured at a distance. Sitting there in a state of solitude little congenial to his nature, Hātim lifted his eyes and saw a caravan approaching. It was the caravan of three great poets who were travelling to the court of the King of El-Hīra. Hātim begged them to alight and to accept of refreshment after the hot and dreary journey. He killed them a camel each, though one would have more than sufficed for the three; and in return they wrote him verses in praise of himself and his kindred. Overjoyed at the honour, Hātim insisted on the poets each accepting a hundred camels; and they departed with their gifts. When the grandfather came to the pasturing and asked where the camels were gone, Hātim answered, "I have exchanged them for a crown of honour, which will shine for all time on the brow of thy race. The lines in which great poets have celebrated our house will pass from mouth to mouth, and will carry our glory over all Arabia." *

This story well illustrates the Arab's passionate love of poetry. He conceived his language to be the finest in the world, and he prized eloquence and poetry as the goodliest gifts of the gods. There were three great events in Arab life, when the clan was called together and great feastings and rejoicings ensued. One was the birth of a son to a chief; another the foaling of a generous mare; the third was the discovery that a great poet had risen up among them. The advent of the poet meant the immortality of the deeds of the clansmen and the everlasting contumely of their foes; it meant the uplifting of the glory of the tribe over all the clans of Arabia, and the winning of triumphs by bitterer weapons than

---

* For these and other stories about Hātim, see Caussin de Perceval's "Essai sur l'Histoire des Arabes," ii. 607–628 : a treasury of Arab life, abounding in those anecdotes which reveal more of the character of the people than whole volumes of ethnological treatise.

sword and spear—the weapons of stinging satire and scurrilous squib. No man might dare withstand the power of the poets among a people who were keenly alive to the point of an epigram, and who never forgot an ill-natured jibe if it were borne upon musical verse. Most of the great heroes of the desert were poets as well as warriors, and their poesy was deemed the chief gem in their crown, and, like their courage, was counted a proof of generous birth. The Khalif 'Omar said well, "The kings of the Arabs are their orators and poets, those who practise and who celebrate all the virtues of the Bedawy."

This ancient poetry of the Arabs is the reflection of the people's life. Far away from the trouble of the world, barred by wild wastes from the stranger, the Bedawy lived his happy child's life, enjoying to the uttermost the good the gods had sent him, delighting in the face that Nature showed him, inspired by the glorious breath of the deserts that were his home. His poetry rings of that desert life. It is emotional, passionate, seldom reflective. Not the end of life, the whence and the whither, but the actual present joy of existence, was the subject of his song. Vivid painting of nature is the characteristic of this poetry : it is natural, unpolished, unlaboured. The scenes of the desert—the terrors of the nightly ride through the hill-girdled valley where the Ghūls and the Jinn have their haunts; the gloom of the barren plain, where the wolf, "like a ruined gamester," roams ululating; the weariness of the journey under the noonday sun; the stifling sand-storm, the delusive mirage; or again, the solace of the palm-tree's shade, and the delights of the cool well; —such are the pictures of the Arab poet. The people's life is another frequent theme: the daily doings of the herdsman, the quiet pastoral life, on the one hand; on the other, the deeds of the chiefs—war, plunder, the chase, wassail, revenge, friendship, love. There were satires on rival tribes, panegyrics on chiefs, laments for the dead. This poetry is wholly objective, artless, childlike; it is the outcome of a people still in the freshness of youth, whom the mysteries and complications of life have not yet set a-thinking. "Just as his language knows but the present and the past, so the ancient Arab lived but in to-day and yesterday. The future is nought to him; he seizes the present with too thorough abandonment to have an emotion left for anything beyond. He troubles himself not with what fate the morrow may bring forth, he dreams not of a beautiful future, —only he revels in the present, and his glance looks backward alone. Rich in ideas and impressions, he is poor in thought. He drains hastily the foaming cup of life; he feels deeply and passionately; but it is as if he were never conscious of the coming of the thoughtful age which, while it surveys the past, as often turns an anxious look to the unknown future."*

It is very difficult for a Western mind to enter into the real beauty of the old Arab poetry. The life it

---

* A. von Kremer, "Culturgeschichte des Orients," ii. 352.

depicts is so unlike any we can now witness, that it is almost removed beyond the pale of our sympathies. The poetry is loaded with metaphors and similes, which to us seem far-fetched, though they are drawn from the simplest daily sights of the Bedawy. Moreover, it is only in fragments that we can read it; for the change in the whole character of Arab life and in the current of Arab ideas that followed the conquests of Islām extinguished the old songs, which were no longer suitable to the new conditions of things; and as they were seldom recorded in writing, we possess but a little remnant of them.* Yet " these fragments may be broken, defaced, dimmed, and obscured by fanaticism, ignorance, and neglect; but out of them there arises anew all the freshness, bloom, and glory of desert-song, as out of Homer's epics rise the glowing spring-time of humanity and the deep blue heavens of Hellas. It is not a transcendental poetry, rich in deep and thoughtful legend and lore, or glittering in the many-coloured prisms of fancy, but a poetry the chief task of which is to paint life and nature as they really are; and within its narrow bounds it is magnificent. It is chiefly and characteristically full of manliness, of vigour, and of a chivalrous spirit, doubly striking when compared with the spirit

---

* The later Arabic poets were mostly incapable of the genius of the old singers: the times had changed, and the ancient poetry appeared almost as exotic to their ideas as it does to our own. No greater mistake can be made than to judge of the old poets by such a writer as Behā-ed-dîn Zoheyr, of whom the late Professor E. H. Palmer gave us so beautiful a version.

of abjectness and slavery found in some other Asiatic nations. It is wild and vast and monotonous as the yellow seas of its desert solitudes; it is daring and noble, tender and true." *

There was one place where, above all others, the Kasīdas of the ancient Arabs were recited: this was 'Okādh, the Olympia of Arabia, where there was held a great annual Fair, to which not merely the merchants of Mekka and the south, but the poet-heroes of all the land resorted. The Fair of 'Okādh was held during the sacred months,—a sort of "God's Truce," when blood could not be shed without a violation of the ancient customs and faiths of the Bedawīs. Thither went the poets of rival clans, who had as often locked spears as hurled rhythmical curses. There was little fear of a bloody ending to the poetic contest, for those heroes who might meet there with enemies or blood-avengers are said to have worn masks or veils, and their poems were recited by a public orator at their dictation. That these precautions and the sacredness of the time could not always prevent the ill-feeling evoked by the pointed personalities of rival singers leading to a fray and bloodshed is proved by recorded instances; but such results were uncommon, and as a rule the customs of the time and place were respected. In spite of occasional broils on the spot, and the lasting feuds which these poetic contests must have excited, the Fair of

---

* E. Deutsch, "Literary Remains," 453, 454: cp. Nöldeke, "Beiträge zur Kennt. d. Poesie d. alten Araber," xxiii., xxiv.

'Okādh was a magnificent institution. It served as a focus for the literature of all Arabia : everyone with any pretensions to poetic power came, and if he could not himself gain the applause of the assembled people, at least he could form one of the critical audience on whose verdict rested the fame or the shame of every poet. The Fair of 'Okādh was a literary congress, without formal judges, but with unbounded influence. It was here that the polished heroes of the desert determined points of grammar and prosody; here the seven Golden Songs were recited, although (alas for the charming legend !) they were *not* afterwards "suspended" in the Kaaba; and here "a magical language, the language of the Hijāz," was built out of the dialects of Arabia and made ready to the skilful hand of Mohammad, that he might conquer the world with his Korān.

The Fair of 'Okādh was not merely a centre of emulation for Arab poets : it was also an annual review of Bedawy virtues. It was there that the Arab nation once a year inspected itself, so to say, and brought forth and criticised its ideals of the noble and the beautiful in life and in poetry. For it was in poetry that the Arab—and for that matter each man all the world over—expressed his highest thoughts, and it was at 'Okādh that these thoughts were measured by the standard of the Bedawy ideal. The Fair not only maintained the highest standard of poetry that the Arabic language has ever reached : it also upheld the noblest ideal of life and duty that the Arab nation has yet set forth and obeyed. 'Okādh was the press, the stage, the pulpit, the Parliament, and the Académie Française of the Arab people; and when, in his fear of the infidel poets (whom Imra-el-Keys was to usher to hell), Mohammad abolished the Fair, he destroyed the Arab nation even whilst he created his own new nation of Muslims;—and the Muslims cannot sit in the places of the old pagan Arabs.

It is very difficult for the Western mind to dissociate the idea of Oriental poetry from the notion of amatory odes, and sonnets to the lady's eyebrow: but even the few extracts that have been given in this chapter show that the Arab had many other subjects besides love to sing about, and though the divine theme has its place in almost every poem, it seldom rivals the prominence of war and nature-painting, and it is treated from a much less sensual point of view than that of later Arab poets. Many writers have drawn a gloomy picture of the condition of women in Arabia before the coming of Mohammad, and there is no doubt that in many cases their lot was a degraded one. There are ancient Arabic proverbs that point to the contempt in which woman's judgment and character were held by the Arabs of " the Time of Ignorance," and Mohammad must have derived his mean opinion of women from a too general impression among his countrymen. The marriage tie was certainly very loose among the ancient Arabs. The ceremony itself was often of the briefest. A man said to Umm-Khārija *khitb* (*i.e.* I am an asker-in-marriage), and she answered *nikh* (*i.e.* I am a giver-in-marriage), and the knot was thus tied, only to be undone with equal facility and brevity. The frequency of divorce among the Arabs does not speak well for their constancy, and must have had a degrading effect upon the women. Hence it is argued that women were the objects of contempt rather than of respect among the ancient Arabs.

Yet there is reason to believe that the evidence upon which this conclusion is founded is partial and one-sided. There was a wide gulf between the Bedawy and the town Arab. It is not impossible that the view commonly entertained as to the state of women in preïslamic times is based mainly on what Mohammad saw around him in Mekka, and not on the ordinary life of the desert. To such a conjecture a singularly uniform support is lent by the ancient poetry of the Arabs; and though the poets were then —as they always are—men of finer mould than the rest, yet their example, and still more their poems passing from mouth to mouth, must have created a widespread belief in their principles. It is certain that the roaming Bedawy, like the mediæval knight, entertained a chivalrous reverence for women, although, like the knight, he was not always above a career of promiscuous gallantry. Yet there was a certain glamour of romance even about the intrigues of the Bedawy. He did not regard the object of his love as a chattel to be possessed, but as a divinity to be assiduously worshipped. The poems are full of instances of the courtly respect displayed by the heroes of the desert towards defenceless maidens, and the mere existence of so general an ideal of conduct in the poems is a strong argument for Arab chivalry: for with the Arabs the abyss between the ideal accepted of the mind and the attaining thereof in action was narrower than it is among more advanced nations.

Whatever was the condition of women in the trading cities and villages, it is certain that in the desert woman was regarded as she has never since been viewed among Muslims. The modern harīm system was as yet undreamt of; the maid of the desert was unfettered by the ruinous restrictions of modern life in the East. She was free to choose her own husband, and to bind him to have no other wife than herself. She might receive male visitors, even strangers, without suspicion: for her virtue was too dear to her and too well assured to need the keeper. It was the bitterest taunt of all to say to a hostile clan that their men had not the heart to give nor their women to deny; for the chastity of the women of the clan was reckoned only next to the valour and generosity of the men. In those days bastardy was an indelible stain. It was the wife who inspired the hero to deeds of glory, and it was her praise that he most valued when he came home triumphing. The hero of desert song thought himself happy to die in guarding some women from their pursuers. Wounded to the death, 'Antara halted alone in a narrow pass, and bade the women press on to a place of safety. Planting his spear in the ground, he supported himself on his horse, so that when the pursuers came up they knew not he was dead, and dared not approach within reach of his dreaded arm. At length the horse moved, and the body fell to the ground, and the enemies saw that it was but the corpse of the hero that had held the pass. In death, as in a life, *sans peur et sans reproche*, 'Antara was true to the chivalry of his race.*

There are many instances like this of the knightly courtesy of the Arab chief in "the Time of Ignorance." In the old days, as an ancient writer says, the true Arab had but one love, and her he loved till death. Even when polygamy became commoner, especially in the towns, it was not what is meant by polygamy in a modern Muslim state: it was rather the patriarchal system of Abram and Sarai.

There is much in the fragments of the ancient poetry which reflects this fine spirit. It is ofttimes "tender and true," and even Islām could not wholly root out the real Arab sentiment, which reappears in Muslim times in the poems of Aboo-Firās. Especially valuable is the evidence of the old poetry with regard to the love of a father for his daughters. Infanticide, which is commonly attributed to the whole Arab nation of every age before Islām, was in reality exceedingly rare in the desert. It was probably adopted by poor and weak clans, either from inability to support their children, or in order to protect themselves

---

* Sir F. J. Goldsmid reminds me, in the "Academy," that this story is told of Rabīa ibn Mukaddam in Fresnel's "Lettres sur les Arabes." The point, however, lies in the deed and not in the name of the doer of it.

from the stain of having them dishonoured by stronger
tribes ; and the occasional practice of this barbarous
and suicidal custom affords no ground for assuming
an unnatural hatred and contempt for girls among
the ancient Arabs. These verses of a father to his
daughter tell a different story :—

If no Umeymeh were there, no want would trouble my soul,—
    no labour call me to toil for bread through pitchiest night;
What moves my longing to live is but that well do I know
    how low the fatherless lies,—how hard the kindness of kin.
I quake before loss of wealth lest lacking fall upon her,
    and leave her shieldless and bare as flesh set forth on a
      board.
My life she prays for, and I from mere love pray for her death—
    yea death, the gentlest and kindest guest to visit a maid.
I fear an uncle's rebuke, a brother's harshness for her ;
    my chiefest end was to spare her heart the grief of a word.

Once more, these touching lines breathe a spirit of
faithful love for a lost wife and devotion to her
child :—

Take thou thy way by the grave wherein thy dear one lies
    —Umm-el-'Ala—and lift up thy voice : ah if she could hear !
How art thou come—for very fearful wast thou—to dwell
    in a land where not the most valiant goes but with quaking
      heart ?
God's love be thine and His mercy, O thou dear lost one !
    not meet for thee is the place of shadow and loneliness.
And a little one hast thou left behind—God's ruth on her !
    she knows not what to bewail thee means, yet weeps for thee.
For she misses those sweet ways of thine that thou hadst with her,
    and the long night wails, and we strive to hush her to sleep
      in vain.
When her crying smites in the night upon my sleepless ears,
    straightway mine eyes brimfull are filled from the well of
      tears.

Hitherto we have been looking at but one side of

Arab life. Bedawīs were indeed the bulk of the race, and furnished the swords of the Muslim conquests; but there was also a vigorous town-life in Arabia, and the citizens waxed rich with the gains of their trafficking. For through Arabia ran the trade route between East and West: it was the Arab traders who carried the produce of the Yemen to the markets of Syria; and how ancient was their commerce one may divine from the words of a poet of Judæa spoken more than a thousand years before the coming of Mohammad.

> Wedan and Javan from San'a paid for thy produce :
>> sword-blades, cassia, and calamus were in thy trafficking.
> Dedan was thy merchant in saddle-cloths for riding;
> Arabia and all the merchants of Kedar, they were the merchants
>> of thy hand :
>> in lambs and rams and goats, in these were they thy
>> merchants.
> The merchants of Sheba and Raamah, they were thy merchants :
>> with the chief of all spices, and with every precious stone,
>> and gold, they paid for thy produce.
> Haran, Aden, and Canneh, the merchants of Sheba, Asshur and
>> Chilmad were thy merchants;
> They were thy merchants in excellent wares,
>> in cloth of blue and broidered work,
>> in chests of cloth of divers colours, bound with cords and
>> made fast among thy merchandize.*

Mekka was the centre of this trading life, the typical Arab city of old times—a stirring little town,

---

* Ezekiel xxvii. 19–24. The identifications of the various names with Arabian towns are partly conjectural, but the general reference is clearly to Arabia. Cf. the Speaker's Commentary, vi. 122; and the interpretations of Hitzig, Movers, Tuch, and Ménant.

with its caravans bringing the silks and woven stuffs of Syria and the far-famed damask, and carrying away the sweet-smelling produce of Arabia, frankincense, cinnamon, sandal-wood, aloe, and myrrh, and the dates and leather and metals of the south, and the goods that come to the Yemen from Africa and even India; with its assemblies of merchant-princes in the Council Hall near the Kaaba; and again its young poets running over with love and gallantry; its Greek and Persian slave-girls brightening the luxurious banquet with their native songs, when as yet there was no Arab school of music, and the monotonous but not unmelodious chant of the camel-driver was the national song of Arabia; and its club, where busy men spent their idle hours in playing chess and draughts, or in gossiping with their acquaintance. It was a little republic of commerce, too much infected with the luxuries and refinements of the states it traded with, yet retaining enough of the free Arab nature to redeem it from the charge of effeminacy.

Mekka was a notable centre of music and poetry, and this characteristic lasted into Muslim times. There is a story of a certain stonemason who had a wonderful gift of singing. When he was at work the young men used to come and importune him, and bring him gifts of money and food to induce him to sing. He would then make a stipulation that they should first help him in his work; and forthwith they would strip off their cloaks, and the stones would gather round him rapidly. Then he would mount a rock and begin to sing, whilst the whole hill was coloured red and yellow with the garments of his audience. Singers were then held in high admiration, and the greatest chiefs used to pay their court to ladies of the musical profession. One of these used to give receptions, open to the whole city, in which she would appear in great state, surrounded by her ladies-in-waiting, each dressed magnificently and wearing " an elegant artificial chignon." It was in this town-life that the worse qualities of the Arab came out; it was here that his raging passion for dicing and his thirst for wine were most prominent. In the desert there was little opportunity for indulging in either luxury; but in a town which often welcomed a caravan bringing goods to the value of twenty thousand pound, such excesses were to be looked for. Excited by the song of the Greek slave-girl and the fumes of mellow wine, the Mekkan would throw the dice till, like the Germans of Tacitus, he had staked and lost his own liberty.

But Mekka was more than a centre of trade and of song. It was the focus of the religion of the Arabs. Thither the tribes went up every year to kiss the black stone which had fallen from heaven in the primæval days of Adam, and to make the seven circuits of the Kaaba naked,—for they would not approach God in the garments in which they had sinned,—and to perform the other ceremonies of the pilgrimage. The Kaaba, a cubical building in the centre of Mekka, was the most sacred temple in all Arabia, and it gave its sanctity to all the district around. It was first built, saith tradition, by Adam from a heavenly model, and then rebuilt from time to time by Seth and Abraham and Ishmael, and less reverend personages, and it contained the sacred things of the land. Here was the black stone, here the great god of red agate, Hubal, and the three hundred and sixty idols, one for each day of the year, which Mohammad afterwards destroyed in one day. Here was Abraham's stone, and that other which marked the tomb of Ishmael; and hard by was Zemzem, the god-sent spring which gushed from the sand when the forefather of the Arabs was perishing of thirst.

The religion of the ancient Arabs, little as we know of it, is especially interesting, inasmuch as the Arabs longest retained the original Semitic character, and hence probably the original Semitic religion : and thus in the ancient cultus of Arabia we may see the religion once professed by Chaldeans, Canaanites, and Phœnicians. This ancient religion " rises little higher than animistic polydæmonism. It is a collection of tribal religions standing side by side, only loosely united, though there are traces of a once closer connection." * The great objects of worship were the sun and the stars and the three moon-goddesses— El-Lāt, the bright moon; Menāh, the dark; and El-'Uzzà, the union of the two : whilst a lower cultus of trees, stones, and mountains, supposed to be tenanted

---

* C. P. Tiele, " Outlines of the History of Religion " : tr. J. E. Carpenter, p. 63.

by souls, shows that the religion had not yet quite risen above simple fetishism.   At the time of Mohammad the Arabs worshipped numerous images, which may have been merely a development of the previous stone-worship, or may have been introduced from intercourse with Christians. There are traces of a belief in a supreme God behind this pantheon, and the moon-goddesses and other divinities were regarded as daughters of *the most high God* (Allāh ta'āla). The various deities (but not the Supreme Allah) had their fanes, where human sacrifices, though rare, were not unknown; and their cultus was superintended by a hereditary line of seers, who were held in great reverence, but never developed into a priestly caste.

Besides the tribal gods, individual households had their special Penates, to whom was due the first and the last salām of the returning or outgoing host. But in spite of all this superstitious apparatus the Arabs were never a religious people.   In the old days, as now, they were reckless, skeptical, materialistic. They had their gods and their divining-arrows, but they were ready to demolish both if the responses proved contrary to their wishes.   A great majority believed in no future life nor in a reckoning-day of good and evil.   If some tied camels to the graves of the dead that the corpse might ride mounted to the judgment-seat, they must have been the exceptions; and if there are some doubtful traces of the doctrine of metempsychosis, this again must have been the creed of the very few.

Christianity and Judaism had made but small

impress upon the Arabs. There were Jewish tribes in the north, and there is evidence in the Korān and elsewhere that the traditions and rites of Judaism were widely known in Arabia. But the creed was too narrow and too exclusively national to commend itself to the majority of the people. Christianity fared even worse. Whether or not St. Paul journeyed there, it is at least certain that very little effect was produced by the preaching of Christianity in Arabia. We hear of Christians on the borders, and even two or three among the Mekkans, and bishops and churches are spoken of at Dhafār and Nejrān. But the Christianity that the Arabs knew was, like the Judaism of the northern tribes, a very imperfect reflection of the faith it professed to set forth. It had become a thing of the head instead of the heart, and the refinements of monophysite and monothelite doctrines gained no hold upon the Arab mind.

Thus Judaism and Christianity, though they were well known, and furnished many ideas and ceremonies to Islām, were never able to effect any general settlement in Arabia. The common Arabs did not care much about any religion, and the finer spirits found the wrangling dogmatism of the Christian and the narrow isolation of the Jew little to their mind. For there were before the time of Mohammad men who were dissatisfied with the low fetishism in which their countrymen were plunged, and who protested emphatically against the idle and even cruel superstitions of the Arabs. Not to refer to the prophets, who, as the Korān relates, were sent in old time to the tribes of

Ād and Thamood to convert them, there was, immedi‑
ately before the preaching of Mohammad, a general
feeling that a change was at hand ; a prophet was
expected, and women were anxiously hoping for male
children if so be they might mother the Apostle of
God; and the more thoughtful minds, tinged with
traditions of Judaism, were seeking for what they
called " the religion of Abraham." These men were
called " *Hanīfs*," or skeptics, and their religion
seems to have consisted chiefly in a negative position,
—in denying the superstition of the Arabs, and only
asserting the existence of one sole-ruling God whose
absolute slaves are all mankind, without being able
to decide on any minor doctrines, or to determine in
what manner this one God was to be worshipped. So
long as the Hanīfs could give their countrymen no
more definite creed than this, their influence was
limited to a few inquiring and doubting minds. It
was reserved for Mohammad to formulate the faith
of the Hanīfs in the dogmas of Islām. For the
leader of these few " skeptics " was Zeyd ibn 'Amr,
to whom Mohammad often resorted, and another was
the cousin of the Prophet and his near neighbour.
Thus the Hanīfs were the forerunners of the man
who was to change the destinies of the Arabs.

We can no longer see the true Arab as he was in
" the Time of Ignorance," and we cannot but regret
our loss ; for the Pagan Arab is a noble type of man,
though there be nobler. There is much that is
admirable in his high mettle, his fine sense of honour,
his knightliness, his " open-handed, both-handed "

generosity, his frank friendship, and his manly independent spirit; and the faults of this wild reckless nature are not to be weighed against its many excellencies. When Mohammad turned abroad the current of Arab life, he changed the character of the people. The mixture with foreign nations, and the quiet town-life that succeeded to the tumult of conquest, gradually effaced many of the leading ideas of the old Arab nature, and the remnant that still dwell in the land of their fathers have lost much of that nobleness of character which in their ancestors covered a multitude of sins. Mohammad in part destroyed the Arab when he created the Muslim. The last is no amends for the first. The modern Bedawy is neither the one nor the other; he has lost the greatness of the old type without gaining that of the new. As far as the Arabs alone are concerned, Mohammad effected a temporary good and a lasting harm. As to the world at large, that is matter for another chapter.

CHAPTER II.

MOHAMMAD.

A PROPHET for the Arabs must fulfil two conditions if he will bring with his good tidings the power of making them accepted: he must spring from the traditional centre of Arabian religion, and he must come of a noble family of pure Arab blood. Mohammad fulfilled both. His family was that branch of the Kureysh which had raised Mekka to the dignity of the undisputed metropolis of Arabia, and which, though impoverished, still held the chief offices of the sacred territory. Mohammad's grandfather was the virtual chief of Mekka; for to him belonged the guardianship of the Kaaba, and he it was who used the generous privilege of giving food and water to the pilgrims who resorted to the "House of God." His youngest son, after marrying a kinswoman belonging to a branch of the Kureysh settled at Yethrib (Medīna), died before the birth of his son (571), and this son, Mohammad, lost his mother when he was only six years old. The orphan was adopted by his grandfather, 'Abd-El-Muttalib, and a tender affection sprang up between the chief of eighty years and his little grandson. Many a day the old man might be seen sitting at his wonted place near the Kaaba, and sharing his mat with his favourite. He lived but two years more; and at his dying request, his son Abū-Tālib took charge of Mohammad, for whom he too ever showed a love as of father and mother.

Such is the bare outline of Mohammad's childhood; and of his youth we know about as little, though the Arabian biographies abound in legends, of which some may be true and most are certainly false. There are stories of his journeyings to Syria with his uncle, and his encounter with a mysterious monk of obscure faith; but there is nothing to show for this tale, and much to be brought against it. All we can say is, that Mohammad probably assisted his family in the war of the Fijār, and that he must many a time have frequented the annual Fair of 'Okādh, hearing the songs of the desert chiefs and the praise of Arab life, and listening to the earnest words of the Jews and Christians and others who came to the Fair. He was obliged at an early age to earn his own living; for the noble family of the Hāshimīs, to which he belonged, was fast losing its commanding position, whilst another branch of the Kureysh was succeeding to its dignities. The princely munificence of Hāshim and 'Abd-El-Muttalib was followed by the poverty and decline of their heirs. The duty of providing the pilgrims with food was transferred to the rival branch of Umeyya, whilst the Hāshimīs retained only the lighter office of serving water to the worshippers. Mohammad must take his share in the labour of the family,

and he was sent to pasture the sheep of the Kureysh
on the hills and valleys round Mekka; and though the
people despised the shepherd's calling, he himself was
wont to look back with pleasure to these early days,
saying that God called never a prophet save from
among the sheep-folds. And doubtless it was then
that he developed that reflective disposition of mind
which at length led him to seek the reform of his
people, whilst in his solitary wanderings with the
sheep he gained that marvellous eye for the beauty
and wonder of the earth and sky which resulted in
the gorgeous nature-painting of the Korān. Yet he
was glad to change this humble work for the more
lucrative and adventurous post of camel-driver to the
caravans of his wealthy kinswoman Khadīja; and he
seems to have taken so kindly to the duty, which
involved responsibilities, and to have acquitted himself so worthily, that he attracted the notice of his
employer, who straightway fell in love with him, and
presented him with her hand. The marriage was a
singularly happy one, though Mohammad was scarcely
twenty-five and his wife nearly forty, and it brought
him that repose and exemption from daily toil which
he needed in order to prepare his mind for his great
work. But beyond that, it gave him a loving woman's
heart, that was the first to believe in his mission,
that was ever ready to console him in his despair
and to keep alive within him the thin flickering
flame of hope when no man believed in him—not
even himself—and the world was black before his
eyes.

We know very little of the next fifteen years. Khadīja bore him sons and daughters, but only the daughters lived. We hear of his joining a league for the protection of the weak and oppressed, and there is a legend of his having acted with wise tact and judgment as arbitrator in a dispute among the great families of Mekka on the occasion of the rebuilding of the Kaaba. During this time, moreover, he relieved his still impoverished uncle of the charge of his son 'Aly—afterwards the Bayard of Islām—and he freed and adopted a certain captive, Zeyd; and these two became his most devoted friends and disciples. Such is the short but characteristic record of these fifteen years of manhood. We know very little about what Mohammad did, but we hear only one voice as to what he was. Up to the age of forty his unpretending modest way of life had attracted but little notice from his townspeople. He was only known as a simple, upright man, whose life was severely pure and refined, and whose true desert sense of honour and faith-keeping had won him the high title of El-Amīn, " the Trusty."

Let us see what fashion of man this was, who was about to work a revolution among his countrymen, and change the conditions of social life in a great part of the world. The picture * is drawn from an older man than we have yet seen ; but Mohammad at forty and Mohammad at fifty or more were probably very little different. " He was of the middle height,

---

* E. Deutsch, " Literary Remains," pp. 70–72.

rather thin, but broad of shoulders, wide of chest, strong of bone and muscle. His head was massive, strongly developed. Dark hair, slightly curled, flowed in a dense mass down almost to his shoulders. Even in advanced age it was sprinkled by only about twenty grey hairs—produced—by the agonies of his 'Revelations.' His face was oval-shaped, slightly tawny of colour. Fine, long, arched eyebrows were divided by a vein which throbbed visibly in moments of passion. Great black restless eyes shone out from under long, heavy eyelashes. His nose was large, slightly aquiline. His teeth, upon which he bestowed great care, were well set, dazzling white. A full beard framed his manly face. His skin was clear and soft, his complexion 'red and white,' his—hands were as 'silk and satin,' even as those of a woman. His step was quick and elastic, yet firm, and as that of one 'who steps from a high to a low place.' In turning his face he would also turn his full body. His whole gait and presence were dignified and imposing. His countenance was mild and pensive. His—laugh was rarely more than a smile.

"In his habits he was extremely simple, though he bestowed great care on his person. His eating and drinking, his dress and his furniture, retained, even when he had reached the fulness of power, their almost primitive nature. The only luxuries he indulged in were, besides arms, which he highly prized, a pair of yellow boots, a present from the Negus of Abyssinia. Perfumes, however, he loved passionately, being most sensitive of smell. Strong drinks he abhorred.

" His constitution was extremely delicate. He was nervously afraid of bodily pain; he would sob and roar under it. Eminently unpractical in all common things of life, he was gifted with mighty powers of imagination, elevation of mind, delicacy and refinement of feeling. 'He is more modest than a virgin behind her curtain,' it was said of him. He was most indulgent to his inferiors, and would never allow his awkward little page to be scolded, whatever he did. 'Ten years,' said Anas, his servant, 'was I about the Prophet, and he never said as much as "uff" to me.' He was very affectionate towards his family. One of his boys died on his breast in the smoky house of the nurse, a blacksmith's wife. He was very fond of children. He would stop them in the streets and pat their little cheeks. He never struck any one in his life. The worst expression he ever made use of in conversation was 'What has come to him?—may his forehead be darkened with mud!' When asked to curse some one, he replied, 'I have not been sent to curse, but to be a mercy to mankind.' 'He visited the sick, followed any bier he met, accepted the invitation of a slave to dinner, mended his own clothes, milked his goats, and waited upon himself,' relates summarily another tradition. He never first withdrew his hand out of another man's palm, and turned not before the other had turned. . . . He was the most faithful protector of those he protected, the sweetest and most agreeable in conversation; those who saw him were suddenly filled with reverence; those who came near him loved him; they who described him would say, 'I have never seen his like either before or after.' He was of great taciturnity; but when he spoke it was with emphasis and deliberation, and no one could ever forget what he said. He was, however, very nervous and restless withal, often low-spirited, downcast as to heart and eyes. Yet he would at times suddenly break through these broodings, become gay, talkative, jocular, chiefly among his own. He would then delight in telling little stories, fairy tales, and the like. He would romp with the children and play with their toys."

" He lived with his wives in a row of humble cottages, separated from one another by palm-branches, cemented together with mud. He would kindle the fire, sweep the floor, and milk the goats himself. 'Āïsha tells us that he slept upon a leathern mat, and that he mended his clothes, and even clouted his shoes, with his own hand. For months together . . . he did not get a sufficient meal. The little food that he had was always shared with those who dropped in to partake of it. Indeed, outside the Prophet's house was a bench or gallery, on which were always to be found a number of the poor, who lived entirely on his generosity, and were hence called the ' people of the bench.' His ordinary food was dates and water or barley-bread; milk and honey were luxuries of which he was fond, but which he rarely allowed himself. The fare of the desert seemed most congenial to him, even when he was sovereign of Arabia." *

Mohammad was fully forty before he felt himself called to be an apostle to his people. If he did not actually worship the local deities of the place, at least he made no public protest against the fetish worship of the Kureysh. Yet in the several phases of his life, in his contact with traders, in his association with Zeyd and other men, he had gained an insight into better things than idols and human sacrifices, divining-arrows, fetish mountains and stars. He had heard a dim echo of some "religion of Abraham"; he had listened to the stories of the Haggadah; he knew a very little about Jesus of Nazareth. He seems to have suffered long under the burden of doubt and self-distrust. He used to wonder about the hills alone, brooding over these things; he shunned the society of men, and "solitude became a passion to him."

At length came the crisis. He was spending the sacred months on Mount Hirā, "a huge barren rock, torn by cleft and hollow ravine, standing out solitary in the full white glare of the desert sun, shadowless, flowerless, without well or rill." Here, in a cave, Mohammad gave himself up to prayer and fasting. Long months or even years of doubt had increased his nervous excitable disposition. He had, they say, cataleptic fits during his childhood, and was

---

* R. Bosworth Smith, "Mohammed and Mohammedanism," 2nd ed. p. 131.

evidently more delicately and finely constituted than those around him. Given this nervous nature, and the grim solitude of the hill where he had wandered for long weary months, blindly feeling after some truth upon which to rest his soul, it is not difficult to believe the tradition of the cave, that Mohammad heard a voice say, " Cry!"   "What shall I cry?" he answers—the question that has been burning his heart during all his mental struggles—

> Cry*! in the name of thy Lord, who created—
> Created man from blood.
> Cry! for thy Lord is the Bountifullest,
> Who taught the pen,
> Taught man what he knew not.

Mohammad arose trembling, and went to Khadīja, and told her what he had seen; and she did her woman's part, and believed in him and soothed his terror, and bade him hope for the future. Yet he could not believe in himself. Was he not perhaps mad, possessed by a devil? Were these indeed voices from God? And so he went again on his solitary wanderings, hearing strange sounds, and thinking them at one time the testimony of Heaven, at another the temptings of Satan or the ravings of madness. Doubting, wondering, hoping, he had fain put an end to a life which had become intolerable in its changings from the heaven of hope to the hell of despair, when again he heard the voice, " Thou art the messenger of God, and I am Gabriel." Conviction

---

* Or " read," " recite." These lines are the beginning of Sūra xcvi. of the Korān. Those on the opposite page are from lxxiv.

at length seized hold on him; he was indeed to bring a message of good tidings to the Arabs, the message of God through His angel Gabriel. He went back to Khadīja exhausted in mind and body. "Wrap me, wrap me," he said; and the word came unto him—

> O thou who art wrapped, arise up and warn!
> And thy Lord magnify,
> And thy raiment purify,
> And shun abomination!
> And grant not favours to gain increase!
> And wait for thy Lord.

There are those who see imposture in all this; for such I have no answer. Nor does it matter whether in a hysterical fit or under any physical disease soever Mohammad saw these visions and heard these voices. We are not concerned to draw the lines of demarcation between enthusiasm and ecstasy and inspiration. It is sufficient that Mohammad *did* see these things—the subjective creations, if you will, of a tormented mind. It is sufficient that he believed them to be a message from on high, and that for years of neglect and persecution, and for years of triumph and conquest, he acted upon his belief.

Mohammad now (A.D. 612) came forward as the Apostle of the One God to the people of Arabia: he was at last well assured that his God was of a truth *the* God, and that He had indeed sent him with a message to his people, that they too might turn from their idols and serve the living God. He was almost alone, but he was no longer afraid; he had learnt that self-trust which is the condition of all true work.

At first he spoke to his near kinsmen and friends; and it is impossible to overrate the importance of the fact that his closest relations and those who lived under his roof were the first to believe and the staunchest of faith. The prophet who is *with* honour in his own home need appeal to no stronger proof of his sincerity, and that Mohammad *was* "a hero to his own valet" is an invincible argument for his earnestness. The motherly Khadīja had at once, with a woman's instinct, divined her husband's heart and confirmed his fainting hope by her firm faith in him. His dearest friends, Zeyd and 'Aly, were the next converts; and though, to his grief, he could never induce his lifelong protector, Abū-Tālib, to abandon the gods of his fathers, yet the old man loved him none the less, and said, when he heard of 'Aly's conversion, "Well, my son, he will not call thee to aught save what is good; wherefore thou art free to cleave unto him." A priceless aid was gained in the accession of Abū-Bekr, who was destined to succeed Mohammad as the first Khalif of Islām, and whose calm judgment and quick sagacity, joined to a gentle and compassionate heart, were of incalculable service to the faith. Abū-Bekr was one of the wealthiest merchants of Mekka, and exercised no small influence among his fellow-citizens, as much by his character as his position. Like Mohammad, he had a nickname, Es-Siddīk, "The True": *The True* and *The Trusty*,—auspicious names for the future of the religion !

Five converts followed in Abū-Bekr's steps; among

them 'Othmān, the third Khalif, and Talha, the man of war. The ranks of the faithful were swelled from humbler sources. There were many negro slaves in Mekka, and of them not a few had been predisposed by earlier teaching to join in the worship of the One God; and of those who were first converted was the Abyssinian Bilāl, the original Muëddin of Islām, and ever a devoted disciple of the Prophet. These and others from the Kureysh raised the number of Muslims to more than thirty souls by the fourth year of Mohammad's mission—thirty in three long years, and few of them men of influence!

This small success had been achieved with very little opposition from the idolaters. Mohammad had not spoken much in public; and when he did speak to strangers, he refrained from directly attacking their worship, and only enjoined them to worship the One God who had created all things. The people were rather interested, and wondered whether he were a soothsayer or madman, or if indeed there were truth in his words. But now (A.D. 615) Mohammad entered upon a more public career. He summoned the Kureysh to a conference at the hill of Es-Safā, and said, " I am come to you as a warner, and as the forerunner of a fearful punishment. . . . I cannot protect you in this world, nor can I promise you aught in the next life, unless ye say, There is no God but Allāh." He was laughed to scorn, and the assembly broke up; but from this time he ceased not to preach to the people of a punishment that would come upon the unbelieving city. He told them, in the fiery language of the early sūras, how God had punished the old tribes of the Arabs who would not believe in His messengers, how the Flood had swallowed up the people who would not hearken to Noah. He swore unto them, by the wonderful sights of nature, by the noonday brightness, by the night when she spreadeth her veil, by the day when it appeareth in glory, that a like destruction would assuredly come upon them if they did not turn away from their idols and serve God alone. He enforced his message with every resource of language and metaphor, till he made it burn in the ears of the people. And then he told them of the Last Day, when a just reckoning should be taken of the deeds they had done; and he spoke of Paradise and Hell with all the glow of Eastern imagery. The people were moved, terrified; conversions increased. It was time the Kureysh should take some step. If the idols were destroyed, what would come to them, the keepers of the idols, and their renown throughout the land? How should they retain the allegiance of the neighbouring tribes who came to worship their several divinities at the Kaaba? That a few should follow the ravings of a madman or magician who preferred one god above the beautiful deities of Mekka was little matter; but that the leading men of the city should join the sect, and that the magician should terrify the people in open day with his denunciations of the worship which *they* superintended, was intolerable. The chiefs were seriously alarmed, and resolved on a more active policy. Hitherto they had merely ridiculed the professors of this new faith; they would now take stronger measures. Mohammad himself they dared not touch; for he belonged to a noble family, which, though it was reduced and impoverished, had deserved well of the city, and which, moreover, was now headed by a man who was reverenced throughout Mekka, and was none other than the adoptive father and protector of Mohammad himself. Nor was it safe to attack the other chief men among the Muslims, for the blood-revenge was no light risk. They were thus compelled to content themselves with the sorry satisfaction of torturing the black slaves who had joined the obnoxious faction. They exposed them on the scorching sand, and withheld water till they recanted —which they did, only to profess the faith once more when they were let go. The first Muëddin alone remained steadfast: as he lay half-stifled he would only answer "Ahad! Ahad!"—"One [God]! One!" —till Abū-Bekr came and bought his freedom, as he was wont to do for many of the miserable victims. Mohammad was very gentle with these forced renegades: he knew what stuff men are made of, and he bade them be of good cheer for their lips, so that their hearts were sound.

At last, moved by the sufferings of his lowly followers, he advised them to seek a refuge in Abyssinia —"a land of righteousness, wherein no man is wronged"; and in the fifth year of his mission (616) eleven men and four women left Mekka secretly, and were received in Abyssinia with welcome and peace. These first emigrants were followed by more the next year, till the number reached one hundred. The Kureysh were very wroth at the escape of their victims, and sent ambassadors to the Nejāshy, the Christian king of Abyssinia, to demand that the refugees should be given up to them. But the Nejāshy assembled his bishops, and sent for the Muslims and asked them why they had fled; and one of them answered and said—

"O king! we lived in ignorance, idolatry, and unchastity; the strong oppressed the weak; we spoke untruth; we violated the duties of hospitality. Then a prophet arose, one whom we knew from our youth, with whose descent and conduct and good faith and morality we are all well acquainted. He told us to worship one God, to speak truth, to keep good faith, to assist our relations, to fulfil the rights of hospitality, and to abstain from all things impure, ungodly, unrighteous. And he ordered us to say prayers, give alms, and to fast. We believed in him; we followed him. But our countrymen persecuted us, tortured us, and tried to cause us to forsake our religion; and now we throw ourselves upon thy protection. Wilt thou not protect us?" And he recited a chapter of the Korān, which spoke of Christ; and the king and the bishops wept upon their beards. And the king dismissed the messengers, and would not give up the men.

The Kureysh, foiled in their attempt to recapture the slaves, vented their malice on those believers who remained. Insults were heaped upon the Muslims, and persecution grew hotter each day. For a moment

Mohammad faltered in his work. Could he not spare his people these sufferings? Was it impossible to reconcile the religion of the city with the belief in one supreme God? After all, was the worship of those idols so false a thing? did it not hold the germ of a great truth? And so Mohammad made his first and last concession. He recited a revelation to the Kureysh, in which he spoke respectfully of the three moon-goddesses, and asserted that their intercession with God might be hoped for: " Wherefore bow down before God and serve Him "; and the whole audience, overjoyed at the compromise, bowed down and worshipped at the name of the God of Mohammad—the whole city was reconciled to the double religion. But this Dreamer of the Desert was not the man to rest upon a lie. At the price of the whole city of Mekka he would not remain untrue to himself. He came forward and said he had done wrong—the devil had tempted him. He openly and frankly retracted what he had said : and " As for their idols, they were but empty names which they and their fathers had invented."

Western biographers have rejoiced greatly over " Mohammad's fall." Yet it was a tempting compromise, and few would have withstood it. And the life of Mohammad is not the life of a god, but of a man : from first to last it is intensely human. But if for once he was not superior to the temptation of gaining over the whole city and obtaining peace where before there was only bitter persecution, what can we say of his manfully thrusting back the rich prize he had gained, freely confessing his fault, and resolutely giving himself over again to the old indignities and insults ? If he was once insincere—and who is not? —how intrepid was his after-sincerity! He was untrue to himself for a while, and he is ever referring to it in his public preaching with shame and remorse; but the false step was more than atoned for by his magnificent recantation.

Mohammad's influence with the people at large was certainly weakened by this temporary change of front, and the opposition of the leaders of the Kureysh, checked for the moment by the Prophet's concession, now that he had repudiated it, broke forth into fiercer flame. They heaped insults upon him, and he could not traverse the city without encountering a curse. They threw unclean things at him, and vexed him in his every doing. The protection of Abū-Tālib alone saved him from personal danger. This refuge the Kureysh determined to remove. They had attempted before, but had been turned back with a soft answer. They now went to the aged chief, bowed with the weight of fourscore years, and demanded that he should either compel his nephew to hold his peace, or else that he should withdraw his protection. Having thus spoken they departed. The old man sent for Mohammad, and told him what they had said. "Now therefore save thyself and me also, and cast not upon me a burden heavier than I can bear"; for he was grieved at the strife among his kindred, and would fain have seen Mohammad temporize with the Kureysh. But though the Prophet believed that at length his uncle was indeed about to abandon him, his courage and high resolve never faltered. "Though they should set the sun on my right hand and the moon on my left to persuade me, yet while God commands me I will not renounce my purpose." But to lose his uncle's love! —he burst into tears, and turned to go. But Abū-Tālib called aloud, "Son of my brother, come back." So he came. And he said, "Depart in peace, my nephew, and say whatsoever thou desirest; for, by the Lord, I will never deliver thee up."

The faithfulness of Abū-Tālib was soon to be tried. At first, indeed, things looked brighter. The old chief's firm bearing overawed the Kureysh, and they were still more cowed by two great additions that were now joined to the Muslim ranks. One was Mohammad's uncle, Hamza, "the Lion of God," a mighty hunter and warrior of the true Arab mettle, whose sword was worth twenty of weaker men to the cause of Islām. The other was 'Omar, afterwards Khalif, whose fierce impulsive nature had hitherto marked him as a violent opponent of the new faith, but who presently proved himself one of the main-stays of Islām. The gain of two such men first frightened, then maddened the Kureysh. The leaders met together and consulted what they should do. It was no longer a case of an enthusiast followed by a crowd of slaves and a few worthy merchants; it was a faction led by stout warriors, such as Hamza, Talha, 'Omar—half a dozen picked swordsmen; and the Muslims, emboldened by their new allies, were boldly surrounding the Kaaba, and performing the rites of their religion in the face of all the people. The Kureysh resolved on extreme measures. They determined to shut off the obnoxious family of the Hāshimīs from the rest of their kindred. The chiefs drew up a document, in which they vowed that they would not marry with the Hāshimīs, nor buy and sell with them, nor hold with them any communication soever; and this they hung up in the Kaaba.

The Hāshimīs were not many enough to fight the whole city, so they went, every man of them, save one, to the shi-b (or quarter) of Abū-Tālib,—a long, narrow mountain defile on the eastern skirts of Mekka, cut off by rocks or walls from the city, except for one narrow gateway,—and there they shut themselves up. For though the ban did not forbid them to go about as heretofore, they knew that no soul would speak with them, and that they would be subject to the maltreatment of the common crowd. So they collected their stores and waited. Every man of the family, Muslim or Pagan, cast in his lot with his kinsman, Mohammad, saving only his own uncle, Abū-Lahab, a determined enemy to Islām, to whom a special denunciation is justly consecrated in the Korān.

For two long years the Hāshimīs remained shut up in their quarter. Only at the pilgrimage-time— when the blessed institution of the sacred months made violence sacrilege—could Mohammad come forth and speak unto the people of the things that were in his heart to say. Scarcely any converts were made during this weary time; and most of those who had previously been converted, and did not belong to the doomed clan, took refuge in Abyssinia; so that in the seventh year of Mohammad's mission there were probably not more than twelve Muslims of any weight who remained by him. Still the Hāshimīs remained in their quarter. It seemed as if they must all perish: their stores were almost gone, and the cries of starving children could be heard outside. Kind-hearted neighbours would sometimes smuggle-in a camel's load of food, but it availed little. The Kureysh themselves were growing ashamed of their work, and were wishing for an excuse for releasing their kinsmen. The excuse came in time. It was discovered that the deed of ban was eaten up by worms, and Abū-Tālib turned the discovery to his advantage. The venerable chief went out and met the Kureysh at the Kaaba, and pointing to the crumbling leaf he bitterly reproached them with their hardness of heart towards their brethren: then he departed. And straightway there rose up five chiefs, heads of great families, and, amid the murmurs of the fiercer spirits who were still for no quarter, they put on their armour, and going to the shi-b of Abū-Tālib, bade the Hāshimīs come forth in peace. And they came forth.

It was now the eighth year of Mohammad's mission; and for the last two years, wasted in excommunication, Islām had almost stood still, at least externally. For though Mohammad's patient bearing under the

ban had gained over a few of his imprisoned clan to
his side, he had made no converts beyond the walls
of his quarter. During the sacred months he had
gone forth to speak to the people,—to the caravans
of strangers and the folk at the fairs,—but he had
no success ; for hard behind him followed Abū-Lahab,
the squinter, who mocked at him, and told the people
he was only "a liar and a sabean." And the people
answered that his own kindred must best know what
he was, and they would hear nothing from him. The
bold conduct of the five chiefs had indeed secured
for Mohammad a temporary respite from persecution ;
but this relief was utterly outweighed by the troubles
that now fell upon him and fitly gave that year the
name of "The Year of Mourning." For soon after
the revoking of the ban Abū-Tālib died, and five
weeks later Khadīja. In the first Mohammad lost
his ancient protector, who, though he would never
give up his old belief, had yet faithfully guarded the
Prophet from his childhood upwards, and, with the
true Arab sentiment of kinship, had subjected himself
and his clan to years of persecution and poverty in
order to defend his brother's son from his enemies.
The death of Khadīja was even a heavier calamity
to Mohammad. She first had believed in him, and
she had ever been his angel of hope and consolation.
To his death he cherished a tender regret for her ;
and when his young bride 'Āïsha, the favourite of
his declining years, jealously abused "that toothless
old woman," he answered with indignation, "When
I was poor, she enriched me ; when they called me a

liar, she alone believed in me ; when all the world was against me, she alone remained true."

Mohammad might well feel himself alone in the world. Most of his followers were in Abyssinia; only a few tried friends remained at Mekka. All the city was against him; his protector was dead, and his faithful wife. Dejected, almost hopeless, he would try a new field. If Mekka rejected him, might not Et-Tāïf give him welcome ? He set out on his journey of seventy miles on foot, taking only Zeyd with him; and he told the people of Et-Tāïf his simple message. They stoned him out of the city for three miles. Bleeding and fainting, he paused to rest in an orchard, to recover strength before he went back to the insults of his own people. The owners of the place sent him some grapes; and he gathered up his strength once more, and bent his weary feet towards Mekka. On the way, as he slept, his fancy called up a strange dream : men had rejected him, and now he thought he saw the Jinn, the spirits of the air, falling down and worshipping the One God, and bearing witness to the truth of Islām. Heartened by the vision, he pushed on : and when Zeyd asked him if he did not fear to throw himself again into the hands of the Kureysh, he answered, " God will protect His religion and help His prophet."

So this lonely man came back to dwell among his enemies. Though a brave Arab gentleman, compassionating his isolation, gave him the Bedawy pledge of protection, yet he well knew that the power of his foes made such protection almost useless, and at any time he might be assassinated. But the Kureysh had not yet come to think of this last resource, and meanwhile a new prospect was opening out for Mohammad. The same year, as he was visiting the caravans of the pilgrims who had come from all parts of Arabia to worship at the Kaaba, he found a group of men of Yethrib who were willing to listen to his words. He expounded to them the faith he was sent to preach, and he told them how his people had rejected him, and asked them whether Yethrib would receive him. The men were impressed with his words and professed Islām, and promised to bring news the next year; then they returned home and talked of this matter to their brethren. Now at Yethrib, besides two pagan tribes that had migrated upwards from the south, there were three clans of Jewish Arabs. Between the pagans and Jews, and then between the two pagan clans, there had been deadly wars; and now there were many parties in the city, and no one was master. The Jews, on the one hand, were expecting their Messiah; the pagans looked for a prophet. If Mohammad were not the Messiah, the Jews thought that he might at least be their tool to subdue their pagan rivals. "Whether he is a prophet or not," said the pagans, "he is our kinsman by his mother, and will help us to overawe the Jews; and if he is the coming prophet, it is our policy to recognise him before those Jews who are always threatening us with their Messiah." The teaching of Mohammad was so nearly Jewish, that a union of the two creeds might be hoped for; whilst to the pagan Arabs of Yethrib monotheism was no strange doctrine. All parties were therefore willing to receive Mohammad and at least try the experiment of his influence. As a peace-maker, prophet, or messiah, he would be equally welcome in a city torn asunder by party jealousies.

When the time of pilgrimage again came round, Mohammad waited at the appointed place in a secluded glen, and there met him men from the two pagan tribes of Yethrib—the clans of Khazraj and Aws—ten from one and two from the other. They told him of the willingness of their people to embrace Islām, and their hope to make ready the city for his welcome. They plighted their faith with him in these words : "We will not worship save one God; we will not steal, nor commit adultery, nor kill our children ; we will in no wise slander, nor will we disobey the prophet in anything that is right." This is the first pledge of the 'Akaba.

The twelve men of Yethrib went back and preached Islām to their people. " So prepared was the ground, so zealous the propagation, and so apt the method, that the new faith spread rapidly from house to house and from tribe to tribe. The Jews looked on in amazement at the people, whom they had in vain endeavoured for generations to convince of the errors of polytheism and dissuade from the abominations of idolatry, suddenly and of their own accord casting away their idols and professing belief in God alone." They asked Mohammad to send them a teacher versed in the Korān, so anxious were they to know Islām truly ; and Mus'ab was sent, and taught them and conducted their worship; so that Islām took deep root at Yethrib.

Meanwhile Mohammad was still among the Kureysh at Mekka. His is now an attitude of waiting; he is listening for news from his distant converts. Resting his hopes upon them, and despairing of influencing the Mekkans, he does not preach so much as heretofore. He holds his peace mainly, and bides his time. One hears little of this interval of quietude. Islām seems stationary at Mekka, and its followers are silent and reserved. The Kureysh are joyful at the ceasing of those denunciations which terrified whilst they angered them, yet they are not quite satisfied. The Muslims have a waiting look, as though there were something at hand.

It was during this year of expectation that the Prophet's celebrated " Night Journey " took place. This Mi'rāj has been the subject of extravagant embellishments on the part of the traditionists and commentators, and the cause of much obloquy to the Prophet from his religious opponents. Mohammad dreamed a dream, and referred to it briefly and obscurely in the Korān. His followers persisted in believing it to have been a reality—an ascent to heaven in the body—till Mohammad was weary of repeating his simple assertion that it was a dream. The traditional form of this wonderful vision may be read in any life of Mohammad, and though it is doubtless very different from the story the Prophet himself gave, it is still a grand vision, full of glorious imagery, fraught with deep meaning.

Again the time of pilgrimage came round, and again Mohammad repaired to the glen of the mountain-road. Mus'ab had told him the good tidings of the spread of the faith at Yethrib, and he was met at the rendezvous by more than seventy men. They came by twos and threes secretly for fear of the Kureysh, "waking not the sleeper, nor tarrying for the absent." Then Mohammad recited to them verses from the Korān, and in answer to their invitation that he should come to them, and their profession that their lives were at his service, he asked them to pledge themselves to defend him as they would their own wives and children. And a murmur of eager assent rolled round about from the seventy, and an old man, one of their chiefs, stood forth and said, "Stretch out thy hand, O Mohammad." And the chief struck his own hand into Mohammad's palm in the frank Bedawy fashion, and thus pledged his fealty. Man after man the others followed, and struck their palms upon Mohammad's. Then he chose twelve of them as leaders over the rest, saying, "Moses chose from among his people twelve leaders. Ye shall be the sureties for the rest, even as the apostles of Jesus were; and I am the surety for my people." The voice of some stranger was heard near by, and the assembly hastily dispersed and stole back to their camp. This is the second pledge of the 'Akaba.

The Kureysh knew that some meeting had taken place, and though they could not bring home the offence to any of the Yethrib pilgrims, they kept a stricter watch on the movements of Mohammad and his friends after the pilgrims had returned homeward. It was clear that Mekka was no longer a safe place for the Muslims, and a few days after the second pledge Mohammad told his followers to betake themselves secretly to Yethrib. For two months at the beginning of the eleventh year of the mission (622) the Muslims were leaving Mekka in small companies to make the journey of 250 miles to Yethrib. One hundred families had gone, and whole quarters of the city were deserted, left with empty houses and locked doors, " a prey to woe and wind." There were but three believers now remaining in Mekka—these were Mohammad, Abū-Bekr, and 'Aly. Like the captain of a sinking ship, the Prophet would not leave till all the crew were safe. But now they were all gone save his two early friends, and everything was ready for the journey; still the Prophet did not go. The Kureysh, who had been too much taken by surprise to prevent the emigration, now prepared measures for a summary vengeance on the disturber of their peace and the emptier of their city. They set a watch on his house, and, it is said, commissioned a band of armed youths of different families to assassinate him, that the blood recompense might not fall on one household alone. But Mohammad had warning of his danger, and leaving 'Aly to deceive the enemy, he was concealed with Abū-Bekr in a narrow-mouthed cave on Mount Thōr, an hour-and-a-half's journey from Mekka, before the Kureysh knew of his escape. For three days they remained hidden there, while their enemies were searching the

ountry for them. Once they were very near, and
ıbū-Bekr trembled :—" We are but two." " Nay,"
nswered Mohammad, " we are three, for God is with
ıs." And a spider, they say, wove its web over the
ntrance of the cave, so that the Kureysh passed on,
hinking that no man had entered there.

On the third night the pursuit had been almost
given over, and the two fugitives took up their
ourney again. Mounted on camels they journeyed
;o Yethrib. In eight days they reached the outskirts
of the city (September, A.D. 622). Mohammad was
received with acclamation, and took up his residence
among his kindred. The seat of Islām was transferred from Mekka to Yethrib, henceforward to be
known as Medīna,—*Medīnet-en-Neby*, " the city of
the Prophet."

This is the *Hijreh*, or Flight of Mohammad, from
which the Muslims date their history. Their first
year began on the 16th day of June of the Year of
Grace 622.

A great change now comes over the Prophet's life.
He is still the same man, but his surroundings are
totally different ; the work to be done is on a wider,
rougher stage. Thus far we have seen a gentle,
thoughtful boy tending the sheep round Mekka ;—
a young man of little note, of whom the people only
knew that he was pure and upright and true ;—then
a man of forty whose solitary communion with his
soul has pressed him to the last terrible questions
that each man, if he will think at all, must some time

ask himself—What is life? What does this worl
mean? What is reality, what is truth? Lon;
months, years perhaps, we know not how long an
weary, filled with the tortures of doubt and th
despair of ever attaining to the truth, filled with th
dreary thought of his aloneness iñ the relentles
universe, and the longing to end it all, brought at las
their fruits—sure conviction of the great secret o
life, a firm belief in the Creator in whom all thing
live and move and have their being, whom to serv
is man's highest duty and privilege, the one thing
to be done. And then ten years of struggling witl
careless, unthinking idolaters ; ten years of slov
results, the gaining over of a few close friends, the
devoted attachment of some slaves and men of the
meaner rank ; finally, the conversion of half-a-dozer
great citizen chiefs, ending in the flight of the whole
brotherhood of believers from their native city anc
their welcome to a town of strangers, where the faith
had forced itself home to the hearts of perhaps twc
hundred citizens. It was but little that was done;
so many years of toil, of indomitable courage and
perseverance and long-suffering, and only a few
hundred converts at the end ! But it was the seed of
a great harvest. Mohammad had shown men what
he was ; the nobility of his character, his strong
friendship, his endurance and courage, above all, his
earnestness and fiery enthusiasm for the truth he
came to preach,—these things had revealed the hero,
the master whom it was alike impossible to disobey
and impossible not to love. Henceforward it is only

a question of time. As the men of Medīna come to know Mohammad, they too will devote themselves to him body and soul; and the enthusiasm will catch fire and spread among the tribes till all Arabia is at the feet of the Prophet of the One God. "No emperor with his tiaras was obeyed as this man in a cloak of His own clouting." He had the gift of influencing men, and he had the nobility only to influence them for good.

We have now to see Mohammad as king. Though he came as a fugitive, rejected as an impostor by his own citizens, yet it was not long before his word was supreme in his adopted city. He had to rule over a mixed and divided people, and this must have helped him to the supreme voice. There were four distinct parties at Medīna. First, the "Refugees" (Muhājirūn), who had fled from Mekka; on these Mohammad could always rely with implicit faith. But he attached equal importance to the early converts of Medīna, who had invited him among them and given him a home when the future seemed very hopeless before him, and who were thenceforward known by the honourable title of the "Helpers" (Ansār). How devoted was the affection of these men is shown by the well-known scene at El-Ji'rāneh, when the Helpers were discontented with their share of the spoils, and Mohammad answered, "Why are ye disturbed in mind because of the things of this life wherewith I have sought to incline the hearts of these men of Mekka into Islām, whereas ye are already steadfast in the faith? Are ye not satisfied that others should obtain the flocks and the camels, while ye carry back the Prophet of the Lord unto your homes? Nay, I will not leave you for ever. If all mankind went one way, and the men of Medīna went another way, verily I would go the way of the men of Medīna. The Lord be favourable unto them, and bless them, and their sons, and their sons' sons, for ever!" And the "Helpers" wept upon their beards, and cried with one voice, "Yea, we are well satisfied, O Prophet, with our lot." To retain the allegiance of the Refugees and the Helpers was never a trouble to Mohammad; the only difficulty was to rein in their zeal and hold them back from doing things of blood and vengeance on the enemies of Islām. To prevent the danger of jealousy between the Refugees and the Helpers, Mohammad assigned each Refugee to one of the Ansār to be his brother; and this tie of gossipry superseded all nearer ties, till Mohammad saw the time of its usefulness was over. The third party in Medīna was that of the "Disaffected," or in the language of Islām the "Hypocrites" (Munāfikūn). This was composed of the large body of men who gave in their nominal allegiance to Mohammad and his religion when they saw they could not safely withstand his power, but who were always ready to turn about if they thought there was a chance of his overthrow. Mohammad treated these men and their leader 'Abdallah ibn Ubayy (who himself aspired to the sovranty of Medīna) with patient courtesy and friendliness, and, though they actually deserted him more than once at vitally critical moments, he never retaliated, even when he was strong enough to crush them, but rather sought to win them over heartily to his cause by treating them as though they were what he would have them be. The result was that this party gradually diminished and became absorbed in the general mass of earnest Muslims, and though up to its leader's death it constantly called forth Mohammad's powers of conciliation, it finally vanished from the history of parties.

The fourth party was the real thorn in the Prophet's side. It consisted of the Jews, of whom three tribes were settled in the suburbs of Medīna. They had at first been well disposed to Mohammad's coming. He could not indeed be the Messiah, because he was not of the lineage of David; but he would do very well to pass off upon their neighbours, the pagan Arabs, as, if not the Messiah, at least a great prophet; and by his influence the Jews might regain their old supremacy in Medīna. Mohammad's teaching was very nearly Jewish—they had taught him the fables of their Haggadah, and he believed in their prophets —why should he not be one of them and help them to the dominion? When Mohammad came, they found out their mistake ; instead of a tool they had a master. He told the people, indeed, the stories of the Midrash, and he professed to revive the religion of Abraham : but he added to this several damning articles ; he taught that Jesus *was* the Messiah, and that no other Messiah was to be looked for ; and, moreover, whilst reverencing and inculcating the doctrine of the Hebrew prophets and of Christ, as he knew it, he yet insisted on his own mission as in nowise inferior to theirs—as, in fact, the seal of prophecy by which all that went before was confirmed or abrogated. The illusion was over; the Jews would have nothing to say to Islām: they set themselves instead to oppose it, ridicule it, and vex its Preacher in every way that their notorious ingenuity could devise.

The step was false: the Jews missed their game, and they had to pay for it. Whether it was possible to form a coalition,—whether the Jews might have induced Mohammad to waive certain minor points if they recognised his prophetic mission,—it is difficult to say. It seems most probable that Mohammad would not have yielded a jot to their demands, and would have accepted nothing short of unconditional surrender to his religion. And it is at least doubtful whether Islām would have gained anything by a further infusion of Judaism. It already contained all that it could assimilate of the Hebrew faith; the rest was too narrow for the universal scope of Islām. The religion of Mohammad lost little, we may be sure, by the standing aloof of the Arabian Jews; but the Jews themselves lost much. Mohammad, indeed, treated them kindly so long as kindness was possible. He made a treaty with them, whereby the rights of the Muslims and the Jews were defined. They were to practise their respective religions unmolested; protection and security were promised to all the parties to the treaty, without distinction of creed; each was to help the other if attacked; no alliance was to be made with the Kureysh; war was to be made in common, and no war could be made without the consent of Mohammad: crime alone could do away with the protection of this treaty.

But the Jews could not content themselves with standing aloof; they must needs act on the offensive. They began by asking Mohammad hard questions out of their law, and his answers they easily refuted from their books. They denied all knowledge of the Jewish stories in the Korān—though they knew that they came from their own Haggadah, which was ever in their mouths in their own quarter,—and they showed him their Bible, where, of course, the Haggadistic legends were not to be found. Mohammad had but one course open to him—to say they had suppressed or changed their books; and he denounced them accordingly, and said that his was the true account of the patriarchs and prophets, revealed from heaven. Not satisfied with tormenting Mohammad with questions on that Tōrah which they were always wrangling about themselves, they took hold of the everyday formulas of Islām, the daily prayers and ejaculations, and, " twisting their tongues," mispronounced them so that they meant something absurd or blasphemous. When asked which they preferred, Islām or idolatry, they frankly avowed that they preferred idolatry. To lie about their own religion and to ridicule another religion that was doing a great and good work around them was not enough for these Jews; they must set their poets to work to lampoon the women of the believers in obscene verse, and such outrages upon common decency, not to say upon the code of Arab honour and chivalry, became a favourite occupation among the poets of the Jewish clans.

These were offences against the religion and the persons of the Muslims. They also conspired against the state. Mohammad was not only the preacher of Islām, he was also the king of Medīna, and was responsible for the safety and peace of the city. As a prophet, he could afford to ignore the jibes of the Jews, though they maddened him to fury; but as the chief of the city, the general in a time of almost continual warfare, when Medīna was kept in a state of military defence and under a sort of military discipline, he could not overlook treachery. He was bound by his duty to his subjects to suppress a party that might (and nearly did) lead to the sack of the city by investing armies. The measures he took for this object have furnished his European biographers with a handle for attack. It is, I believe, solely on the ground of his treatment of the Jews that Mohammad has been called " a bloodthirsty tyrant ": it would certainly be difficult to support the epithet on other grounds.

The bloodthirstiness consists in this: some half-dozen Jews, who had distinguished themselves by their virulence against the Muslims, or by their custom of carrying information to the common enemy of Medīna, were executed; two of the three Jewish clans were sent into exile, (just as they had previously come into exile,) and the third was exterminated—the men killed, and the women and children made slaves.

The execution of the half-dozen marked Jews is generally called assassination, because a Muslim was sent
secretly to kill each of the criminals. The reason is
almost too obvious to need explanation. There were
no police or law-courts or even courts-martial at
Medīna ; some one of the followers of Mohammad
must therefore be the executor of the sentence of
death, and it was better it should be done quietly, as
the executing of a man openly before his clan would
have caused a brawl and more bloodshed and retaliation, till the whole city had become mixed up in the
quarrel. If secret assassination is the word for such
deeds, secret assassination was a necessary part of the
internal government of Medīna. The men must be
killed, and best in that way. In saying this I assume
that Mohammad was cognisant of the deed, and that
it was not merely a case of private vengeance ; but in
several instances the evidence that traces these execu-
tions to Mohammad's order is either entirely wanting
or is too doubtful to claim our credence.

Of the sentences upon the three whole clans, that
of exile, passed upon two of them, was clement
enough. They were a turbulent set, always setting
the people of Medīna by the ears ; and finally a brawl
followed by an insurrection resulted in the expulsion
of one tribe ; and insubordination, alliance with
enemies, and a suspicion of conspiracy against the
Prophet's life, ended similarly for the second. Both
tribes had violated the original treaty, and had endeavoured in every way to bring Mohammad and his
religion to ridicule and destruction. The only ques-

tion is whether their punishment was not too light. Of the third clan a fearful example was made, not by Mohammad, but by an arbiter appointed by themselves. When the Kureysh and their allies were besieging Medīna, and had well-nigh stormed the defences, this Jewish tribe entered into negotiations with the enemy, which were only circumvented by the diplomacy of the Prophet. When the besiegers had retired, Mohammad naturally demanded an explanation of the Jews. They resisted in their dogged way, and were themselves besieged and compelled to surrender at discretion. Mohammad, however, consented to the appointing of a chief of a tribe allied to the Jews as the judge who should pronounce sentence upon them. The man in question was a fierce soldier, who had been wounded in the attack on the Jews, and indeed died from his wound the same day. This chief gave sentence that the men, in number some six hundred, should be killed, and the women and children enslaved; and the sentence was carried out. It was a harsh, bloody sentence, worthy of the episcopal generals of the army against the Albigenses, or of the deeds of the Augustan age of Puritanism; but it must be remembered that the crime of these men was high treason against the State, during time of siege; and those who have read how Wellington's march could be traced by the bodies of deserters and pillagers hanging from the trees, need not be surprized at the summary execution of a traitorous clan.

Whilst Mohammad's supremacy was being established and maintained among the mixed population of Medīna, a vigorous warfare was being carried on outside with his old persecutors, the Kureysh. On the history of this war, consisting as it did mainly of small raids and attacks upon caravans, I need not dwell; its leading features were the two battles of Bedr and Ohud, in the first of which three hundred Muslims, though outnumbered at the odds of three to one, were completely victorious (A.D. 624, A.H. 2); whilst at Ohud, being outnumbered in the like proportion and deserted by the "Disaffected" party, they were almost as decisively defeated (A.H. 3). Two years later the Kureysh, gathering together their allies, advanced upon Medīna and besieged it for fifteen days; but the foresight of Mohammad in digging a trench, and the enthusiasm of the Muslims in defending it, resisted all assaults, and the coming of the heavy storms for which the climate of Medīna is noted drove the enemy back to Mekka. The next year (A.H. 6) a ten years' truce was concluded with the Kureysh, in pursuance of which a strange scene took place in the following spring. It was agreed that Mohammad and his people should perform the Lesser Pilgrimage, and that the Kureysh should for that purpose vacate Mekka for three days. Accordingly, in March 629, about two thousand Muslims, with Mohammad at their head on his famous camel El-Kaswā—the same on which he had fled from Mekka —trooped down the valley and performed the rites which every Muslim to this day observes.

"It was surely a strange sight which at this time presented itself in the vale of Mekka,—a sight unique in the history of the world. The ancient city is for three days evacuated by all its inhabitants, high and low, every house deserted; and, as they retire, the exiled converts, many years banished from their birth-place, approach in a great body, accompanied by their allies, revisit the empty homes of their childhood, and within the short allotted space fulfil the rites of pilgrimage. The ousted inhabitants, climbing the heights around, take refuge under tents or other shelter among the hills and glens; and, clustering on the overhanging peak of Abū-Kubeys, thence watch the movements of the visitors beneath, as with the Prophet at their head they make the circuit of the Kaaba and the rapid procession between Es-Safā and Marwa; and anxiously scan every figure if per-chance they may recognise among the worshippers some long-lost friend or relative. It was a scene rendered possible only by the throes which gave birth to Islām." *

When the three days were over, Mohammad and his party peaceably returned to Medīna; and the Mekkans re-entered their homes. But this pilgrimage, and the self-restraint of the Muslims therein, advanced the cause of Islām among its enemies. Converts increased daily, and some leading men of the Kureysh now went over to Mohammad. The clans around were sending in their deputations of homage. But the final keystone was set in the eighth year of the Flight (A.D. 630), when a body of Kureysh broke the

---

* Sir W. Muir, "Life of Mahomet," (one vol. ed.) 402.

truce by attacking an ally of the Muslims; and Mohammad forthwith marched upon Mekka with ten thousand men, and the city, despairing of defence, surrendered. Now was the time for the Prophet to show his bloodthirsty nature. His old persecutors are at his feet. Will he not trample on them, torture them, revenge himself after his own cruel manner? Now the man will come forward in his true colours: we may prepare our horror, and cry shame beforehand.

But what is this? Is there no blood in the streets? Where are the bodies of the thousands that have been butchered? Facts are hard things; and it is a fact that the day of Mohammad's greatest triumph over his enemies was also the day of his grandest victory over himself. He freely forgave the Kureysh all the years of sorrow and cruel scorn they had inflicted on him: he gave an amnesty to the whole population of Mekka. Four criminals, whom justice condemned, made up Mohammad's proscription list when he entered as a conqueror the city of his bitterest enemies. The army followed his example, and entered quietly and peaceably; no house was robbed, no woman insulted. One thing alone suffered destruction. Going to the Kaaba, Mohammad stood before each of the three hundred and sixty idols and pointed to it with his staff, saying, "Truth is come and falsehood is fled away," and at these words his attendants hewed it down; and all the idols and household gods of Mekka and round about were destroyed.

It was thus that Mohammad entered again his native city. Through all the annals of conquest, there is no triumphal entry like this.

The taking of Mekka was soon followed by the adhesion of all Arabia. Every reader knows the story of the spread of Islām. The tribes of every part of the peninsula sent embassies to do homage to the Prophet. Arabia was not enough: the Prophet had written in his bold uncompromising way to the great Kings of the East, to the Persian Khusrū, and the Greek Emperor; and these little knew how soon his invitation to the faith would be repeated, and how quickly Islām would be knocking at their doors with no faltering hand.

The Prophet's career was near its end. In the tenth year of the Flight, twenty years after he had first felt the Spirit move him to preach to his people, he resolved once more to leave his adopted city and go to Mekka to perform a farewell pilgrimage. And when the rites were done in the valley of Minā, the Prophet spoke unto the multitude—the forty thousand pilgrims—with solemn last words.*

"Ye People! Hearken to my words; for I know not whether after this year I shall ever be amongst you here again.

"Your Lives and your Property are sacred and inviolable amongst one another until the end of time.

"The Lord hath ordained to every man the share

---

* The following is an abridgment: cp. Muir 485, and the "Sīret-er-Rasūl," tr. Weil, ii. 316, 317.

of his inheritance : a Testament is not lawful to the prejudice of heirs.

"The child belongeth to the Parent : and the violator of Wedlock shall be stoned.

"Ye people! Ye have rights demandable of your Wives, and they have rights demandable of you. Treat your women well.

"And your Slaves, see that you feed them with such food as ye eat yourselves, and clothe them with the stuff ye wear. And if they commit a fault which ye are not willing to forgive, then sell them, for they are the servants of the Lord, and are not to be tormented.

"Ye people! Hearken unto my speech and comprehend it. Know that every Muslim is the brother of every other Muslim. All of you are on the same equality : ye are one Brotherhood."

Then, looking up to heaven, he cried, "O Lord! I have delivered my message and fulfilled my mission." And all the multitude answered, "Yea, verily hast thou!"—"O Lord! I beseech Thee, bear Thou witness to it!" and, like Moses, he lifted up his hands and blessed the people.

Three months more and Mohammad was dead.

A.H. 11. June 632.

It is a hard thing to form a calm estimate of the Dreamer of the Desert. There is something so tender and womanly, and withal so heroic, about the man, that one is in peril of finding the judgment unconsciously blinded by the feeling of reverence and well-nigh love that such a nature inspires. He who, standing alone, braved for years the hatred of his people, is the same who was never the first to withdraw his hand from another's clasp, the beloved of children, who never passed a group of little ones without a smile from his wonderful eyes and a kind word for them, sounding all the kinder in that sweet-toned voice. The frank friendship, the noble generosity, the dauntless courage and hope of the man, all tend to melt criticism in admiration.

In telling in brief outline the story of Mohammad's life, I have endeavoured to avoid controversial points. I have tried to convey in the simplest manner the view of that life which a study of the authorities must force upon every unbiassed mind. Many of the events of Mohammad's life have been distorted and credited with ignoble motives by European biographers; but on the facts they mainly agree, and these I have narrated, without encumbering them with the ingenious adumbrations of their learned recorders. But there are some things in the Prophet's life which have given rise to charges too weighty to be dismissed without discussion. He has been accused of cruelty, sensuality, and insincerity; he has been called a bloodthirsty tyrant, a voluptuary, and an impostor.

The charge of cruelty scarcely deserves consideration. I have already spoken of the punishment of the Jews, which forms the ground of the accusation. One has but to refer to Mohammad's conduct to the prisoners after the battle of Bedr, to his patient tolerance towards his enemies at Medīna, his gentleness to his people, his love of children and the dumb

creation, and above all, his bloodless entry into
Mekka, and the complete amnesty he gave to those
who had been his bitter enemies during eighteen years
of insult and persecution and finally open war, to
show that cruelty was no part of Mohammad's
nature.

To say that Mohammad, or any other Arab, was
sensual in a higher degree than an ordinary European
is simply to enounce a well-worn axiom : the passions
of the men of the sunland are not as those of the chill
north. But to say that Mohammad was a voluptuary
is false. The simple austerity of his daily life, to the
very last, his hard mat for sleeping on, his plain food,
his self-imposed menial work, point him out as an
ascetic rather than a voluptuary in most senses of the
word. Two things he loved, perfume and women ;
the first was harmless enough, and the special case of
his wives has its special answer. A great deal too
much has been said about these wives. It is a melancholy spectacle to see professedly Christian biographers gloating over the stories and fables of Mohammad's domestic relations like the writers and readers
of " society " journals. It is, of course, a fact that
whilst the Prophet allowed his followers only four
wives he took more than a dozen himself ; but be it
remembered that, with his unlimited power, he need
not have restricted himself to a number insignificant
compared with the harīms of some of his successors,
that he never divorced one of his wives, that all of
them save one were widows, and that one of these
widows was endowed with so terrific a temper

that Abū-Bekr and 'Othmān had already politely declined the honour of her alliance before the Prophet married her.   Several of these marriages must have been entered into from the feeling that those women whose husbands had fallen in battle for the faith, and who had thus been left unprotected, had a claim upon the generosity of him who prompted the fight.   Other marriages were contracted from motives of policy, in order to conciliate the heads of rival factions.   It was not a high motive, but one does not look for very romantic ideas about love-matches from a man who regarded women as " crooked ribs," and whose system certainly does its best to make marriage from love impossible ; yet, on the other hand, it was not a sensual motive.   Perhaps the strongest reason —one of which it is impossible to over-estimate the force—that impelled Mohammad to take wife after wife was his desire for male offspring.   It was a natural wish that he should have a son who should follow in his steps and carry on his work ; but the wish was never gratified, Mohammad's sons died young.

After all, the overwhelming argument is his fidelity to his first wife.   When he was little more than a boy he married Khadīja, who was fifteen years older than himself, with all the added age that women gain so quickly in the East.   For five-and-twenty years Mohammad remained faithful to his elderly wife, and when she was sixty-five, and they might have celebrated their " silver wedding," he was as devoted to her as when first he married her.   During all those years there was never a breath of scandal.   Thus far

Mohammad's life will bear microscopic scrutiny. Then Khadīja died; and though he married many women afterwards, some of them rich in youth and beauty, he never forgot his old wife, and loved her best to the end: "when I was poor she enriched me, when they called me a liar she alone believed in me, when all the world was against me she alone remained true." This loving, tender memory of an old wife laid in the grave belongs only to a noble nature; it is not to be looked for in a voluptuary.*

When, however, all has been said, when it has been

---

* An attempt has been made to explain away Mohammad's fidelity to Khadīja, by adducing the motive of pecuniary prudence. Mohammad, they say, was a poor man, Khadīja rich and powerfully connected; any *affaire de cœur* on the husband's part would have been followed by a divorce and the simultaneous loss of property and position. It is hardly necessary to point out that the fear of poverty—a matter of little consequence in Arabia and at that time—would not restrain a really sensual man for five-and-twenty years; especially when it is by no means certain that Khadīja, who loved him with all her heart in a motherly sort of way, would have sought a divorce for any cause soever. And this explanation leaves Mohammad's loving remembrance of his old wife unaccounted for. If her money alone had curbed him for twenty-five years, one would expect him at her death to throw off the cloak, thank Heaven for the deliverance, and enter at once upon the rake's progress. He does none of those things. The story of Zeyneb, the divorced wife of Zeyd, is a favourite weapon with Mohammad's accusers. It is not one to enter upon here; but I may say that the lady's own share in the transaction has never been sufficiently considered. In all probability Zeyd, the freed slave, was glad enough to get rid of his too well-born wife, and certainly he bore no rancour against Mohammad. The real point of the story is the question of forged revelations, which is discussed below.

shown that Mohammad was not the rapacious voluptuary some have taken him for, and that his violation of his own marriage-law may be due to motives reasonable and just from his point of view rather than to common sensuality, there remains the fact that some of the sūras of the Korān bear unmistakable marks of self-accommodation and personal convenience; that Mohammad justified his domestic excesses by words which he gave as from God. And hence the third and gravest charge, the charge of imposture. We must clearly understand what is meant by this accusation. It is meant that the Prophet *consciously* fabricated speeches, and palmed them off upon the people as the very word of God. The question, it will at once be perceived, has nothing whatever to do with the truth or untruth of the revelations. Many an earnest enthusiast has uttered prophecies and exhortations which he firmly believed to be the promptings of the Spirit, and no man can charge such with imposture. He thoroughly believes what he says, and the fault is in the judgment, not the conscience. The question is clearly narrowed to this: Did Mohammad believe he was speaking the words of God equally when he declared that permission was given him to take more wives, as when he proclaimed, "There is no god but God"? It is a question that concerns the conscience of man; and each must answer it for himself. How far a man may be deluded into believing everything he says is inspired it is impossible to define. There are men to-day who would seem to claim infallibility;

and in Mohammad's time it was much easier to believe in one's self. Now, one never lacks a friend to remind him of his weakness; then, there were hundreds who would fain have made the man think himself God. It is wonderful, with his temptations, how great a humility was ever his, how little he assumed of all the god-like attributes men forced upon him. His whole life is one long argument for his loyalty to truth. He had but one answer for his worshippers, "I am no more than a man, I am only human." "Do none enter Paradise save by the mercy of God?" asked Āisha. "None, none, none," he answered. "Not even thou by thy own merits?" "Neither shall I enter Paradise unless God cover me with His mercy." He was a man like unto his brethren in all things save one, and that one difference served only to increase his humbleness, and render him the more sensitive to his shortcomings. He was sub-limely confident of this single attribute, that he was the messenger of the Lord of the Worlds, and that the words he spake came verily from Him. He was fully persuaded—and no man dare dispute his right to the belief—that God had sent him to do a great work among his people in Arabia. Nervous to the verge of madness, subject to hysteria, given to wild dreamings in solitary places, his was a temperament that easily lends itself to religious enthusiasm. He felt a subtle influence within him which he believed to be the movings of the Spirit: he thought he heard a voice; it became real and audible to him, awed and terrified him, so that he fell into frantic fits. Then he would arise and utter some noble saying; and what wonder if he thought it came straight from highest heaven? It was not without a sore struggle that he convinced himself of his own inspiration; but once admitted, the conviction grew with his years and his widening influence for good, and nothing then could shake his belief that he was the literal mouth-piece of the All-Merciful. When a man has come to this point, he cannot be expected to discriminate between this saying and that. As the instrument of God he has lost his individuality; he believes God is ever speaking through his lips; he dare not question the inspiration of the speech lest he should seem to doubt the Giver.

Yet there must surely be a limit to this delusion. There are some passages in the Korān which it is difficult to think Mohammad truly believed to be the voice of the Lord of the Worlds. Mohammad's was a sensitive conscience in the early years of his teaching, and it is hard to think that it could have been so obscured in later times that he could really believe in the inspired source of some of his revelations. He may have thought the commands they conveyed necessary, but he could hardly have deemed them divine. In some cases he could scarcely fail to be aware that the object of the " revelation " was his own comfort .or pleasure or reputation, and not the *major Dei gloria*, nor the good of the people.

The truth would seem to be that in the latter part of his life Mohammad was forced to enlarge the limits of his revelations as the sphere of his influence increased. From a private citizen of Mekka he had become the Emīr, the chief of the Arabs, the ruler of a factious, jealous, turbulent people; and the change must have had its effect upon his character. The man who from addressing a few devout followers in a tent in the desert finds himself the head of a nation of many tribes, king of a country twice the size of France, will find many things difficult that before seemed easy. As a statesman Mohammad was as great as he was as a preacher of righteousness; but when his field of work enlarged, his mind had to accommodate itself to the needs of commoner minds. He learnt to see the expedient where before he knew only the right. His revelations now deal with the things of earth, when before they looked only towards the things of heaven; and petty social rules, "general orders," selfish permissions, are promulgated with the same authority and as from the same divine source as the command to worship one God alone. He governed the nation as a prophet and not as a king, and as a prophet his ordinances must be endorsed with the divine afflatus. He found he must regulate the meanest details of the people's life, and he believed he could only do this by using God's name for his decrees. He doubtless argued himself into the belief that even these petty, and to us sometimes immoral, regulations, being for the good of the people, as he conceived the good, were really God's ordinances; but even thus he had lowered the standard of his teaching, and alloyed with base metal the pure gold of his early ideal. It was a temptation that few men have withstood, but it was, nevertheless, a falling-off from the

Mohammad we loved at Mekka, the simple truth-loving bearer of good tidings to the Arabs.

Yet behind this engrafted character, formed by the difficulties of his position, by the invincible jealousy and treachery of the tribes he governed, the old nature still lived, and ever and anon broke forth in fervid words of faith and hope in the cause and the promises that had been the light and support of his early years of trial. In the later chapters of the Korān, among complicated directions for the Muslim's guidance in all the circumstances of life, we suddenly hear an echo of the old fiery eloquence and the expression of the strong faith which never deserted him.

Surely the character of Mohammad has been misjudged. He was not the ambitious schemer some would have him, still less the hypocrite and sham prophet others have imagined. He was an enthusiast in that noblest sense when enthusiasm becomes the salt of the earth, the one thing that keeps men from rotting whilst they live. Enthusiasm is often used despitefully, because it is joined to an unworthy cause, or falls upon barren ground and bears no fruit. So was it not with Mohammad. He was an enthusiast when enthusiasm was the one thing needed to set the world aflame, and his enthusiasm was noble for a noble cause. He was one of those happy few who have attained the supreme joy of making one great truth their very life-spring. He was the messenger of the One God, and never to his life's end did he forget who he was, or the message which was the marrow of his being. He brought his tidings to his people with a grand dignity, sprung from the consciousness of his high office, together with a most sweet humility, whose roots lay in the knowledge of his own weakness. Well did Carlyle choose him for his prophet-hero! There have been purer lives and higher aspirations than Mohammad's; but no man was ever more thoroughly filled with the sense of his mission or carried out that mission more heroically.

CHAPTER III.

ISLAM.

WHEN it was noised abroad that the Prophet was dead, 'Omar, the fiery-hearted, the Simon Peter of Islām, rushed among the people, and fiercely told them they lied, it could not be true, Mohammad was not dead. And Abū-Bekr came and said, " Ye people ! he that hath worshipped Mohammad, let him know that Mohammad is dead; but he that hath worshipped God,—that the Lord liveth, and doth not die."

Many have sought to answer the questions—Why was the triumph of Islām so speedy and so complete ? Why have so many millions embraced the religion of Mohammad, and scarcely a hundred ever recanted ? Why do a thousand Christians became Muslims to one Muslim who adopts Christianity ? Why do a hundred and fifty millions of human beings still cling to the faith of Islām ? Some have attempted to explain the first overwhelming success of the Mohammadan religion by the argument of the sword. They forget Carlyle's laconic reply, " First get your sword." You must win men's hearts before you can induce them to peril their lives for you, and the first conquerors of Islām must have been made Muslims before they were made " fighters on the path of God."   Others allege the low morality of the religion and the sensual paradise it promises as a sufficient cause for the zeal of its followers; but even were these admitted to the full, to say that such reasons could win the hearts of millions of men, who have the same hopes and longings after the right and the noble as we, is to libel mankind.   No religion has ever gained a lasting hold upon the souls of men by the force of its sensual permissions and fleshly promises.   It is urged, again, that Islām met no fair foe, that the worn-out forms of Christianity and Judaism it encountered were no test of its power as a quickening faith, and that it prevailed simply because there was nothing to prevent it ; and this was undoubtedly a help to the progress of the new creed, but could not have been the cause of its victory.

In all these reasons the religion itself is left out of the question.   Decidedly Islām itself was the main cause of its triumph.   By some strange intuition Mohammad succeeded in finding the one form of monotheism that has ever commended itself to any wide section of the Eastern world.   It was only a remnant of the Jews that learned to worship the one God of the prophets after the hard lessons of the Captivity. Christianity has never gained a firm hold upon the East.   Islām not only was at once accepted (partly in earnest, partly in name, but accepted) by Arabia, Syria, Persia, Egypt, Northern Africa, and Spain at its first outburst, but, with the exception of Spain, it has never lost its vantage-ground ; it has seen no country that has once embraced its doctrine turn to another faith; it has added great multitudes in India and China and Turkestan to its subjects ; and in quite recent times it has been spreading in wide and swiftly-following waves over Africa, and has left but a small part of that vast continent unconverted to its creed. Admitting the mixed causes that contributed to the rapidity of the first torrent of Mohammadan conquest, they do not account for the duration of Islām. There must be something in the religion itself to explain its persistence and increase, and to account for its present hold over so large a proportion of the dwellers on the earth.

Men trained in European ideas of religion have always found a difficulty in understanding the fascination which the Muslim faith has for so many minds in the East. " There is no god but God, and Mohammad is His Prophet." There is nothing in this, they say, to move the heart. Yet this creed has stirred an enthusiasm that has never been surpassed. Islām has had its martyrs, its self-tormentors, its recluses, who have renounced all that life offered and have accepted death with a smile for the sake of the faith that was in them. It is idle to say that the eternity of happiness will explain this. The truest martyrs of Islām, as of Christianity, did not die to gain paradise. And if they did, the belief in the promises of the creed must follow the hearty acceptance of the religion. Islām must have possessed a power of seizing men's belief before it could have inspired them with such a love of its paradise.

Mohammad's conception of God has, I think, been misunderstood, and its effect upon the people consequently under-estimated. The God of Islām is commonly represented as a pitiless tyrant, who plays with humanity as on a chessboard, and works out his game without regard to the sacrifice of the pieces ; and there is a certain truth in the figure. There is more in Islām of the potter who shapes the clay than of the father pitying his children. Mohammad conceived of God as the Semitic mind has always preferred to think of Him : his God is the All-Mighty, the All-Knowing, the All-Just. Irresistible Power is the first attribute he thinks of : the Lord of the Worlds, the Author of the Heavens and the Earth, who hath created Life and Death, in whose hand is Dominion, who maketh the Dawn to appear and causeth the Night to cover the Day, the Great, All-Powerful Lord of the glorious Throne; the Thunder proclaimeth His perfection, the whole earth is His handful, and the Heavens shall be folded together in His right hand. And with the Power He conceives the Knowledge that directs it to right ends. God is the Wise, the Just, the True, the Swift in Reckoning, who knoweth every ant's weight of good and of ill that each man hath done, and who suffereth not the reward of the faithful to perish.

God! There is no God but He, the Living, the Steadfast! Slumber seizeth Him not, nor sleep. Whatsoever is in the Heavens, and whatsoever is in the Earth, is His. Who is there that shall plead with Him, save by His leave? He knoweth what was before and what shall come after, and they compass not aught of His knowledge, but what He willeth. His Throne overspreadeth the Heavens and the Earth, and the keeping of both is no burden to Him: and He is the High, the Great.—Korān, ii. 256.

But with this power there is also the gentleness that belongs only to great strength. God is the Guardian over His servants, the Shelterer of the orphan, the Guider of the erring, the Deliverer from every affliction ; in His hand is Good, and He is the Generous Lord, the Gracious, the Hearer, the Near-at-Hand. Each sūra of the Korān begins with the words, " In the name of God, the Compassionate, the Merciful," and Mohammad was never tired of telling the people how God was Very-Forgiving, that his love for man was more tender than the mother-bird's for her young.

It is too often forgotten how much there is in the Korān of the loving-kindness of God, but it must be allowed that this is not the main thought in Mohammad's teaching. The doctrine of the Might of God most held his imagination, and impressed itself most strongly upon Muslims of all ages. The fear rather than the love of God is the spur of Islām. There can be no question which is the higher incentive to good ; but it is nearly certain that the love of God is an idea foreign to most of the races that have accepted Islām, and to preach such a doctrine would have been to mistake the character of the Semitic mind.

The leading doctrine of Mohammad, then, is the

belief in One All-Powerful God. Islām is the "self-surrender" of every man to the will of God. Its danger lies in the stress laid on the power of God, which has brought about the stifling effects of fatalism. Mohammad taught the foreknowledge of God, but he did not lay down precisely the doctrine of Predestination. He found it, as all have found it, a stumbling-block in the way of man's progress. It perplexed him, and he spoke of it, but often contradicted himself; and he would become angry if the subject were mooted in his presence: "Sit not with a disputer about fate," he said, "nor begin a conversation with him." Mohammad vaguely recognised that little margin of Free Will which makes life not wholly mechanical.

This doctrine of one Supreme God, to whose will it is the duty of every man to surrender himself, is the kernel of Islām, the truth for which· Mohammad lived and suffered and triumphed. But it was no new teaching, as he himself was constantly saying. His was only the last of revelations. Many prophets—Abraham, Moses, and Christ—had taught the same faith before; but people had hearkened little to their words. So Mohammad was sent, not different from them, a simple messenger, yet the last and greatest of them, the "seal of prophecy," the "most excellent of the creation of God." This is the second dogma of Islām: "Mohammad is the apostle of God." It is well worthy of notice that it is not said, "Mohammad is the only apostle of God." Islām is more tolerant in this matter than other religions. Its prophet is not the sole commissioner of the Most High, nor is his teaching the only true teaching the world has ever received. Many other messengers had been sent by God to guide men to the right, and these taught the same religion that was in the mouth of the preacher of Islām. Hence Muslims reverence Moses and Christ only next to Mohammad. All they claim for their founder is that he was the last and best of the messengers of the one God.*

After the belief in God and His prophets and scriptures, the Muslim must believe in angels, good and evil genii, in the resurrection and the judgment, and in future rewards and punishments. These doctrines form a very common weapon of attack on the ground of their superstition, their anthropomorphism, and their sensuality. Yet similar minor beliefs have their place in all religions, and they are conceived in scarcely more absurdly realistic a manner in Islām than in any other creed. Every religion seems to need an improbable, almost a ludicrous, side, in order to provide material for the faith of the foolish. Mohammad himself was what is called a superstitious man, and the improbable side thus found its way easily into his creed. With all the fancies floating in Arabia in his time, it would have been strange if he had introduced nothing of

---

* "The Prophet said: Whosoever shall bear witness that there is one God; and that Mohammad is His servant and messenger; and that Jesus Christ is His servant and messenger, and that he is the son of the handmaid of God, and that he is the Word of God, the word which was sent to Mary, and Spirit from God; and [shall bear witness] that there is truth in Heaven and Hell, will enter into paradise, whatever sins he may be chargeable with."— "Mishkāt-el-Masābīh," i. 11.

the superstitious into Islām. The Jinn, the Afrīts, and the other beings of the air and water, have not done much harm to the Mohammadan mind; and they have given so many a delightful fable to the West, that we must feel a certain grateful respect for them. The realistic pictures of paradise and hell have exercised an influence more serious. The minute details of these celestial and infernal pictures must move alternately the disgust and the contemptuous amusement of a Western reader; yet these same things were very real facts to Mohammad, and have been of the utmost importance to generation after generation of Muslims. In the present day there are cultured men who receive these descriptions in the same allegorical sense as some Christians accept the Revelation of S. John—which, indeed, in some respects offers a close parallel to the pictorial parts of the Korān; but the vast majority of believers (like many Christians in the parallel case) take the descriptions literally, and there can be no doubt that the belief founded on such pictures, accepted literally, must work an evil effect on the professors of the faith of which these doctrines form a minor, but a too prominent, part; and it is the aim of rational Muslims to sweep away such cobwebs from their sky.

Islām lies more in doing than in believing. That "faith without works is dead" is a doctrine which every day's routine must bring home to the mind of the devout Muslim. The practical duties of the Mohammadan religion, beyond the actual profession of faith, are the performance of prayer, giving alms, keeping the fast, and accomplishing the pilgrimage. Mr. Lane has so minutely described the regular prayers used over all the Mohammadan East, that it is only necessary here to refer to his account of them in the " Modern Egyptians." There it will be seen that they form no light part of the religious duties of the Muslim, especially since they involve careful preparatory ablutions; for Mohammad impressed upon his followers the salutary doctrine that cleanliness is an essential part of godliness, and the scrupulous cleanliness of the Mohammadan, which contrasts so favourably with the unsavoury state of Easterns of other creeds, is an excellent feature in the practical influence of Islām. The charge which missionaries and the like are fond of bringing against the Muslim prayers, that they are merely lifeless forms and vain repetitions, is an exaggeration. There is a vast deal of repetition in the Mohammadan ritual, just as the paternoster is repeated again and again in the principal Christian liturgies; but iteration does not necessarily kill devotion. There is plenty of real fervour in the prayers of the Mosque, and they are joined-in by the worshippers with an earnest attention which shames the listless sleepy bearing of most congregations in England. It is true the greater part of the prayers are laid down in prescribed forms; but there is an interval set apart for private supplication, and the original congregations in the mosques availed themselves of this permission more generally than is now the case, when the old fervour has become comparatively cool. Mohammad frequently enjoins

private prayer at home, and specially praises him who
" passes his night worshipping God."

Almsgiving was originally compulsory, and the tax
was collected by the officers of the Khalif; but now
the Muslim is merely expected to give voluntarily
about a fortieth part of his income in charity each
year. The great fast of Ramadān is too well known
to need more than a passing mention here; but it is
not so well known that Mohammad, ascetic as he was
himself in this as in many other matters, whilst he
ordained the month of fasting for the chastening of
his able-bodied followers, was a determined enemy to
useless mortification of the flesh, and boldly affirmed
that God took no pleasure in a man's wantonly injur-
ing himself; hence if one that was weakly and sick
could not keep the fast without bodily detriment he
was to omit it. And the same wise leniency was
shown by the Arab prophet in respect of prayer,—
which may be curtailed or omitted in certain cases,—
and with regard to the pilgrimage, which no one was
to perform to his hurt. This same pilgrimage is
often urged as a sign of Mohammad's tendency to
superstition and even idolatry. It is asked how the
destroyer of idols could have reconciled his conscience
to the circuits of the Kaaba and the veneration of
the black stone covered with adoring kisses. The
rites of the pilgrimage cannot certainly be defended
against the charge of superstition; but it is easy to
see why Mohammad enjoined them. They were
hallowed to him by the memories of his ancestors,
who had been the guardians of the sacred temple,

and by the traditional reverence of all his people; and besides this tie of association, which in itself was enough to make it impossible for him to do away with the rites, Mohammad perceived that the worship in the Kaaba would prove of real value to his religion. He swept away the more idolatrous and immoral part of the ceremonies, but he retained the pilgrimage to Mekka and the old veneration of the temple for reasons of which it is impossible to dispute the wisdom. He well knew the consolidating effect of a centre to which his followers could gather; and hence he reasserted the sanctity of the black stone that "came down from Heaven"; he ordained that everywhere throughout the world, the Muslim should pray looking towards the Kaaba, and he enjoined him to make the pilgrimage thither. Mekka is to the Muslim what Jerusalem is to the Jew. It bears with it all the influence of centuries of associations. It carries the Muslim back to the cradle of his faith, the childhood of his prophet; it reminds him of the struggle between the old faith and the new, of the overthrow of the idols, and the establishment of the worship of the One God. And, most of all, it bids him remember that all his brother Muslims are worshipping towards the same sacred spot; that he is one of a great company of believers, united by one faith, filled with the same hopes, reverencing the same things, worshipping the same God. Mohammad showed his knowledge of the religious emotions in man when he preserved the sanctity of the temple of Mekka.

It would take too much space to look closely into the lesser duties of Islām, many of which suggest exceedingly wholesome lessons to Western civilisation. But we must not pass over one of these minor duties, for it reflects the highest credit upon the founder and the professors of Mohammadanism—I mean the humane treatment of animals.

"There is no religion which has taken a higher view in its authoritative documents of animal life, and none wherein the precept has been so much honoured by its practical observance. 'There is no beast on earth,' says the Korān, 'nor bird which flieth with its wings, but the same is a people like unto you—unto the Lord shall they return'; and it is the current belief that animals will share with men the general resurrection, and be judged according to their works. At the slaughter of an animal, the Prophet ordered that the name of God should always be named; but the words, 'the Compassionate, the Merciful,' were to be omitted; for, on the one hand, such an expression seemed a mockery to the sufferer, and, on the other, he could not bring himself to believe that the destruction of any life, however necessary, could be altogether pleasing to the All-Merciful. 'In the Name of God,' says a pious Musalman before he strikes the fatal blow; 'God is most great; God give thee patience to endure the affliction which He hath allotted thee!' In the East there has been no moralist like Bentham to insist in noble words on the extension of the sphere of morality to all sentient beings, and to be ridiculed for it by people who call themselves religious; there has been no naturalist like Darwin, to demonstrate by his marvellous powers of observation how large a part of the mental and moral faculties which we usually claim for ourselves alone we share with other beings; there has been no Oriental 'Society for the Prevention of Cruelty to Animals.' But one reason of this is not far to seek. What the legislation of the last few years has at length attempted to do, and, from the mere fact that it is legislation, must do ineffectually, has been long effected in the East by the moral and religious sentiment which, like almost everything that is good in that part of the world, can be traced back, in part at least, to the great Prophet of Arabia. In the East, so far as it has not been hardened by the West, there is a real sympathy between man and the domestic animals; they understand one another; and the cruelties which the most humane of our countrymen unconsciously effect in the habitual use, for instance, of the muzzle or the bearing-rein on the most docile, the most patient, the most faithful, and the most intelligent of their companions, are impossible in the East. An Arab *cannot* ill-treat his horse; and Mr. Lane bears emphatic testimony to the fact that in his long residence in Egypt he never saw an ass or a dog (though the latter is there looked upon as an unclean animal) treated with cruelty, except in those cities which were overrun by Europeans." *

* R. Bosworth Smith: "Mohammed and Mohammedanism," 2nd ed., 255-257.

There are some very beautiful traditions of the Prophet, showing the tenderness with which he always treated animals and which he ever enjoined on his people. A man once came to him with a carpet and said, "O Prophet, I passed through a wood and heard the voices of the young of birds, and I took and put them into my carpet, and their mother came fluttering round my head." And the Prophet said, " Put them down "; and when he had put them down the mother joined the young. And the Prophet said, " Do you wonder at the affection of the mother towards her young? I swear by Him who has sent me, Verily God is more loving to his servants than the mother to these young birds. Return them to the place from which ye took them, and let their mother be with them." "Fear God with regard to animals," said Mohammad ; " ride them when they are fit to be ridden, and get off when they are tired. Verily there are rewards for our doing good to dumb animals, and giving them water to drink."

Such, in brief outline, is the religion of Mohammad. It is a form of pure theism, simpler and more austere than the theism of most forms of modern Christianity, lofty in its conception of the relation of man to God, and noble in its doctrine of the duty of man to man, and of man to the lower creation. There is little in it of superstition, less of complexity of dogmas ; it is an exacting religion, without the repulsiveness of asceticism ; severe, but not merciless. On the other hand, it is over-rigid and formal ; it leaves too little to the believer and too much to his ritual ; it places a prophet and a book between man and God, and practically discourages the desire for a direct relation between the Deity and his servant; it draws the picture of that God in over-harsh outlines, and leaves out too much of the tenderness and loving-kindness of the God of Christ's teaching, and hence it has been the source of more intolerance and fanatical hatred than most creeds.

This religion is Islām as understood and taught by its Prophet, so far as we can gather it from the Korān, aided by those traditions which seem to have the stamp of authenticity. It need hardly be said that it is not identical with the Islām with which the philosophers of Baghdād amused themselves, nor with the fantastic creed which the Fātimī Khalifs of Egypt represented, and brought in the person of El-Hākim to its limit of extravagance ; nor is it the Islām with which as much as with their ferocity the Karmatīs aroused the fear and abhorrence of all good Muslims. Neither the Sūfism of Persia nor the sensational religion of the dervīshes of Turkey conforms to this ancient Islām, to which perhaps a modification of Wahhāby puritanism would be the nearest approach. The original faith of Mohammad has not gained by its development in foreign lands and alien minds, and perhaps the best we can hope for modern Islām is that it may try the experiment of retrogression, and seek to regain the simplicity of the old form without losing the advantages (if there be any) which it has acquired from contact with Western civilisation.

Islâm is unfortunately a social system as well as a religion; and herein lies the great difficulty of fairly estimating its good and its bad influence on the world. It is but in the nature of things that the teacher who lays down the law of the relation of man to God should also endeavour to appoint the proper relation between man and his neighbour. Christianity was undoubtedly a social even more than a religious reform, but the social regulations were too indefinite, or at all events too impracticable, for any wide acceptance among the professors of the religion. Islâm was less fortunate. Mohammad not only promulgated a religion; he laid down the elements of a social system, containing minute regulations for a man's conduct in various circumstances of life, with due rewards or penalties according to his fulfilment of these rules. As a religion Islâm is great; it has taught men to worship one God with a pure worship who formerly worshipped many gods impurely. As a social system Islâm is a complete failure : it has misunderstood the relation of the sexes, upon which the whole character of a nation's life hangs, and, by degrading women, has degraded each successive generation of their children down an increasing scale of infamy and corruption, until it seems almost impossible to reach a lower level of vice.

The fatal spot in Islâm is the degradation of women. The true test of a nation's place in the ranks of civilisation is the position of its women. When they are held in reverence, when it is considered the most infamous of crimes to subject a woman to dishonour, and the highest distinction to protect her from wrong; when the family life is real and strong, of which the mother-wife is the heart; when each man's pulse beats loyal to womanhood, then is a nation great. When women are treated as playthings, toys, drudges, worth anything only if they have beauty to be enjoyed or strength to labour; when sex is considered the chief thing in a woman, and heart and mind are forgotten; when a man buys women for his pleasure and dismisses them when his appetite is glutted, then is a nation despicable.

And so is it in the East. Yet it would be hard to lay the blame altogether on Mohammad. The real roots of the degradation of women lie much deeper. When Islám was instituted, polygamy was almost necessitated by the number of women and their need of support; and facility of divorce was required by the separation of the sexes, and the consequence that a man could not know or even see the woman he was about to marry before the marriage ceremony was accomplished. It is not Mohammad whom we must blame for these great evils, polygamy and divorce; it is the state of society which demanded the separation of the sexes, and in which it was not safe to allow men and women freely to associate; in other words, it was the sensual constitution of the Arab that lay at the root of the matter. Mohammad might have done better. He might boldly have swept away the traditions of Arab town-life, unveiled the women, intermingled the sexes, and punished by the most severe measures any license which such association might at first encourage. With his boundless influence, it is possible that he might have done this, and, the new system once fairly settled and the people accustomed to it, the good effects of the change would show themselves. But such an idea could never have occurred to him. We must always remember that we are dealing with a social system of the seventh century, not of the nineteenth. Mohammad's ideas about women were like those of the rest of his contemporaries. He looked upon them as charming snares to the believer, ornamental articles of furniture difficult to keep in order, pretty playthings; but that a woman should be the counsellor and companion of a man does not seem to have occurred to him. It is to be wondered that the feeling of respect he always entertained for his first wife, Khadīja, (which, however, is partly accounted for by the fact that she was old enough to have been his mother,) found no counterpart in his general opinion of womankind: "Woman was made from a crooked rib, and if you try to bend it straight, it will break; therefore treat your wives kindly." Mohammad was not the man to make a social reform affecting women, nor was Arabia the country in which such a change should be made, nor Arab ladies perhaps the best subjects for the experiment. Still he did something towards bettering the condition of women: he limited the number of wives to four; laid his hand with the utmost severity on the incestuous marriages that were then rife in Arabia; compelled husbands to support their divorced wives during their four months of probation; made hasty divorce less common by adding the rough, but deterring, condition that a woman triply divorced could not return to her husband without first being married to some one else; and required four witnesses to prove a charge of adultery against a wife—a merciful provision, difficult of fulfilment.

The evil permitted by Mohammad in leaving the number of wives four instead of insisting on monogamy was not great. Without considering the sacrifice of family peace which the possession of a large harīm entails, the expense of keeping several wives, each of whom must have a separate suite of apartments or a separate house, is so great that not more than one in twenty can afford it. It is not so much in the matter of wives as in that of concubines that Mohammad made an irretrievable mistake. The condition of the female slave in the East is indeed deplorable. She is at the entire mercy of her master, who can do what he pleases with her and her numerous companions : for the Muslim is not restricted in the number of his concubines, as he is in that of his wives. The female white slave is kept solely for the master's sensual pleasure, and is sold when he is tired of her, and so she passes from master to master, a very wreck of womanhood. Her condition is a little improved if she bear a son to her tyrant; but even then he is at liberty to refuse to acknowledge the child as his own, though it must be owned he seldom does this. Kind as the Prophet was himself towards bondswomen, one cannot forget the unutterable brutalities which his followers inflicted upon conquered nations in the taking of slaves. The Muslim soldier was allowed to do as he pleased with any "infidel" woman he might meet on his victorious march. When one thinks of the thousands of women, mothers and daughters, who must have suffered untold shame and dishonour by this license, he cannot find words to express his horror. And this cruel indulgence has left its mark on the Muslim character, nay, on the whole character of Eastern life. Now, as at the first, young girls are dragged away from their homes and given over to the unhallowed lusts of a Turkish voluptuary; and not only to Turks, but to Englishmen; for the contagion has spread, and Englishmen, even those who by their sacred order should know better, instead of uttering their protest, as men of honour and Christians, against the degradation, have followed the example of the Turk, and helped in the ruin of women. Concubinage is the black stain in Islām. With Mohammad's views of women, we could hardly expect him to do better; but, on the other hand, he could scarcely have done worse. There are, however, one or two alleviating circumstances. One is the fact that the canker has not eaten into the whole of Eastern society; it is chiefly among the rich that the evil effects of the system are felt. And another fact which shows that the Mohammadan system, bad as it is, is free from a defect which social systems better in other respects than Mohammad's are subject to is the extreme rarity of prostitution in Muslim towns. The courtesan forms a very small item in the census of a Mohammadan city, and is retained more for strangers from Europe than for the Muslim inhabitants. Instances are frequently occurring in the Indian law courts which show the strong feeling that exists on the subject among the Mohammadans of India. They consider it quite inconceivable that a Muslim should have illicit intercourse with a free Muslima woman, and this inconceivableness of the action is urged as evidence in trials of the legitimacy of children. But whilst admitting the importance of this remarkable feature in Islām, it must not be forgotten that the liberty allowed by their law to Muslims in the matter of concubines does not very materially differ from prostitution, and whilst the latter is directly forbidden by the dominant religion of Europe, concubinage is as directly permitted by Islām.

One would think that long intercourse with Europeans might have somewhat raised the estimation of women in the East; but either because travellers in the East are not always the best specimens of Western morality, or because the Eastern mind has an unequalled aptitude for assimilating the bad and rejecting the good in any system it meets, it is certain that women are no better off now than they were, in the East. A well-known correspondent of a leading daily print writes thus of Turkish home-life:

It is obvious that the home-life of any people will depend almost entirely on the position which is assigned to women. It is not necessary to inquire what this position is according to the teaching of the sacred books of a race. Between Christianity and

Islām it is enough to notice that there is apparently no country where the first is the prevailing religion in which woman is hindered by religion from obtaining a position almost, if not quite, on an equality with man, and similarly, no country where the second prevails where woman is not in a degraded position. . . . Under Christianity she is everywhere free. Under Islām she is everywhere a slave. The pious Mohammadan, like the pious Jew, thanks God that he has not been made a woman. The pious Mohammadan woman, like the pious Jewess, thanks God that she has been made according to the Creator's will. Man and woman alike recognise that to be a woman is to be in an inferior condition. This feeling of the degradation of woman so pervades Turkey that the poorer classes of Christians have even become infected by it. When a son is born there is nothing but congratulations. When a daughter, nothing but condolences. A polite Turk, if he has occasion to mention his wife, will do so with an apology. He regards it as a piece of rudeness to mention the fact to you, and it would be equally rude for him to inquire after your wife, or to hint that he knew you were guilty of anything so unmentionable as to have one. Charles the Twelfth told his queen that she had been chosen to give children, and not advice. The Turk regards woman as destined solely for the same purpose and for his pleasure. Probably polygamy is of itself sufficient to account for the way in which Mohammadans regard woman. But whether this is so or not, there is one influence which polygamy asserts which accounts for the low ideal of woman prevalent in all Muslim countries. When a man has a number of wives it is impossible that they can all become his companions and his confidantes, or that one of them can become his companion or confidante to the same extent as if the man had only one wife. Hence a man who is limited to one will not be contented with beauty alone. He must have a certain amount of intelligence and education. The Turk, on the other hand, has no reason whatever to think of anything except beauty. As he never means to see much of his wife, intelligence or education is a matter of small account. If he can afford it he will have a Circassian wife, a woman who has been reared with the intention of being sold, who has not an idea in her head, who has seen nothing, and knows nothing. Such a woman would be as objectionable as a wife to the great majority of Europeans as a South Sea Island beauty. But she satisfies the ideal of the Turk. She is beautiful, and beauty is all that he requires.

It is this sensual and degraded view of woman that destroys to so great an extent the good influence which the better part of the teaching of Islām might exert in the East. So long as women are held in so light an esteem, they will remain vapid, bigoted, and sensual ; and so long as mothers are what most Muslim mothers are now, their children will be ignorant, fanatical, and vicious. In Turkey there are other influences at work besides the Mohammadan social system ; but Turkish women may serve as an instance of the state of things which that system encourages. "In those early years spent at home, when the child ought to have instilled into him some germ of those principles of conduct by which men must walk in the world if they are to hold up their heads among civilised nations, the Turkish child is only taught the first steps towards those vicious habits of mind and body which have made his race what it is. The root of the evil is partly found in the harīm system. So long as that system keeps Turkish women in their present depressed state, so long will Turkish boys and girls be vicious and ignorant." As I have said elsewhere,* " It is quite certain that there is no hope for the Turks so long as Turkish women remain what they are, and home-training is the initiation of vice." If the mother is ignorant and vicious, the son cannot form a high ideal of womanhood, and thus is

---

* "The People of Turkey," preface, xxii.

barred off from the chivalrous spirit wherewith alone a man may reach to the highest love :—that

> subtle master under heaven,
> Not only to keep down the base in man,
> But teach high thought, and amiable words,
> And courtliness, and the desire of fame,
> And love of truth, and all that makes a man.

The Muslim has no ideal of chivalry like this to make his life pure and honourable: his religion encourages an opposite view, and the women among whom he is brought up only confirm it.

If Islām is to be a power for good in the future, it is imperatively necessary to cut off the social system from the religion. At the beginning, among a people who had advanced but a little way on the road of civilisation, the defects of the social system were not so apparent ; but now, when Easterns are endeavouring to mix on equal terms with Europeans, and are trying to adopt the manners and customs of the West, it is clear that the condition of their women must be radically changed if any good is to come of the Europeanising tendency. The difficulty lies in the close connection between the religious and social ordinances in the Korān ; the two are so intermingled that it is hard to see how they can be disentangled without destroying both. The theory of revelation would have to be modified. Muslims would have to give up their doctrine of the syllabic inspiration of the Korān and exercise their moral sense in distinguishing between the particular and the general, the temporary and the permanent; they would have to recognise that there was much in Mohammad's teaching which, though useful at the time, is inapplicable to the present conditions of life ; that his knowledge was often partial, and his judgment sometimes at fault ; that the moral sense is capable of education as much as the intellect, and, therefore, that what was apparently moral and wise in the seventh century may quite possibly be immoral and suicidal in a society of the nineteenth century. Mohammad himself said, according to tradition, " I am no more than a man ; when I order you anything respecting religion, receive it : and when I order you about the affairs of the world, then I am nothing more than man." And he seemed to foresee that the time would come when his minor ordinances would call for revision ; " Ye are in an age," he said, " in which, if ye abandon one-tenth of what is ordered, ye will be ruined. After this, a time will come when he who shall observe one-tenth of what is now ordered will be redeemed."*

If Muslims would take these warnings of their prophet to heart, there would be some hope for Islām. Some few of the higher intellects among them have already admitted the principle of moral criticism applied to the Korān ; but it is very doubtful whether " rational Islām " will ever gain a wide following, any more than " rational Christianity." People in general do not care to think for themselves in matters religious. They like their creed served up to them as cooked meat, not raw flesh. They must have definite texts and hard-and-fast commandments to appeal to. They

---

* " Mishkāt-el-Masābīh," i. 46, 51.

will not believe in the spirit, but prefer the letter. They will have nothing to say to tendencies, but must have facts. It is of no avail to speak to them of the spirit of a life or of a whole book; they must hang their doctrine on a solitary sentence. They will either believe every letter of their scripture, or they will believe nothing.

Such people make up the majority of the professors of Islām; and with them no reform, within Islām, seems possible. Among the upper (I will not call them the higher) classes, they are either fanatics or concealed infidels; and their lives are a proof of the incompatibility of ordinary Mohammadanism, real or nominal, with a high social and national life. Among the poorer classes, the social system has a more restricted field of operation, for the poor are naturally less able to avail themselves of the permissions of their Prophet. In a poor community Islām exerts an eminently salutary influence, as the condition of the Mohammadan converts in Western Africa conclusively proves. An able observer,* whose African birth and training qualify him in a high degree for properly understanding the true state of his countrymen, whilst his Christian profession serves as a guarantee against excessive prejudice in favour of Islām, has recorded his experience of the work of Mohammadan missionaries in Liberia and the neighbouring parts of Africa. "All careful and candid observers," he remarks, "agree that the influence of Islām in Central and West

---

* Dr. E. Blyden, "The People of Africa." (New York, 1871.)

Africa has been, upon the whole, of a most salutary character. . . . As an eliminatory and subversive agency, it has displaced or unsettled nothing as good as itself." It has inculcated habits of moderation and temperance over the whole of the vast region covered by its emissaries ; and so great is the influence of its teaching, that where there are Muslim inhabitants, even in pagan towns, it is a very rare thing to see a person intoxicated. The Mohammadan converts drink nothing but water. " From Senegal to Lagos, over two thousand miles, there is scarcely an important town on the seaboard where there is not at least one mosque and active representatives of Islām, side by side with the Christian teacher. And as soon as a pagan, however obscure or degraded, embraces the Muslim faith, he is at once admitted as an equal to the society. . . . The pagan village possessing a Muslim teacher is always found to be in advance of its neighbours in all the elements of civilisation. . . . The introduction of Islam into Central and West Africa has been the most important, if not the sole, pre- servative against the desolations of the slave trade. Mohammadanism furnished a protection to the tribes who embraced it, by effectually binding them together in one strong religious fraternity, and enabling them by their united efforts to baffle the attempts of powerful slave-hunters. Enjoying this comparative immunity from sudden hostile incursion, industry was stimulated among them ; industry diminished their poverty ; and as they increased in worldly substance, they also increased in desire for knowledge. Receiving a desire of letters by a study of the Arabic language, they acquired loftier views, wider tastes, and those energetic habits which so pleasingly distinguish them from their pagan neighbours." Students often travel on foot from the west coast right across Africa to study at the great mosque of the Azhar in Cairo. It must be remembered that these results were observed in the very centre of African Christianity, in Sierra Leone and other coast settlements. It is said that in Sierra Leone three-fourths of the Muslim population were not born Muslims, but were converted from Christianity or paganism; and this, although " all liberated Africans are always handed over to Christian missionaries for instruction, and their children are baptized and brought up at the public expense in Christian schools, and are thus, in a sense, ready-made Christians."

These facts show that, even in the present day, and with the competition of Christian missionary societies, Islām may be a power for good in poor communities —that it can not only give them a pure instead of a degraded faith, but can raise them socially and intellectually. The effects of a simple form of Islām on these African converts may give one some notion of its influence on its hearers in the early days, before the theologians had corrupted it.

But this good influence is very partial and limited, even among the poorer classes. In communities where all are poor, Islām is an excellent agent for improvement; but in countries where there are many grades of wealth and rank, the poor only ape in a humble manner the vices of those whom they are taught to regard as their " betters."   In all civilised and wealthy countries the social system of Islām exerts a ruinous influence on every class, and if there is to be any great future for the Mohammadan world, that system of society must be done away.

THE WOMAN'S CAUSE IS MAN'S; THEY RISE OR SINK
TOGETHER, DWARFED OR GODLIKE, BOND OR FREE.

CHAPTER IV.

THE KORAN.

THERE is probably no book that is more talked about and less read than the Korān. As one of the great classics of the world, the Mohammadan Bible commands the same superficial acquaintance as " Paradise Lost," and, like the English epic, is the subject of those commonplaces of conversation which people think are due to standard books which they have not read. There are very few educated persons who have not an opinion about the Korān, but not one of a thousand who cheerfully criticise it has ever given it an hour of ordinary study. It is not unusual to hear the rare beings who have actually read the Korān through take to themselves considerable credit for their perseverance ; but the difficulty of the task hardly justifies this self-gratulation. The whole Korān, estimated by the number of verses, is only two-thirds the length of the New Testament, and, if we omit the numerous stories of the Jewish patriarchs, we have no more to read than the Gospels and Acts together. On the score of length there is no excuse for not reading the Korān: it is rather the style and character of the contents that deter ordinary readers. The Korān has suffered, just as the Bible has gained, by an authorised version. Sale's translation has hitherto been practically the sole source of our knowledge, or ignorance, of the Korān in England. It had the advantage of a century of priority over all other English translations, and even when others appeared, it still held its place as the accepted version for general reading. It is not a bad translation, but it is an insufferably dull one. The renderings are, as a rule, fairly accurate ; but Sale's want of literary skill, his inability to reproduce in the smallest degree the effect of the Arabic, and his dreary manner of arranging the verses and paragraphs— wherein the tired eye searches vainly for a pause or resting-place, the well-prized white line which shows that the writer took fresh breath now and then, and gives the reader leave to do likewise—make his translation one of the most wearisome of all books, even among those " which every gentleman's library should possess." It is difficult to read, and impossible to understand, Sale's Korān, if to understand is to grasp the drift and character of a book ; and on Sale's well-meaning but prosaic work must be laid much of the responsibility for the prevailing distaste for the Korān.

This cause, however, ought not to continue still in effect. There are now versions of the Korān which are not only easy to read, but replete with poetic inspiration. Mr. Rodwell's translation is full of beauty, and ought to be much wider known than it is.

In this for the first time the results of German criticism are utilised for the arrangement of the various chapters of the Korān in an approximately chronological order. One of the chief drawbacks to Sale's version is the order of the chapters, in which he retained the arrangement, universal among Mohammadans, which the most superficial student perceives at once to be unscientific and destructive to the proper comprehension of the Sacred Book. The Mohammadan arrangement is regulated by the simple principle of putting the long chapters first, and gradually fining down to the shortest chapters. In other words, the Mohammadan arrangement inverts the true order of the chapters, for the shortest are almost universally the oldest, and the longest the latest. But as this general rule does not hold good in every instance, chapters of the most diverse dates are placed side by side, to the ruin of all sequence in style or thought. It was this preposterous arrangement that made Carlyle think the Korān "a wearisome, confused jumble, crude, incondite; endless iterations, long-windedness, entanglement; most crude, incondite;—unsupportable stupidity, in short!" As soon as the mechanical arrangement is set aside, and a fairly chronological order substituted, the chaotic impression disappears. For ourselves we do not think the Korān at all an incomprehensible jumble, but believe we can trace a clearly progressive development in thought and language. But we admit that this could not be traced in Sale's version, and at present Mr. Rodwell's alone presents the approximately true order. One might have thought that this decided advance in translation would have made the Korān more generally known, and that readers would have been attracted by the bold imagery and fine bursts of real poetry which Mr. Rodwell's version brings into prominence. Such, however, has not been the case.

Another attempt was made, in a different direction, to induce those who had been deterred from the study of Sale's Korān by its length and confusion to acquire some knowledge of the sacred book in a less troublesome manner. Lane's " Selections " were arranged under subjects ; all that was objectionable in general reading was excised ; and the interminable histories of the Israelite patriarchs were reduced to a connected narrative. Many who had been foiled in their laudable efforts to master Sale were able to learn something of the Korān and its author from these " Selections " ; but it may be doubted whether the loss which is entailed by the neglect of the chronological order is quite repaid by the convenience in reference and analysis which undoubtedly belongs to the arrangement according to subjects. Lane's "Selections " are the best means of learning the ordinary contents of the Korān that the general reader possesses : but he cannot gain from them that insight into the development of Mohammad's thought and the growth of Islām which a chronologically arranged book of extracts or typical chapters would have afforded.

Finally, Professor E. H. Palmer, who had a rare gift of language, and understood the art of reproducing Arabian effects in English words as no other

Englishman does, translated the Korān for Professor Max Müller's series of "Sacred Books of the East." Palmer's version is undoubtedly the best that has yet appeared. His intimate acquaintance with the modes of thought and expression of the modern Bedawīs—an acquaintance which, alas, did not avert his tragic and lamentable fate—enabled him to give a peculiar life and reality to his translation. His Korān reads like the words of a living Arab—words which we might hear ourselves any day in the desert—not dead utterances of the past. There is a stiffness about the earlier versions which mars their effect. One feels that they are the result of laborious study of a difficult language, which no longer lives in men's lips, but is as dead as the tongue of the Vedas. It is quite different with Palmer's work. He almost knew the people to whom the Korān was spoken, for the modern Arab still represents to a great degree his forefather of Mohammad's day. He knew the language of the Korān as a medium of common everyday intercourse, for an Arab now will speak in moments of excitement and enthusiasm the same burning words that came red-hot from Mohammad's lips. Palmer realised the fact that, though all language changes—and Arabic has undergone many corruptions since the first promulgation of Islām—the continuity is not broken, and the Arabic of the Korān still exists in its essential characteristics in the present day. It is this which gives his translation a freshness and buoyancy which we may seek in vain elsewhere. For the first time we feel that the words we read in the Korān came straight from a

man's heart, and begin to understand the power of
Mohammad's influence, and the fascination of his
voice.　It is no longer a standard classic that we
study, but a living revelation that we hear.*

Apart from the Eastern glow which is for the first
time retained in a translation, Palmer's unrivalled

---

* Palmer's principle of translating the Korān as if it were the
speech of a modern Bedawy has its drawbacks.　Although it has
always been held up as the model of Arabic style, the Korān
contains many expressions which it is difficult to regard as anything else than vulgarisms.　Mohammad, as an unlettered man,
naturally addressed his countrymen in their common everyday
speech, and it is not surprising to find a certain proportion of
what is called "slang" in his language.　Palmer's mistake was
not in admitting this, but in trying to reproduce it.　The impression produced upon an audience in Mekka by certain vulgar
expressions which were in everyday use is quite different from that
produced upon the educated readers for whom Palmer's translation is intended by corresponding vulgarisms in English.　To
us the occurrence of such phrases as Palmer intentionally intro-
duces has something of the effect that the insertion of a music-
hall melody in a symphony of Beethoven's would produce.　To
the original audience the "slang" expressions were part of their
own speech and excited no remark.　We, however, do not use
"slang" expressions, and when we meet with them in books,
especially sacred books, they jar upon our literary sense.　Palmer
attempted the task—an impossible one we admit—of producing
the same impression upon English readers as was produced upon
the original audience by Mohammad's own rhetoric; and he failed
in the attempt because he forgot that the audiences are wholly
dissimilar, and that what would strike a rude Arab in a given
manner would have a totally different effect upon a cultivated
reader.　Palmer's theory would only apply if the readers of his
translation were entirely of the lowest classes; as they are obviously almost wholly restricted to the educated classes, the theory
breaks down and offers an impediment, instead of an aid, to the
due appreciation of the Korān.

instinct for the thoughts and ideas of the Arab has led him often to a new and luminous rendering of a passage which his predecessors had failed to bring out. Scholars will not invariably accept his innovations, but as a rule they impress us with their clear common sense and reasonableness. Without throwing off entirely the influence of traditional interpretation, the translator releases himself from the narrow bonds of commentators' intelligence, and lets his own clear sense and his knowledge of the speech and thought of modern Arabs throw their practical light upon the subject. And as a result he has produced a translation of the Korān which, with not a few faults, and in our opinion certain radically erroneous principles, is yet the first successful reproduction in tone and spirit of the sacred book of the Muslims that has been done in English. We see the Arabian Prophet and his preaching, it is true, " in a mirror, darkly " ; but, in spite of a badly polished surface and many specks and dints, it is still a mirror, and reflects the Korān in its due proportions. Previous translations, excellent in many ways, and in some superior to this one, have been rather copies or adaptations than true reflections.

We have read several important treatises on what the Korān borrowed from earlier sources and like subjects of theologico-antiquarian interest, but we do not remember to have seen anywhere a clear reckoning of the net result of Mohammad's teaching in the Korān, which is practically the main point for the world at large. How much of the present Mohammadan religion is clearly laid down in the Korān ;

how far modern Mohammadan law is definitely enacted in the Korān; did Mohammad in the Korān recognise the necessity of the adaptation of his religion to changed circumstances?—these are among the questions that most deeply concern us, and these can be answered by a moderately industrious study of the book. To understand, however, the drift of Mohammad's teaching, and avoid the danger of falling into the pernicious habit of taking isolated "texts" for doctrine, which has been the destruction of too many Muslim as well as Christian divines, it is essential to view the Korān as far as possible as a connected whole, and judge each sentence by its context, and each chapter by its neighbours. This, however, cannot be done in the unreasonable and confusing order in common use among Muslims, and retained in Sale's and Palmer's versions.

The Arabic text was collected in a purely haphazard fashion, in which the only discoverable merit is fidelity. We may safely assert that the present text contains nothing but the words of Mohammad; but we can assert nothing else in its favour. The original editors deserve all credit for their honesty and scrupulous care in gathering all that could be surely proved to have been spoken by Mohammad, and adding nothing of their own; but beyond this it is impossible to congratulate them. Their task was undoubtedly a difficult one. Mohammad's revelations were spoken during a long period, and often in short fragments. Sometimes the whole of a chapter (as we now have it) was spoken at one time, but very often only a few verses were uttered, and other fragments were afterwards added, occasionally with instructions from the Prophet himself that they were to be inserted in such or such a chapter, but frequently without any such instructions. These verses and chapters were not arranged, or even in many cases written down, at the time of the Prophet's death, and it was not till war began to diminish the number of those who had committed portions of the Korān to memory that the Muslims perceived on how perishable a foundation their sacred book was built. It was then, after much misgiving at so serious an innovation, that they determined to collect the fragments of the Korān "from palm-leaves, skins, blade-bones, and the hearts of men." The Prophet's amanuensis, Zeyd ibn Thābit, undertook this important task under the rule of Abū-Bekr, the first Khalif. He gathered together all that could be remembered, or found in written form, of Mohammad's words, and determined (on what principles it is now impossible to ascertain) what verses belonged to any given chapter. The date at which most of the chapters were spoken was apparently forgotten; at all events, Zeyd could think of no better arrangement than that of length, and he accordingly placed the longest chapters first and the shortest last, prefixing the short prayer known as the Fātiha, as Chapter I. It may be doubted whether Zeyd would have adopted a chronological order even if the precise date of every chapter had been known to him; for he did know that certain chapters were spoken at Mekka and others at Medīna—that is to say, in the first and the second half of Mohammad's career—yet he mixed them indiscriminately together, and generally placed the Medīna or later chapters in the earlier part of the book. Zeyd's edition is practically the Korān as we have it now. A second redaction was indeed made some twenty years later, in which Zeyd himself took part, but this was rather to settle some disputed points of pronunciation and dialectal differences than to amend the substance of the text; and no subsequent alterations have been made. We may therefore take it for granted that the present Arabic Korān is practically identical with the edition which was drawn up a few years after Mohammad's death, and which commended itself to the majority of his companions and disciples.

These disciples and friends, however, had various advantages over modern readers. They knew the Prophet personally, and did not require to be told how his teaching developed and his style changed. Indeed they would have repudiated any theory of development. Their Prophet was always infallible to them, and they would allow neither progress nor deterioration in his revelations. All equally came down from God, copied from the great "Mother of the Book" which lies open before the Throne and was written before all ages. To them there was no importance in determining the age of the various portions of the revelation. It all came from the same divine source, and what did a few years earlier or later signify? The same opinion would be expressed by almost every Muslim in the present day. With the exception of a few commentators, whose business is to find matter to comment on, Mohammadans care no more for the date of a chapter in the Korān than a good Evangelical Christian does for the age of Deuteronomy or the Canticles. But because the faithful decline to pry into the constitution and growth of their sacred books, is it necessary that students who are not believers in the particular revelation should be compelled to bewilder themselves with the unscientific and chaotic arrangement which satisfies the believer? To us the interest of the Korān is many-sided, and not the least important side is the light it throws on the character of Mohammad. In the common arrangement, however, it is almost impossible to glean any impressions on the Prophet's character and mental changes ; it is even difficult to conceive of the strange medley as the work of one man.

That a scientific order is possible has been conclusively shown by a German professor, who possesses in a peculiar degree the instinct of language, and may without flattery be acknowledged the most remarkable genius among Arabic scholars that Germany has produced. Nöldeke's " Geschichte des Qorâns " settled practically for ever the question of the chronological order of the Korān; it is not probable that any very marked advance will be made beyond his profound and well-considered work. To detail the evidences upon which his conclusions are based would carry us too far ; but it may be stated that they consist chiefly of indications derived from a minute study of the style and vocabulary of the Korān. External evidence is almost wholly wanting except in respect of the later or Medīna chapters ; nor are the apparent references within the work to passing events sufficiently explicit to prove of much service. The language is the only test which may be trusted thoroughly and throughout. A very cursory reading of the Korān will show anyone that there is a marked difference of style between some chapters and others. It is this difference that Prof. Nöldeke laid hold of and examined until a definite progression of style became visible. An aid in this investigation is found in the rhyme. Mohammad did not speak in poetry, nor precisely in prose. Poetry indeed he detested, and the only verse he ever uttered, and that involuntarily, is a very bad one. No part of the Korān conforms to the exigencies of Arabian prosody. Yet it is not plain prose, but rather a rhetorical form of prose which has much of the character of poetry without its metrical restraints. The words fall into short clauses (in the earlier chapters) which balance one another more or less musically, and the last words generally rhyme together. As time went on these clauses became longer and longer, and the rhyme underwent various modifications, till the latest chapters become almost plain prose. It is easy to understand how valuable a guide the variations in the rhyme and the length of the verses must be in an investigation into the dates of the component parts of the Korān. From these evidences Prof. Nöldeke has not only been able to determine the chronological position of most of the chapters, but even to decide when verses have been interpolated (by the original editor) in a chapter of a different date. In very few cases, however, is it possible to fix the precise sequence of the chapters, or the exact year in which they were first spoken. All that can be done is to arrange them in certain groups, each of which belongs to a limited period; but we cannot as a rule state the position each chapter should occupy within its proper group. The four groups, however, into which Nöldeke divides the 114 chapters enable the student to gain nearly as coherent an impression of the gradual development of the doctrine and style of Mohammad as if the order were more minutely detailed.*

During the years of struggle and persecution at Mekka, which have been briefly described in Chapter II., ninety out of the 114 chapters of the Korān were revealed, amounting to about two-thirds of the whole book. All these chapters are inspired with but one great design, and are in strong contrast with the complicated character of the later chapters issued at Medīna. In the Mekka chapters Mohammad appears in the unalloyed character of a prophet; he has not yet assumed the functions of a statesman and law-giver. His object is not to give men a code or a constitution, but to call them to the worship of the One God. This is the only aim of the Mekkan

---

* This order is preserved in the selected chapters from the Korān published in my " Speeches and Table Talk of the Prophet Mohammad " (Macmillan, 1882), where I have endeavoured to present all that was permanent in the teaching of Mohammad in the smallest possible compass.

speeches. There is hardly a word of other doctrines, scarcely anything of ritual, or social or penal regulations. Every chapter is directed simply to the grand design of the Prophet's life, to convince men of the unutterable majesty of the One God, who brooks no rivals. Mohammad appeals to the people to credit the evidence of their own eyes; he calls to witness the wonders of nature, the stars in their courses, the sun and the moon, the dawn cleaving asunder the dark veil of night, the life-giving rain, the fruits of the earth, life and death, change and decay, beginning and ending—all are "signs of God's power, if only ye would understand." Or he tells the people how it happened to older generations, when prophets came to them and exhorted them to believe in One God and do righteousness, and they rejected them, and there fell upon the unbelieving nation grievous woe. How was it with the people of Noah? he asks—they were drowned in the flood because they would not hearken to his words. And the people of the Cities of the Plain? And Pharaoh and his host? And the old tribes of the Arabs would not hear the warnings of their prophets? One answer follows each—there came upon them a great calamity: "These are the true stories," he cries, "and there is only One God! and yet ye turn aside!" Eloquent appeals to the signs of nature, threats of a day of reckoning to come, warnings drawn from the legends of the prophets, arguments for the truth and reality of the revelation, make up the substance of this first division of the Korān.

The whole series of Mekkan chapters, however, is

by no means uniform. Nöldeke has traced three successive stages in the speeches before the Flight, gradually approximating the style of the chapters which were published at Medīna, or rather during the Medīna period, for the names Mekkan and Medīnite chapters must be understood merely in the sense of belonging to the periods before and after the Flight respectively, and do not imply the precise locality of their utterance. The first of the three stages contains the forty-eight chapters which Nöldeke, on various grounds, already briefly indicated, refers to the first four years of Mohammad's mission—from his first sermon to the date of the Abyssinian emigration. The second consists of the speeches of the fifth and sixth years, twenty-one in number; and the third includes the remaining twenty-one which were spoken between the sixth year of the Prophet's mission and his flight to Medīna.

The chapters—or speeches as we prefer to call them, for at this period every chapter is a masterpiece of rhetoric—of the first group are the most striking in the whole Korān. It is in them that the poetry of the man comes out most articulately. Mohammad had not lived among the sheepfolds in vain, and spent long solitary nights gazing at the silent heaven and watching the dawn break over the mountains. This earliest portion of the Korān is one long blazonry of nature's beauty. How can you believe in aught but the one omnipotent God when you see this glorious world around you and this wondrous tent of heaven above you? is Mohammad's frequent question to his countrymen. "Lift up thine eyes to the heavens: dost thou see any flaw therein? Nay, lift up thine eyes again: thy sight returneth dim and dazed." We find little else than this appeal to the witness of nature in the first group of Mekkan orations. The Prophet was in too exalted a state during these early years to stoop to argument; he rather seeks to dazzle the sense with brilliant images of God's workings in creation: "Verily in the creation of the heavens and the earth are signs to you if ye would understand." His sentences have a rhythmical ring, though they are not in true metre. The lines are very short, yet with a musical fall; and the meaning is often but half expressed. The Prophet seems impatiently to stop, as if he despaired of explaining himself: one feels the speaker has essayed a thing beyond words, and has suddenly discovered the impotence of language, and broken off with the sentence unfinished. The style is throughout fiery and impassioned. The words are those of a man whose whole heart is bent on convincing, and they carry with them even now the impression of the burning vehemence with which they were originally hurled forth. These earliest speeches are generally short. They are pitched too high to be long maintained at their original level. We feel we have here to do with a poet, as well as a preacher, and that his poetry costs him too much to be spun out.

The simple creed of this early stage of Islām is set forth in many of these short speeches. Complicated dogma is nowhere to be found in the Korān, but its teaching is never more plain and simple than in such a chapter as that of " The Territory " (*i.e.* of Mekka) (ch. xc.).

*In the name of God, the Compassionate, the Merciful,**
I swear by this country—
And thou art a dweller in this country—
And by father and child!
Verily We have created man amid trouble :—
Doth he think that no one shall prevail against him?
He saith—" I have squandered riches in abundance."
Doth he think that no one seeth him?
Have We not made him two eyes?
And a tongue and two lips?
And pointed him out the two highways?
Yet doth he not attempt the steep one.
And what shall teach thee what the steep one is?
The ransoming of captives,
Or feeding on the day of famine
The orphan of thy kindred
Or the poor that lieth in the dust;
Finally to be of those who believe, and enjoin steadfastness on
    each other, and enjoin mercy on each other :—
These are the people of the right hand.
While they who disbelieve our signs, they are the people of the
    left :
Over them a Fire closeth!

In exhorting to good deeds and the fear of God, Mohammad's great weapon is the certainty of a day of retribution, and his great inducement to believers is the promise of reward in Paradise. The happiness of those who shall have the books of the records of their deeds given them in their right hands, and the baleful misery of those who shall receive their books

---

* This formula precedes every chapter of the Korān save one. The translations, unless otherwise specified, are my own as published in my " Speeches and Tabletalk of the Prophet Mohammad " (Macmillan's " Golden Treasury Series ").

in the left hand, are continually held before the eyes of the people. The judgment day is an ever-present reality to Mohammad. He is never weary of describing it in words of terror and abasement. He cannot find names enough to define it. It is the Hour, the mighty Day, the Inevitable, the great Calamity, the Smiting, the Overwhelming, the Difficult Day, the True Promised Day, the Day of Decision. Images fail him when he tries to describe its awfulness :—

In the name of God, the Compassionate, the Merciful.
The Smiting !   What is the Smiting ?
And what shall teach thee what is the Smiting ?
The Day when men shall be like moths adrift
And the hills shall be like woolflocks rift !
Then as for him whose scales are heavy,—his shall be a life of
    bliss.
And as for him whose scales are light, a place in the Pit is his !
And what shall teach thee what that place is ?—
"A Fire that blazes ! "   (ci.)*

And again :—

In the name of God, the Compassionate, the Merciful.
When the heaven is rent asunder,
And when the stars are scattered,

---

* I have attempted in this instance to preserve the system of rhymes of the original, which are shown in the following transliteration of the Arabic :—

Bismi-llāhi-r-rahmāni-r-rahīm
El-kāri'atu mā-l-kāri'ah
Wa-mā adrāka mā-l-kāri'ah
Yawma yekūnu-n-nāsu ke-l-farāsi-l-mabthūth
Wa-tekūnu-l-jibālu ke-l-ihni-l-manfūsh
Fe-amma men thekulet mawāzīnuhu fe-huwa fee 'ishetin rādiyeh
Wa-amma men khaffet mawāzīnuhu fe-ummuhu hāwiyeh
Wa-mā adrāka mā hiyeh
Nārun hāmiyeh.

And when the seas are let loose,
And when the tombs are turned upside-down,
The soul shall know what it hath done and left undone.
O man! what hath deceived thee respecting thy Lord, the
    Generous;
Who created thee, and fashioned thee, and moulded thee aright?
It what form it pleased him He builded thee.
Nay, but ye take the Judgment for a lie!
But verily there are Watchers over you—
Worthy reporters
Knowing what ye do!
Verily the righteous shall be in delight,
And the wicked in Hell-Fire:
They shall be burnt at it on the day of doom,
And they shall not be hidden from it.
What shall teach thee what is the Day of Judgment?
Again, what shall teach thee what is the Day of Judgment?
A day when no soul can avail aught for another soul; for the
    ordering on that day is with God.   (lxxxii.)

Few finer examples of Mohammad's appeal to the testimony of nature can be cited than the " Chapter of the Merciful " (lv.), in which he recounts the every-day sights of the earth and sky, and in a refrain demands of men and genii which of the bounties of their Lord will they two deny? It is the *Benedicite* of Islām.

In the name of God, the Compassionate, the Merciful.
The Merciful hath taught the Korān,
He created man,
Taught him clear speech.
The sun and the moon in their courses,
And the plants and the trees do homage.
And the Heaven, He raised it, and appointed the balance
(That ye should not transgress in the balance :—
But weigh ye justly and stint not the balance).
And the Earth, He prepared it for living things,
Therein is fruit, and the palm with sheaths,

And grain with its husk and the fragrant herb :
Then which of the bounties of your Lord will ye twain deny?
He created man of clay like a pot,
And He created the Jinn of clear fire :
Then which of the bounties of your Lord will ye twain deny?
Lord of the two easts
And Lord of the two wests :
Then which of the bounties of your Lord will ye twain deny?
He hath let loose the two seas that meet together,
Yet between them is a barrier they cannot pass :
Then which of the bounties of your Lord will ye twain deny?
He bringeth up therefrom pearls great and small :
Then which of the bounties of your Lord will ye twain deny?
And His are the ships towering on the sea like mountains :
Then which of the bounties of your Lord will ye twain deny?
All on the earth passeth away,
But the face of thy Lord abideth endued with majesty and honour :
Then which of the bounties of your Lord will ye twain deny?
All things in Heaven and Earth supplicate Him : every day is He
    at work :
Then which of the bounties of your Lord will ye twain deny? . . .
Blessed be the name of thy Lord, endued with majesty and
    honour !   (lv.)

Warnings of a judgment to come, threats of hell
and promises of heaven, with eloquent descriptions of
God's works, form the chief themes of the first group
of Mekkan speeches ; but there are also many passages
devoted to a personal defence of the Prophet himself.
The sixty-eighth chapter begins : " By the pen and
what they write, verily thou art not, by God's grace,
mad !"   It must be remembered that throughout the
Korān it is God who is supposed to speak *in propriâ
personâ*, and Mohammad is only the mouthpiece of
the revelation.   It is natural, therefore, that the
Deity who sent the Prophet should sometimes put
words of self-defence into his lips.   The Mekkans

commonly regarded Mohammad as a madman or one possessed with a devil (jinny); and the words in the sixty-eighth chapter are intended to refute this calumny. It goes on, " But thou shalt see and they shall see which of you is the infatuated. ' Wait awhile, I too am waiting,' saith the Lord; 'let me alone with him who calls this new discourse a lie!—I will let them have their way, for my device is sure!' " Sometimes these personal chapters show the pathetic side of the Prophet's lonely struggle; it must have been at a time of deep depression that the " Splendour of Morning " (xciii.) was spoken:—

In the name of God, the Compassionate, the Merciful.
By the splendour of morning,
And the still of night!
Thy Lord hath not forsaken thee nor hated thee!
And the future will surely be better for thee than the present,
And thy Lord will surely give to thee and thou wilt be well
    pleased.
Did He not find thee an orphan and sheltered thee,
And found thee erring and guided thee,
And found thee poor and enriched thee ?
Then as for the orphan, oppress him not,
And as for him who asketh of thee, chide him not away,
And as for the bounty of thy Lord, tell of it.

Other chapters evince a very different spirit. Mohammad could be vehement in cursing individual scoffers as well as in threatening unbelief in the abstract. This is how he curses his uncle Abū-Lahab ('Father of flame,' a name which his nephew grimly plays upon), who was the most bitter of his enemies:—

In the name of the merciful and compassionate God.
Abū-Lahab's two hands shall perish, and he shall perish!
His wealth shall not avail him, nor what he has earned!

He shall broil in a fire that flames, and his wife carrying faggots !
—On her neck a cord of palm fibres.　(cxi. Palmer.)

Again cowardly slanders whispered behind the back stir up in Mohammad a wrath that approaches the sacred indignation of " Woe to you, Scribes and Pharisees, hypocrites !　Ye shall receive the greater damnation ! "　After the usual invocation of the merciful God, which sounds strangely as a prelude to a curse, he bursts forth :—

Woe to every Backbiter, slanderer !
Who hath heaped up riches and counted them over !
He thinketh that his riches have made him everlasting :
Nay ! he shall surely be cast into Blasting Hell !
And what shall teach thee what Blasting Hell is ?
The fire of God kindled :
Which reaches over the hearts ;
Verily, it is closed over them [like a tent]
With stays well-stretched.　(civ.)

To the first group of Mekkan chapters belongs the famous credo :—

Say : He is One God ;
God the Eternal.
He begetteth not, nor is begotten ;
Nor is there one like unto Him.　(cxii.)

—and also some invocations against charms and spells, and, omitting less important utterances, the prayer, called the Fātiha, which is prefixed to the Korān in the usual arrangement, and which forms a prominent feature in the everyday devotions as well as the public ritual of all Mohammadans :—

In the name of God, the Compassionate, the Merciful.
Praise to God, the Lord of the Worlds,
The Compassionate, the Merciful,

> King of the day of judgment!
> Thee we worship, and Thee we ask for help.
> Guide us in the right way,
> The way of those to whom Thou art gracious;
> Not of those upon whom is Thy wrath, nor of the erring.   (i.)

The second group of Mekkan speeches is markedly different from the first.   Poetic fire is not always long-lived; " whether there be prophecies, they shall fail; whether there be tongues they shall cease "; and in the second period we find that much of the poetry of the Korān is gone out.   The verses and the chapters become longer and more diffuse. The Prophet wanders from his point more frequently, and has lost the power of effective peroration which characterised the earlier speeches.   The wonderful oaths of the first group, where Mohammad swears by everything that is in heaven and earth—

> By the sun and its noonday brightness!
> And the moon when it follows him!
> And the day when it displays him!
> And the night when it covers him!
> And the heaven and what built it!
> And the earth and what spread it!—

have now almost disappeared, and the mild asseveration " By the Korān " takes their place.   A certain formality is noticeable in the custom now introduced of beginning a speech with the statement "this is the revelation of God," and emphasising the words of the Deity, as it were by inverted commas, by the initial verb " say," which never appears in the earlier chapters except in certain formulas.   The signs of nature still hold a prominent place in Mohammad's argument, but the evidence he most frequently appeals to is the history of former prophets. These legends, derived from the Jewish Haggadah, but considerably corrupted, constitute a very important, but also an uninteresting part of the Korān. More than fifteen hundred verses, forming a quarter of the whole work, are occupied with endless repetitions of the same wearisome tales. They may be found arranged methodically in the second part of Lane's "Selections," where the repetitions are omitted and the main incidents prominently brought out. From the story of the Creation, the rebellion of Iblīs, or the devil, and the expulsion from Paradise, these legends extend to the miraculous birth of the Messiah. Adam and Eve, Cain and Abel, Enoch, Noah, Abraham, Ishmael, Isaac, Jacob, Joseph and his brethren, Job, Jethro, Moses, Saul, David, Solomon, Jonah, Ezra, and Christ, are the chief characters who figure in the Korānic Lives of the Saints, and the events recorded are often as puerile and absurd as any related in mediæval hagiology. To Mohammad, however, they possessed a high value. "God has sent down the best of legends, a book uniform, repeating, whereat the skins of those that fear their Lord do creep!" His doctrine of the continuity of revelation required the support of such legends. He held that all these preceding prophets were true messengers of God. Each brought his message to his people, and each was rejected and disbelieved. He puts words into the mouths of the patriarchs which are almost identical with his own speeches; and the family likeness between Abraham, and Moses, and other Hebrew teachers, and Mohammad, as depicted in the Korān, cannot escape the most superficial reader. Mohammad believed that all these early prophets were sent by God to bring precisely the same message as was contained in the Korān; he believed in a species of apostolic succession; and the only ground of pre-eminence he claimed for himself was that of finality. Abraham and Moses, and David and Christ, had all come with a portion of God's truth; but Mohammad came with the final revelation, which superseded, whilst it confirmed, all that went before. He is the "seal of prophecy," the last apostle whom God sends before the day of retribution. Beyond this he differs no whit from his predecessors; and he is ever striving to impress upon his audience that his doctrine is nothing new, but simply the teaching of all good men who have gone before him. No doubt there were times when his frequent recitals of the revelations which he attributed to Moses and Christ had the special motive of converting Jews and Christians: but many of these stories were told before he came into any intimate contact with either, and can only be attributed to his theory of the unity of prophecy.

To enter into the details of these curious legends would carry us beyond reasonable limits. Their interest is mainly antiquarian, and beyond the evidence they give of the view held by Mohammad with respect to revelation in general, they have little bearing on our subject—the practical gist of the Korān. They form indeed an obstacle to the student, who, if he is amused now and then by a good story—

like that of the Seven Sleepers of Ephesus, or of Abraham and the Idols—grows weary of reading the same dreary anecdotes of the same venerated patriarchs over and over again. It was in the nature of Mohammad's unsystematic preaching that he should constantly repeat himself. The practice is not confined to the legends of the prophets, for almost every simile and every threat and every doctrine occurs again and again in the Korān. It is, of course, possible, and indeed probable, when we consider the time that elapsed before the Korān was collected as a whole, that many of these repetitions are due to different oral reports of the same speech, and that Mohammad's hearers sometimes confused one oration with another and inserted the words belonging to the one in the wrong chapter, whilst other traditionists placed them in the right one. Whatever the source of the repetition, it forms a serious obstacle to the progress of the reader.

The manner in which the legends of former prophets are used may be seen from a single extract. Mohammad's argument is very simple : Formerly apostles were sent to other nations ; they preached what I am preaching to you now,—exhorted the people to worship but one God, and to work righteousness; but their people rejected them and turned to idols; so God sent down upon them a terrible punishment :— even so will it be with you, if ye reject my words. "Ye walk in the very steps of those who were destroyed for unbelief," says Mohammad ; "how many a generation before them have We destroyed!

Canst thou find any one of them, or hear a whisper of them?"

The Chapter of "the Moon" (liv.) contains a short summary of prophetic antecedents, which will serve to show briefly how Mohammad introduced his "tales of the elders," without the prolixity of the more detailed legends. After reproaching the people for their disbelief and hardness of heart, he exclaims :—

The people of Noah before them, called it a lie; and they called
    our servant a liar, and said " Mad ! " and he was rejected.
Then he besought his Lord, " Verily, I am overpowered : defend
    me ! "
So we opened the gates of heaven with water pouring forth,
And we made the earth break out in springs, and the waters met
    by an order foreordained ;
And we carried him on a vessel of planks and nails,
Which sailed on beneath our eyes,—a reward for him who had
    been disbelieved.
And we left it as a sign : but doth anyone mind ?
And what was my torment and warning ?
And we have made the Korān easy for reminding, but doth anyone
    mind ?
And called it a lie ; *and what was my torment and warning ?*
Lo, we sent against them a biting wind on a day of settled
    ill-luck,
It tore men away as though they were trunks of palm-trees
    torn up.
But what was my torment and warning ?
We have made the Korān easy for reminding, but doth anyone mind ?

.   .   .   .   .   .

Nay, but the Hour is their threatened time, and the Hour shall be
    most grievous and bitter,
Verily the sinners are in error and madness !
One day they shall be dragged into the fire on their faces " *Taste*
    ye the touch of Hell !"
Verily, all things have we created by a decree,
And our command is but one moment, like the twinkling of an eye.

And we have destroyed the like of you,—*but doth anyone mind?*
And everything that they do is in the Books,
Everything, little and great, is written down.
Verily the pious shall be amid gardens and rivers,
In the seat of truth before the King Omnipotent.

A great many of the Hebrew legends are brought in, as in the example just quoted, by an allusion to the charge of madness or sorcery, which was then much in vogue as a weapon among the Prophet's opponents. " That is what the people of old said against former Apostles," is Mohammad's retort, " and see what befell them ! " and then he relates the story. He has become much more definite as to his own position and the nature of his revelation. He repudiates all superhuman powers. " I am only inspired that I am a plain warner," is his constant reminder. He will not be held responsible for his people ; they may believe or disbelieve, as they please, or rather as God pleases. " Whoso will, let him take the road unto his Lord: but ye will not will it except God will it." Thus Mohammad ventures on the dangerous ground of free-will and predestination, on which he uttered many contradictory statements, with an unmistakable leaning towards the doctrine of election. " He whom God leads astray," he says, " there is no guide for him." The Korān is not a compulsion to save men against their will; it is only " a memorial—a reminder—a plain Korān to warn him who is living." They may take their choice, if God pleases.

The Hebrew legends occupy nearly half of the contents of the second group of Mekkan chapters ; indeed.

the majority of them belong to this period, and the rest to the third group, none being attributable with certainty to the first division, and very few to the Medīna chapters; but there is plenty of the old themes of judgment, and paradise, and hell, though the descriptions have lost something of their power, and the long verses which are now common weaken the effect of the language. The old eloquence, however, breaks out in its original force now and then, as in the picture of the judgment in the "Chapter of K." (l.) :—

We created man, and we know what his soul whispereth, and we are nearer to him than his jugular vein.

When the two notetakers take note, sitting on the right hand and on the left,

Not a word doth he utter, but a watcher is by him, ready.

And the stupor of death shall come in truth : "this is what thou wouldst have avoided!"

And the trumpet shall be blown: that is the Day of the Threat!

And every soul shall come, along with a driver and a witness—

"Thou didst not heed this; so we have taken away from thee thy veil, and to-day thy sight is keen."

And his companion shall say: "This is what I am ready to witness."—

"Cast ye into Hell every unbelieving rebel, hinderer of the good, transgressor, doubter,

Who setteth other gods with God; cast ye him into the fierce torment."

His companion shall say, "O our Lord! I misled him not; but he was in fathomless error."

God shall say, "Wrangle not before me, for I charged. you before about the threat.

My word doth not change, and I am not unjust to my servants."

On that day will we say to Hell, "Art thou full?" and it shall say, "Is there more?"

And Paradise shall be brought nigh to the righteous, not afar :—

"This is what ye were promised, unto everyone who turneth himself to God, and keepeth his laws,

Who feareth the Merciful in secret, and cometh with a contrite
    heart;
Enter it in peace,"—that is the Day of Eternity!
They shall have what they please therein, and increase at our
    hands.
And how many generations have we destroyed before them,
    mightier than they in valour! then seek through the land—
    is there any refuge?
Verily in that is a warning to him who hath a heart, or giveth ear,
    and is a beholder.

One of the peculiarities of the second group of
Mekkan chapters may be noted in the extract given
above. Mohammad was apparently desirous of giving
a new name to the One God whose gospel he preached.
"Allah" was already known to the Arabs, but Er-
Rahmān, "the Merciful," though employed by the
Hebrews and also by the Himyerites, was not a name
with which the Mekkans were acquainted. The experiment, however, was not successful. The people
seem to have drawn a wrong inference from the use
of the two names, and to have understood them to
refer to two separate gods. At the end of the seventeenth chapter Mohammad removes this confusion in
the words: "Say: call upon Allah, or call upon
Er-Rahmān, whichever ye call him by; for His are
the best of names"; but he judged it advisable to
avoid the double nomenclature, and it seldom occurs
again.

The teaching of Mohammad is still very simple in
the second period. The whole duty of man is summed
up in few words: "Prosperous are the believers who
in their prayers are humble, and who from vain talk
turn aside, and who in almsgiving are active, and who

guard their chastity, and who observe their trusts and covenants, and who guard well their prayers ; these are the heirs who shall inherit Paradise ; they shall dwell therein for aye " (xxiii. 1–10, Palmer). Hardly any definite rules of conduct or ritual are yet laid down, and the little of the kind that does occur is in one chapter—the seventeenth—where the Muslim is enjoined to be steadfast in prayer from sundown to dusk and at dawn ; night prayers are commended as supererogatory works ; hospitality and thrift are counselled in the idiomatic phrase, " Make not thy hand fettered to thy neck, nor yet spread it out quite open " ; infanticide for fear of poverty is forbidden " as a great sin " ; inchastity is denounced as " an abomination ; " homicide is only permitted in the blood revenge, and even then is to be restricted to one person ; the faithful are commanded not to take the wealth of orphans, but to fulfil their covenants, to give full measure, and not to walk proudly on the earth : " Verily thou canst not cleave the earth, and thou shalt not reach the mountains in height." This is how Mohammad sums up his teaching in the eighteenth chapter :—

SAY: I am only a mortal like yourselves : I am inspired that your God is only One God : Then let him who hopes to meet his Lord act righteous acts and join none in the services of his Lord.

This is really all that Mohammad has to tell the people, though his methods of urging it upon their notice are diverse. To worship one God and act righteously is the burden of his speech.

In the third or last Mekkan period we find the characteristics of the second repeated in a tamer style. The language has become still more prosaic; the enumeration of the signs of God in nature wears more and more the aspect of a catalogue; the anecdotes of the patriarchs, though much rarer than in the second period, seem even more tiresome; the constant refutations of the charges of forgery, magic, and poetry—the last now superfluous; the never-ending reiteration of the well-worn arguments—all these weary the reader; and this portion of the Korān is perhaps the least interesting of all. It is more argumentative and less enthusiastic. Years of failure had perhaps damped Mohammad's ardour, and he appears rather as the advocate putting a case to the reason of his hearers than as a prophet filled with the divine afflatus and breathing it forth in unpremeditated music. Mohammad was not a good reasoner, and he has but one method, which we have seen already in the speeches of the second group. The new feature is the frequent answer he makes to the " evil and adulterous generation that seeketh after a sign." Why ask for a sign, he demands, when all nature is a miracle, and bears testimony to its Creator ? It is the old thought, " the heavens declare the glory of God, and the firmament showeth his handiwork." I am only a warner, Mohammad is ever insisting, and I cannot show a sign, except what ye see every day and every night. Signs are with God : He who could make the heavens and the earth could easily show you a sign if he pleased. Beware ! the day will come when you will indeed see a sign, and will bewail your unbelief, and "taste that which ye called a lie." I shall not suffer by your folly : I cannot help it if ye will not save yourselves. Many nations before you have despised the word of truth, and they were grievously punished. It will be so with you in the great day to come, even if God is not pleased to send down upon you an instant punishment as he did upon the unbelieving generations of old. This is the constant moral that Mohammad points again and again. It is needless to give many examples of the style of this period, for the difference between it and the second period is not very striking in an English translation, though the length of the verses is obviously greater. It must not, however, be supposed that Mohammad is always dull and prosaic at this time ; the old eloquence often flashes out—as in the " Chapter of Thunder " (xiii.), where some parts are equal to anything in the earliest speeches. And few passages in the Korān surpass these verses in chapter vi.*:—

Say, " Whose is what is in the heavens and the earth ? "
Say, " God's, who has imposed mercy on himself."
With Him are the keys of the unseen. None knows them save
he ; he knows what is in the land and in the sea ; and
there falls not a leaf save that he knows it ; nor a grain
in the darkness of the earth, nor aught that is moist, nor
aught that is dry, save that is in his perspicuous Book.
He it is who takes you to himself at night, and knows what
you have gained in the day ; then he raises you up again,
that your appointed time may be fulfilled ; then unto Him
is your return, and then will he inform you of what ye
have done.

---

* The late Professor Palmer's translation.

> Verily, God it is who cleaves out the grain and the date-stone;
> he brings forth the living from the dead, and it is he who
> brings the dead from the living. There is God! How then
> can ye be beguiled?
> It is he who cleaves out the morning, and makes night a repose,
> and the sun and the moon two reckonings—that is the
> decree of the mighty, the wise!
> There is God for you, your Lord! There is no God but he,
> the Creator of everything; then worship Him, for he o'er
> everything keeps guard!
> Sight perceives Him not, but he perceives men's sights; for he
> is the subtle, the aware.
> Say, "Verily, my prayers and my devotion and my life and my
> death belong to God, the Lord of the worlds."

Very little is added to the definiteness of the moral teaching in the third period. "Verily God bids you do justice and good, and give to kindred their due, and he forbids you to sin and do wrong and oppress," is as detailed a commandment as Mohammad generally cares to give. A list of prohibited meats, indeed, is given in chapter xvi. ; usury is added to the practices already forbidden ; useless asceticism is discouraged ; certain unimportant Arab customs are abolished ; but nothing of real consequence is added to the moral law or the ritual of Islám. The whole duty of man is still capable of expression in few words :—

> Come! I will recite what your Lord has forbidden you :—that
> ye may not associate aught with Him, and may show kindness
> to your parents, and not kill your children through poverty;—
> we will provide for you and them;—and draw not nigh to
> flagrant sins, either apparent or concealed, and kill not the
> soul, which God hath forbidden, save by right; that is what
> God ordains you, haply ye may understand. And draw not
> nigh to the wealth of the orphan, save so as to better it, until
> he reaches full age; and give weight and measure with justice.
> We do not compel the soul save what it can compass; and

when ye pronounce (judgment) then be just, though it be in the case of a relative. And God's compact fulfil ye: that is what he ordained you, haply ye may be mindful. Verily, this is my right way, follow it then.

Thus a close examination of the earlier of the two main divisions of the Korān reveals no great variety of subjects or treatment. Mohammad's theology is confined to the unity of God, whose power he seeks to illustrate by the recital of the marvels of nature, and whose justice will be vindicated at a great day of reckoning. The complicated ritual familiar to students of modern Mohammadanism is not so far elaborated. The social system and laws of Islām are not yet fixed in their terrible immobility. We hear nothing but a voice crying in the wilderness the words of the prophet of old—" Hear, O Israel! The Lord your God is one Lord."

When we turn to the second great division of the Korān, the twenty-four chapters composed during the ten years after the Flight to Medīna, we begin to understand how the details of Mohammadanism were formed. Hitherto we have only seen an earnest man struggling to bring home to his people the error of their unbelief, and to draw them to the worship of the true God. We have now to see the Prophet as king and legislator. When Mohammad joined his fugitive disciples at Medīna, he found the city prepared to welcome him as its sole ruler, and from this time his plain function of prophet becomes confused with wider and less reconcileable duties. He had to govern a mixed multitude which was little accustomed to submit to authority, and in which were several antagonistic factions. Besides his own fellow-refugees and the converts of Medīna, between whom there was always some jealousy, Mohammad had to deal with a large party of those who judged it politic to profess Islām, but were ready to recant and plot against the Prophet whenever opportunity offered. These are the men whom the Korān frequently attacks under the name of " the Hypocrites." Besides these, the Jews were very numerous in and round Medīna, and though they were at first inclined to palm off Mohammad upon their neighbours as their own promised Messiah, they soon found that he was not the man to make a tool of, and thenceforward they showed themselves his most determined enemies. To keep order among all these sections was no easy task for a born statesman, and to Mohammad, who had no training in the art of governing men, it was peculiarly difficult. His remarkable power of personal influence, which evoked an enthusiastic loyalty from his followers, stood him in good stead, and it must be allowed that he proved himself a strong ruler, as well as a zealous prophet. How far his character as prophet was corrupted by the necessities of government we need not discuss*; for the inspiration of the Korān and the sincerity of its preacher have nothing to do with the present chapter. The point to be considered is merely the variety of causes which produced the comparative complexity of the Medīna chapters. It is intelligible that the nature of the

---

* See above, p. 80 ff.

revelation should change with altered circumstances. Whereas formerly Mohammad merely endeavoured to preach righteousness and the fear of God to an unbelieving city, he was now to wage wars, to subdue rebels, to reconcile rivals, to make treaties, to withstand a siege, to lead a nation to conquest. His words must now not merely speak of a judgment to come, but must encourage the warrior on the battle-field, sing the pæan after victory, animate after defeat, soothe the impatient, curb the rash, rebuke the wrongdoer, reconcile adversaries, and adjust all differences. The Prophet's house at Medīna was practically the court of appeal of the whole body of Muslims. Nothing could be settled without his counsel. Matters of social arrangement, the most delicate domestic details, as well as the larger issues of peace and war, were decided by the Prophet alone. If a man died, the principle of inheritance had to be laid down by Mohammad. If a man quarrelled with his wife, divorce must be explained ; every possible matter of dispute came before the Prophet's carpet, and was then and there considered and pronounced upon ; and these judgments were to last for all time ! Mohammad allowed no difference of degree in inspiration, and his decision, for instance, that he himself might take more than the prescribed number of wives was, in his mind, (or at least in his public declarations,) as much the word of God as the chapter of the Unity. He had, fortunately, a good measure of common sense, and his judgment was generally sound ; else the evil of thus stereotyping the decisions of a particular time and circumstance might have been far greater. But as it is the laws of the Korān represent the modified customs of a rude and uncivilised people, and are often wholly inapplicable to other nations and stages of development. That the laws he approved as suitable to his fellow-countrymen would be intolerable to a different people, who could nevertheless receive his doctrine, was a possibility that was not likely to have occurred to Mohammad, though he seems to have foreseen a time when obedience to all his laws would not be essential.

Under these circumstances it is fortunate that Mohammad never attempted to arrange a code of law, and that his scattered decisions are few and often vague. It is surprising how little definite legislation there is in the Korān. We have seen that there is next to none in the Mekkan speeches; but even in those of Medīna there is singularly little distinct law. The greater portion of the Medīna chapters is concerned with passing events. The conduct of the Muslims in battle and the praise and honour of those who die "in God's way" are frequent topics, and Mohammad is not sparing in abuse of those who show the white feather when there is fighting to be done. A considerable proportion of verses relate to "the Hypocrites," who were constantly giving the prophet-king cause for apprehension. But the chief theme in the Medina orations is the conduct of the Jews, whom Mohammad could never forgive for their rejection of him. He protested that he was foretold in their own scriptures, and that they "knew him as they knew their own children," if only they would admit it; and he promulgated the theory that they had purposely corrupted their sacred books in order to prevent the people from recognising the clear description by which he was portrayed therein. The Jews also repudiated his legends of the patriarchs and prophets, though they came out of their own Haggadah; and Mohammad was obliged to claim a higher origin for his stories. Altogether the Jews were a grievous thorn in the Prophet's side, and when we read in his life how terrible a punishment he allowed to be laid on them, we cannot be surprised at the bitterness of the denunciations with which the pages of the Medīna chapters abound. He taunts them for the little profit their scriptures are to them, and likens them to an ass carrying books :—

Do ye not see those who have been given a portion of the book? They buy error, and they wish that ye may err from the way! But God knows best who your enemies are, and God suffices as a patron, and sufficient is God as a help. And those who are Jews and those who pervert the words from their places, distorting with their tongues and taunting about religion—may God curse them in their unbelief. . . . Behold how they devise against God a lie!

The likeness of those who were charged with the Law and then bore it not is as the likeness of an ass bearing books : sorry is the likeness of the people who say God's signs are lies! but God guides not an unjust people!

Mohammad is less hostile to the Christians, probably because he had not yet come into intimate relations with them, and had therefore not yet tested their stiffneckedness. He frequently repudiates the doctrine of the Trinity and the sonship—" the Messiah,

Jesus the Son of Mary, is but the apostle of God and his word and a spirit from Him : believe then in God and his apostles and say not 'Three'; have done! it were better for you. God is only one God. . . . The Messiah doth surely not disdain to be a servant of God"; but his attitude at first is friendly :—

Thou wilt surely find that the strongest in enmity against those who believe are the Jews and the idolaters; and thou wilt find the nearest in love to those who believe to be those who say "We are Christians"; that is because there are amongst them priests and monks, and because they are not proud. And when they hear what has been revealed to the Prophet, you will see their eyes gush with tears at what they recognise as truth therein; and they will say, "O our Lord, we believe, so write us down among the witnesses . . ." Therefore has God rewarded them, for what they said, with gardens beneath which rivers flow, to dwell therein for aye.

But afterwards Mohammad changed his good opinion of the Christians, and his revulsion of feeling is expressed with vigour :—

The Jews say Ezra is the son of God; and the Christians say that the Messiah is the son of God;—God fight them! how they lie! They take their doctors and their monks for lords rather than God, and the Messiah the son of Mary; but they are bidden to worship but one God, there is no God but he; celebrated be his praise from what they join with Him! They desire to put out the light of God with their mouths, but God will not have it but that we should perfect his light, averse though the misbelievers be! He it is who sent his apostle with guidance and the religion of truth, to make it prevail over every other religion, averse although idolaters may be!

O ye who believe! Verily, many of the doctors and the monks devour the wealth of men openly, and turn folk from God's way; but those who store up gold and silver and expend it not in God's way,—give them glad tidings of grievous woe! On the day when it shall be heated in the fire of hell, and their brows shall be branded therewith, and their sides and their backs!—"This is what ye stored up for yourselves, taste then what ye stored up!"*

These later denunciations probably annul the more favourable judgments elsewhere expressed, for Mohammad distinctly admitted that some verses were to be held as abrogated by others. The statement, therefore, that "Everyone who believes, and the Jews and the Christians and the Sabians, who believe in God and the last day, there shall come no fear upon them, neither shall they grieve," is in the opinion of most Muslims null and void.

Besides these speeches on the political situation and the parties of the State, which occupy so large a part of the Medīna division of the Korān, more words are devoted to the Prophet himself than heretofore. As ruler of a turbulent city, Mohammad found it necessary to maintain his dignity, and there are several indications of this in his utterances. The people are ordered not to approach the Prophet as if he were an ordinary person, and it is solemnly laid down that he who obeys the apostle obeys God. Mohammad's family receive a share of attention; special permissions are accorded him from heaven in respect of his marriages, and the character of one of his wives is divinely vindicated. Such passages are interesting only to the biographer of Mohammad, and to him they form a perplexing problem, which has been solved in very conflicting ways.

---

* Professor Palmer's translation, from which most of the preceding extracts from the Medīna chapters are taken.

Omitting then all that refers merely to temporary matters, that is, the major part of the Medīna chapters, the residue of oratory and law that remains to be considered is not large. In spite of the altered subjects of the revelation and the multitude of uninteresting or ephemeral details treated, it must not be supposed that all the light of eloquence has died out. It is true that the style is dull and protracted, like that of the third Mekkan period; the verses are long, and the chapters bear evidence of being patched up from a large number of fragmentary utterances—answers to questions, outbursts of wrath at some special provocation, and the like. But there are here and there passages exhibiting a beauty and nobility of thought and expression which were surpassed in no period of the Prophet's career. Such is the magnificent imagery in the " Chapter of Light " (xxiv.) :—

God is the light of the heavens and the earth; his light is as a niche in which is a lamp, and the lamp in a glass; the glass is as it were a glittering star: it is lit from a blessed tree, an olive neither of the east nor of the west, the oil thereof would well-nigh shine, though no fire touched it—light upon light— God guideth to His light whom He pleaseth . . .

In the houses God has suffered to be raised for His name to be commemorated therein; men magnify Him at morn and eve;

Men whom neither merchandise nor trafficking divert from remembering God, and being instant in prayer and giving alms, fearing a day when hearts and eyes shall blench;

That God may recompense them for the best that they have wrought, and give them increase of His grace; for God maketh provision for whom He pleaseth without count.

But those who disbelieve are like a vapour in a plain:—the thirsty thinketh it water, till, when he cometh to it, he findeth nothing; but he findeth God with him; and He will settle his account, for God is quick at reckoning:—

Or like black night on a deep sea, which wave above wave doth cover, and cloud over wave—gloom upon gloom—when one putteth out his hand he can scarcely see it; for to whom God giveth not light, he hath no light.

Hast thou not seen that what is in the heavens and the earth magnifieth God, and the birds on the wing? each one knoweth its prayer and its praise, and God knoweth what they do: God's is the empire of the heavens and the earth, and to Him must all things return.

Hast thou not seen that God driveth the clouds, and then joineth them, and then heapeth them up, and thou mayest see the rain coming forth from their midst; and He sendeth down from the heaven mountain-clouds with hail therein, and He maketh it fall on whom He pleaseth, and He turns it away from whom He pleaseth; the flashing of His lightning well-nigh consumeth the eyes!*

The oratorical passages, however, are rare, like the descriptions of nature and the legends of the prophets. The chief remaining section of the Medīna chapters is that occupied by religious, civil, and penal regulations, and these are almost all contained in three chapters (ii., iv., and v.); they are, however, three of the longest, and form an aggregate of nearly 600 verses, or nearly a tenth of the whole Korān.

It is instructive to study this legal section of the Korān carefully in connection with the common statement that the religion of Mohammad is made up of a complicated and harassing ritual and a penal code which takes no count of the relative importance of crimes. Colonel Osborn, among various other mis-

---

* See my " Speeches and Tabletalk of the Prophet Mohammad," Introduction, li., lii.

takes in his clever books on Islām, has said that the same fearful punishment is ordained for a serious sin and a mere trifling infringement of ceremonial regulations. That he is altogether wrong may be proved from the Korān itself—in which it is stated that if the believers avoid *great sins*, God will wipe out their offences, for he is very forgiving. But, in truth, all this complaint of complicated ritual and law is not borne out by the Korān, however true it may be of modern Mohammadan practice. Mohammad had no desire to make a new code of jurisprudence or to bind his followers to a hard and fast ritual. He seldom appears to have volunteered a legal decision, except when a distinct abuse had to be removed: and the legal verses of the Korān are evidently answers to questions put to him in his capacity of Governor of Medīna. In the same way, he laid down but few rules for religious ceremonial, and even these he allowed to be broken in cases of illness or other impediments. "God wishes to make things easy for you," he says, "for man was created weak." He seems to have distrusted himself as a lawgiver, for there is a tradition which relates a speech of his, in which he cautions the people against taking his decision on wordly affairs as infallible. When he speaks on the things of God he is to be obeyed, but when he deals with human affairs he is only a man like those about him. He was contented to leave the ordinary Arab customs in force as the law of the Muslims, except when they were manifestly unjust.

The ritual of the Korān includes the necessary acts

of faith—the recital of the creed, prayer, almsgiving, fasting, and pilgrimage—but lays down scarcely any rules as to how they are to be performed. " Observe the prayers and the middle prayer," Mohammad vaguely directs, " and stand instant before God "; " Seek aid from patience and from prayer; verily God is with the patient " ; but he says nothing of the perplexing alternations of prostrations and formulas which are practised in the mosques. He refers to the Friday prayers, but not in a compulsory tone. " When ye journey about in the earth, it is no crime to you that ye come short in prayer, if ye fear that those who disbelieve will set upon you. God pardons everything but associating aught with Him." The fast is more clearly defined, but with ample reservations :—

There is prescribed for you the fast, as it was prescribed for those before you; maybe ye will fear God for a certain number of days; but he amongst you who is sick or on a journey may fast a (like) number of other days. And for those who are able to fast (and do not), the expiation is feeding a poor man; but he who voluntarily doeth a good act, it is better for him; and to fast is better for you, if ye only knew. The month of Ramadān, wherein the Korān was sent down: . . . whoso amongst you seeth this month, let him fast it; but he who is sick or on a journey, a (like) number of other days—God wisheth for you what is easy.

This reads more like advice than commandment. Turning the face to the Kibla of Mekka is distinctly enjoined in chapter ii., and the pilgrimage to the Kaaba is thus commended : " Verily Safā and Marwa are of the beacons of God, and he who makes the pilgrimage unto the House (Kaaba), or visits it, it is no crime for him to compass it about; and he who obeys his own

impulse to a good work, God is grateful and doth know." Almsgiving is frequently enjoined, but the amount of the alms is merely described as "the surplus." We also find that forbidden food is what has died of itself, and blood, and the flesh of swine, "which is an abomination," and meats which have been offered to idols, to which were added subsequently all animals that had been strangled or gored or preyed upon. Except these, no food was unlawful. "Eat ye of the good things wherewith we have provided you, and give thanks to God." Further, the believers were forbidden to drink wine, and to make statues, and play at games of chance; "in them is sin and profit to men, but the sin is greater than the profit." Usury was strictly prohibited, and classed among the great sins. Ablutions are mentioned, and sand is allowed as a substitute for water; but the details of wudū are not laid down. War against the unbelievers is thus ordained : " Fight in the path of God with those who fight with you, but exceed not. Kill them wheresoever ye find them, and thrust them out from whence they thrust you out, for dissent is worse than slaughter. But if they desist, then verily God is forgiving and merciful. . . . Let there be no hostility save against the unjust; whoso transgresseth against you, transgress against him in like manner "
—a different doctrine from what Mohammad said elsewhere, " Repel evil with what is better." Fighting in the sacred months is a great sin, but is sometimes necessary.

The civil regulations of the Korān are scarcely

more definite than those which refer to the rites of
religion. The law of marriage is capable of more
than one interpretation, and wears the aspect rather
of a recommendation than a statute : " If ye fear that
ye cannot do justice between orphans, then marry such
women as are lawful to you, by twos or threes or
fours ; and if ye fear ye cannot be equitable, then only
one, or what your right hands possess (*i.e.* slaves).
That is the chief thing—that ye be not unfair."
Marriage with unbelievers is forbidden : " Surely a
believing handmaiden is better than an idolatrous
wife." The laws relating to divorce are more explicit
than most regulations of the Korān, and contain most
of the details now in common use in Mohammadan
countries. The laws affecting women are indeed the
most minute and the most considerate in the Korān.
It was here that Mohammad made his principal
reforms, and though to a European these reforms may
seem slight, in contrast with the previous condition of
Arab women they were considerable. The restrictions
of polygamy and recommendation of monogamy, the
institution of prohibited degrees against the horrible
laxity of Arabian marriages, the limitations of divorce,
and stringent rules as to the support of divorced
women during a certain period by their former husbands and as to the maintenance of children, the
innovation of creating women heirs at law, though
only to half the value of men, the abolition of the
custom which treated a man's widow as a part of
his hereditary chattels, form a considerable list of
removed disabilities. Mohammad, indeed, had no

very high opinion of women, as many traditions testify, and the following verse from chapter iv. of the Korān carries with it an unfavourable impression :—

Men stand superior to women in that God hath preferred some of them over others, and in that they expend of their wealth. And virtuous women are devoted, careful in their husbands' absence, as God has cared for them. But those whose perverseness ye fear, admonish them and remove them into bed-chambers and beat them; but if they submit to you, then do not seek a way against them; verily, God is high and great.

But he goes on to advise reconciliation by means of arbiters chosen by the two disputants, and frequently counsels kindness to wives; and it is a fact that no profound legislator ever made such important changes in favour of women as did Mohammad in spite of his narrow outlook and his poor opinion of the sex.

The raising of women to the position of heirs is not the only innovation that Mohammad made in the law of inheritance. It may almost be said that he took away the power of testamentary disposition. The just share of each relative is appointed, and the testator has only the power of disposing as he pleases with one-third of his property. It must not be imagined, however, that the complicated and delicate machinery which Mr. Alaric Rumsey has so ably explained in his " Mohammadan Law of Inheritance " is to be found in full in the Korān. The general principle is given, and certain details, which it needs a Mohammadan lawyer to elucidate (cf. ch. iv., 11–16). One ordinance as to wills deserves to be mentioned : a man is required to provide a year's maintenance for his widows, that they need not be compelled to leave their homes. The main peculiarity of Mohammad's principles of inheritance is the definite institution of an hereditary reserve of two-thirds, which the testator cannot touch, and which devolves upon certain regular heirs, or, in default, upon the state. The system undoubtedly has its merits, and it has been not seldom extolled above the European principle of free disposition; but it may be doubted whether the wide diffusion of property which it involves is, on the whole, advantageous to the state, or has proved successful even under the favourable conditions which certain peculiarities of Eastern life supply.

The penal law of the Korān is extremely fragmentary. Murder is to be dealt with by the Arab custom of vendetta: "retaliation is prescribed for you for the slain, the free for the free, the slave for the slave, the woman for the woman; yet for him who is remitted aught by his brother shall be prosecution in reason, and payment in generosity." Accidental homicide of a Muslim is to be compounded for by the bloodwit and freeing a believing slave. Inchastity in wives was to be punished by immuring the woman until death should release her, " or God make for her a way "; but stoning *both* parties (according to an authentic fragment not included in the ordinary Korān) was afterwards ordained. Four witnesses are required to prove a charge of this gravity. Slaves, in consideration of their disabilities, are to receive one-half the penalty of free women in strokes of the whip. Thieves are punished by cutting off the hands. This is practically all that Mohammad distinctly

11 *

ordained in the matter of criminal law. We do not deny that something more may be extracted from his speeches by inference ; but what has just been epitomised is all that he stands definitely committed to in the Korān.

These facts, drawn from a study of the Medīna chapters, suggest some important conclusions. It is not unusual to compare the Korān to the Pentateuch, and to assert that each forms the law-book as well as the gospel of its sect. The resemblance is stronger than is commonly supposed. Just as the Hebrews deposed their Pentateuch in favour of the Talmud, so the Muslims abolished the Korān in favour of the Traditions and Decisions of the Learned. We do not mean to say that any Mohammadan, if asked what was the text-book of his religion, would answer anything but " the Korān "; but we do mean that practically it is not the Korān that guides his belief or practice. In the middle ages of Christendom it was not the New Testament but the " Summa Theologica " of Thomas Aquinas that decided questions of orthodoxy ; and in the present day does the orthodox churchman usually derive his creed from a personal investigation of the teaching of Christ in the Gospels ? Probably, if he refers to a document at all, the Church Catechism contents him, or if he be of a peculiarly inquiring disposition, a perusal of the Thirty-nine Articles will resolve all doubts. Yet he too would say his religion was drawn from the Gospels, and would not confess to the medium through which it was filtered. In precisely the same way Mohammadanism is constructed on far wider foundations than the Korān alone. The Prophet himself knew that his revelations did not meet all possible contingencies. When he sent Mo'adh to Yemen to collect and distribute alms, he asked him by what rule he would be guided. "By the law of the Korān," said Mo'adh. "But if you find no direction therein?" "Then I will act according to the example of the Prophet." "But if that fails?" "Then I will draw an analogy and act upon that." Mohammad warmly applauded his disciple's intelligence, and very important deductions have been drawn from this approval of the principle of analogy. It is, however, only the last resort. When the Korān supplied no definite decision, the private sayings of Mohammad—a vast body of oral traditions carefully preserved and handed down, and then collected and critically examined—were referred to. And if there was nothing to the purpose in the Sunneh, as this body of traditions is called, then the records of the general consent of the fathers were consulted. "The Law," says Ibn-Khaldūn, "is grounded on the general accord of the Companions of the Prophet and their followers." Finally there was the principle of analogy to guide them if all other sources failed. As a matter of fact, however, Muslims do not go through all this laborious process of investigation, but refer to one of the standard works in which it has all been done for them. It was soon found that "a system which sought to regulate all departments of life, all development of men's ideas and energies by the Sunneh and analogical deductions therefrom, was one which not only gave every temptation a system could give to the manufacture of Tradition, but one which would soon become too cumbersome to be of practical use." Hence, as Mr. Sell has explained in his admirable work on " The Faith of Islām," it became necessary to systematise and arrange this chaotic mass of traditions, decisions, and deductions ; and from this necessity sprang the four great systems of jurisprudence known from their founders as the Hanafite, Mālikite, Shāfi'ite, and Hanbalite, to one of which every orthodox Muslim belongs. The decisions of these four Imāms, Abū-Hanīfa, Ibn-Mālik, Esh-Shāfi'y and Ibn-Hanbal, are binding upon all true Churchmen, in the Mohammadan sense. It is the orthodox belief that since the four Imāms no doctor has arisen who can compare with them in learning and judgment, and whether or not this is true, it is certain that no theologian or jurist has ever superseded their digests of the law. No account is taken of the altered circumstances in which Mohammadans are now placed; the conclusions at which these Imāms arrived in the eighth and ninth centuries are held to be equally applicable in the nineteenth, and a popular theological handbook among our Indian fellow-subjects states that " it is not lawful to follow any other than the four Imāms; in these days, the Kādy must make no order, the Mufty give no fetweh, contrary to the opinions of the four Imāms." *

This is therefore the explanation of the difference

---

* E. Sell, " Faith of Islām," p. 19.

between modern Mohammadanism and the teaching
we have been able to draw from the Korān itself.
Islām rests on many pillars and the Korān is not the
only support. A large part of what Muslims now
believe and practise is not to be found in the Korān
at all. We do not mean to say that the Traditions of
Mohammad are not as good authority as the Korān—
indeed, except that in the latter case the Prophet
professed to speak the words of God and in the former
he did not so profess, there is little to choose between
them—nor do we assert that the early doctors of the
law displayed any imaginative fuculty in drawing their
inferences and analogies, though we have our sus-
picions; all we would insist on is that it is a mistake
to call the Korān either the theological compendium
or the *corpus legis* of Islām. It is neither the one nor
the other. Those who turn over the pages of the
Hedāya, or Khalīl's " Code Musalman," of which
M. Seignette has recently published a French translation in Algiers, will easily see how little help the
Korān is to the Mohammadan legist, and how few
of Khalīl's two thousand clauses can be traced to
the supposed Book of the Law. In the same way,
one may turn the pages of the Korān backwards and
forwards for a lifetime before one finds the smallest
indication of the formidable system of ritual which is
now considered an essential part of the Mohammadan
religion.

For ourselves we prefer the Korān to the religion
as it is now practised, and are glad to think that we
do not owe all the faults of modern Islām to the

sacred book on which it is supposed to rest. There is a peculiar simplicity about the Korān which attracts one in spite of its vain repetitions and dreariness. No book bears more distinctly the impress of its author's mind; of none can it be so positively asserted that it was spoken from the heart without thought or care. Inconsistent, contradictory, tedious, wearisome as it often is, the book has a personality in it which chains the attention. It is not a code of law, nor yet a theological system; but it is something better than these. It is the broken utterance of a human heart wholly incapable of disguise; and the heart was that of a man who has influenced the world as only One other has ever moved it.

CHAPTER V.

AN EASTERN REFORMATION.

THE fast of Ramadān was over, and the exhausted people were assembled in multitudes in the great Mosque of El-Basra. A man stood on the steps of the pulpit, and, throwing away his kaftān, cried aloud, "O, ye who are here met together! Like as I cast away this garment, so do I renounce all that I formerly believed." This man was El-Ash'ary; and this day, three hundred years after the flight of the Arab prophet from Mekka, was an epoch in the history of Islām. For the faith of Mohammad has passed through more phases and experienced greater revolutions than perhaps any other of the religions of the world. In the earliest, the Mekkan phase—the shortest but the noblest of all—we see a simple and singularly lofty Theism, disfigured indeed by a startling realism, but nevertheless possessing a grandeur that Islām never saw again. At Medīna the religion of Mohammad underwent considerable modifications, in correspondence with the altered circumstances of the Prophet's career. Thus far Islām had been a religion of the Arabs. It had yet to learn the influence that culture can exercise upon faith. When the tide of Mohammadan conquest rolled northwards this influence began to be exerted. At the Court of the Khalifs at Damascus was collected whatever of intellectual life the Syrians had attained to under the rule of the Byzantine Emperors; and, low as was the standard reached, it was sublime compared with anything the Arabs had before known, and Islām soon gave signs of its influence. At this time Christianity also came into play. The Syrian Christians were well received at the Court of the Khalifs, and were often encouraged to discuss points of faith with their Muslim antagonists; and the result of the collision of the two creeds is apparent in the doctrines of some of the early Mohammadan sects. When the 'Abbāsy Khalifs established their throne at Baghdād, Islām entered its fourth or Persian phase. Encountered by Parsīs and Buddhists, the Muslim conquerors discovered that there were not a few things in heaven and earth undreamt of in their philosophy, and they forthwith set about supplying the deficiency.

Thus we see Jewish, Christian, Syrian, and Persian elements successively introduced into the simple creed of Mekka. But another influence was brought to bear upon Islām in its third and fourth phases, more potent than any of these; this was the philosophy of Aristotle. Introduced to his works in Syria, the keen-witted Arabs, and more thoughtful and logical Persians, soon began to take a delight in them which would have done credit to any mediæval university.

Plato they never understood, and scarcely tried to understand; but Aristotle speedily created an enthusiasm among the Persian converts to Islām which was fraught with the most momentous results for the Mohammadan religion. The immediate effect of the study of Aristotle's logical writings was the foundation of schools of Freethinkers. Of these the school of the Mo'tezilīs was the most important. They were what may be called the Broad Church of Islām. They repudiated the realistic ideas about the Deity which were rife among other Muslims; denied predestination and asserted the doctrine of individual responsibility ; and scouted the legends of a sensual paradise and of bodily punishments in hell. Armed with all the resources of practised dialecticians, the Mo'tezilīs soon found themselves triumphant. The orthodox divines, unskilled in debate, and able to substantiate their opinions only by vain appeals to Sūrah and Sunnah, were utterly worsted in their encounters with the Broad Church, and eventually declined to discuss matters of faith altogether. Orthodoxy seemed about to be exterminated, at least among the educated classes, and free-thought (of an exceedingly moderate and reasonable kind, be it said) appeared everywhere victorious.

It was at this crisis that El-Ash'ary arose, a prophet in Basra. Born in the two hundred and sixtieth year of the Flight, of an old Arab stock, he was brought up in the strictest orthodoxy; and, as a natural result, on arriving at years of discretion he found the trammels of his childhood's faith too narrow for endurance, and enrolled himself among the disciples of a celebrated doctor of the Mo'tezily heresy. Up to his fortieth year he adhered strictly to the tenets of his master, and was generally regarded as his most distinguished pupil, when a difference arose between them, which was attended with weighty consequences for Islām. Tradition ascribes the origin of this difference to a discussion between pupil and master on the necessity that God should do right, and the impossibility of evil with Him. El-Ash'ary put the case of three brothers, one of whom lived a righteous life, the second was godless, and the third died when a child. The master answered, "The first will be rewarded in heaven, the second punished in hell, and the third neither punished nor rewarded." To this his disciple objected. "But what if the third were to say, O Lord! if thou hadst but let me live I might have become pious, and entered into paradise like my godfearing brother?" The sheykh replied, "God would say, I knew that thou, hadst thou lived, wouldest have been godless and an infidel, and have gone into hell." El-Ash'ary instantly pressed the obvious rejoinder, "Then the second brother would say, "O Lord! why didst thou not let me also die as a child, that I might not have sinned and come into hell?" The professor, fairly driven to bay, exclaimed, "Art thou possessed?" "Nay," said El-Ash'ary, "but the sheykh's ass is stuck fast on the bridge!"

Whatever may be the historical truth that lies beneath this tradition—and questions like these have been asked and left unanswered among others than

Muslims, and in later times than the tenth century—the fact is certain 'that El-Ash'ary, dissatisfied with the liberal school, of which he had been a zealous supporter to his fortieth year, and perhaps filled with that longing after a definite and authorised creed which has brought about the most extraordinary revulsions of faith in men of all times and of all shades of intellect, gave himself up to a minute examination of the Korān and traditions, in order to test the evidences of orthodox Mohammadanism. After a period of severe mental struggle, not without the customary accompaniment of visions with which legend is wont to embellish such states of transition, he satisfied himself of the errors of free-thought, drew up a *Summa Theologica* of his reformed doctrine, and presented it in the great mosque of El-Basra with the words and gesture already narrated.

The mere reaction of religious feeling from scepticism to strict orthodoxy. would in itself be little. History has furnished countless instances of men who, weary of battling in the quicksands of free-thought, have taken refuge beneath the sheltering rock of a traditional Church. But it is not often that these men carry back with them into their peaceful retreat the broad principles and scientific methods which were formerly their greatest pride. They generally look back upon their days of scepticism with horror and affright; and do not dare to approach ever so distantly their former canons of evidence and methods of reasoning. El-Ash'ary's case was different, and it is this that gives it so great an historical importance.

He saw that, without the logical training of their opponents, the orthodox party could not hope to maintain their ground, and he at once introduced into traditional Islām the dialectic system of the heretical sect in which he had been educated. This was his work; not to give the people a heaven-born revelation, not even to elaborate a new interpretation of Mohammad's obscure sayings; but simply to give the orthodox the weapons of the sceptics, to teach the upholders of the traditions how to defend them against the skilful arguments of their adversaries. It seems but a slight thing, this moulding of the Arab material in a foreign form, this grafting of Greek logic on Mekkan dogmas; but it produced astounding results. It effected nothing less than the overthrow of the liberal school, and the establishment of Ash'arite Islām, or at least forms of Islām mainly founded on Ash'arite principles, over the greater part of the Mohammadan world to this day. With us in the present time, the vanquished indeed claim more sympathy than the victors. The defeated liberal party was really nearer to Mohammad's earliest teaching than was El-Ash'ary; and from the point of view of comparative religion there is no question that the Mo'tezilīs were far in advance of the orthodox divines. Yet, whichever way our sympathies may turn, it is impossible not to recognise the importance of El-Ash'ary's place in the history of Mohammadanism.

The remainder of the life of our reformer was spent in disputations at the mosques, where he would hold at bay a ring of sceptics, making them wonder at the keen edge of his replies ; and in composing polemical treatises, of which about a hundred, only one-third of the whole number, have come down to us. After five-and-twenty years thus spent in doing battle with the heretics, he died at El-Basra, in A.D. 935, the most distinguished man of his time. It is not creditable to his charity to have to record that the disciple on whose breast he lay heard the dying man mutter these last words :—" The curse of God be on the Mo'tezilīs ; their work is delusion and lies."

CHAPTER VI.

THE BROTHERHOOD OF PURITY.

THE influence of Arabian Philosophy upon the development of European thought has never been adequately recognised. The older historians of Western culture were shy of owning a debt to infidels, whether Jews or Muslims; and more recent writers have been scarcely more generous, though from a different cause: they have convinced themselves that there is no salvation beyond the Mediterranean, and have treated with a lofty disdain all things Eastern, by a sort of ethnic prejudice which does not widely differ from the Brahman principle of caste. But there is more in this neglect than religious or ethnic prejudice: the obscurity which veils too many oriental studies from ordinary men of culture is deepened in the case of Arabian Philosophy. Even specialists have till recently known very little of the subject, and there is no text-book for the historical student. Renan's two essays—on Greek philosophy in Syria, and on Averroes—may be the alpha and the omega of Arabian philosophy, but there are a score or so of letters between them which are essential to the right understanding of the language. The Aristotelianism

of Averroes is not an epitome of the philosophy of the
Arabs, for it renders no account of those neo-Platonic
elements which produced in the schools of Baghdād
those disputes which were a foretaste of the conflict
between Realists and Nominalists in the universities
of Europe. But Averroes and the little we know of
Avicenna have satisfied the students of philosophy,
and no wider view of the Arabian movement has been
sought. It is not surprising, therefore, that most
people are vague in their conception of the share of
the Arabs in helping on the development of European
culture. They know the common-places—that Greek
philosophy was preserved by the Arabs for the schoolmen's use—that Roger Bacon was a pupil of the
Arabs—that a good many scientific terms beginning
with *al-* are derived from the Arabic, and the like ;
but how the Arabs got that philosophy, how they preserved it, what they made of it, where they studied it,
whither and through what course they transmitted it—
all these are unanswered questions to the most of them,
if they are so much as questions at all. And small
blame is theirs, for no specialist has taken the trouble
to bring this link in the history of thought home to
them. The only worthy book on the subject—the
work of which this chapter is meant to furnish an outline—contains over a thousand pages of a happy mixture of German and Oriental obscurity and disorder ;
and the German translator's summary thereof reaches
four hundred pages ! Ordinary Englishmen of culture,
who ought to know something of the place of the Arabs
in the history of civilisation, cannot be expected to read

a work of this length and character. But the main results can be reduced to a manageable size and an intelligible order; and the following pages are an attempt to make them available for those who are not specialists.

It is well to clear the way at starting by an explanation of the term " Arabian."   There can be no more serious mistake than to imagine that the Arabs came forth from their rude civilisation into the cultured cities of the Greek empire, and speedily became the lamps of learning during the dark ages of Europe. The greater part of what we call Arab culture, Arab science, Arab philosophy, and Arab art, was the work of the strangers who came under the yoke of the conquering Muslims, and, above all, Persians and Spaniards. The Semitic, and perhaps especially the Arab, mind is not given to the departments of study which we are accustomed to associate with the notion of Arabian philosophy. Exact science, and the chains of logical reasoning, are not consonant with the irregular imaginative turn of the Arab intellect ; and few Arabs excelled either in science or philosophy. Their help was hardly needed, for the Persians, who did their culture for them, possessed just that order of mind which lends itself most willingly to those studies, and the immense number of works written by Persians in Arabic, if they only all survived, would leave little for the Arab to do. When, therefore, we speak of Arabian philosophy (and the like), we mean philosophy written in the Arabic tongue, but not necessarily, or even commonly, by Arabs.

Yet there is a certain fitness in applying the term

Arabian to the philosophy which the Arabic-writing Persians studied, for it owed its robustness and its wide prevalence to the religion of the Arabs. If the Korān had not furnished a glorious field for dialectical contest, if orthodoxy had not kindled by the fire of persecution the zeal of the oppressed philosophers, if Islām had not established a general intellectual communion between countries so far apart as Spain and Persia, the high schools of the Middle Age might never have adored their Aristotle, and the later Renaissance of Italy might have reaped all the honours that belong to the earlier Renaissance of Spain; if indeed the latter was not a necessary forerunner of the Humanist movement in the fifteenth century, without which the New Learning would have found no ears open to hear its voice. Islām generally maintained a hold on Arabian philosophy, and its methods were not seldom turned to the advantage of the faith; the relations between the two nearly resembled the tie between the Latin Church and the schoolmen; and the Arabian philosophers usually professed Islām with about as much of the original simple faith of Mohammad in them as some of the fathers of the Church had of the teaching of Christ. By this connection with Islām Arabian philosophy obtained a wider bearing than it could otherwise have gained. It is a noteworthy fact, moreover, which should be remembered by those who deny the Arabs all share in the credit of preserving the learning of the Greeks, that the Persians had that learning in their midst long before the Arabs conquered them, but do not seem to have turned it to much account until their Arab masters set them to work. This is surely a fact to be considered by those who echo G. H. Lewes's wholesale condemnation of the Arabs as mere barbarians.

How Greek philosophy came to be applied to Korānic theology is easily answered by a very superficial study of the history of Islām. We have nothing here to do with the beginnings of the faith, for there was no philosophy there—only one grand dogma, and a strange mixture of Jewish fables and old Arab superstitions kindled to live flame by the enthusiasm of a great man. We have to take up the history of the religion at a little later time, after its prophet's death, when the armies of the Bedawīs were surging over Syria and conquering the kingdom of the Sassanians. This Persia, which the troops of the once-derided "impostor" were now overrunning, was the meeting-place of many creeds and doctrines. Besides the ancient religion of the country, the Parsīism of Zoroaster, which had not much influence upon the invaders, two conflicting streams of thought coming from the west and the east may be distinguished—the Greek philosophic movement from the west, and the Buddhistic pantheism and mysticism from India. The first found its way to Persia chiefly in the hands of the banished Nestorians, who had translated many of the Greek classics into Syriac, and who sought to diffuse a wider knowledge of these treasures of thought in the schools which they founded in the land of their exile, in the cities of the Sassanian kings of Persia. What form of Greek philosophy it was that thus found its way through the Syriac into Persian and then Arab minds, and that was soon to be set forth in the Arabic tongue and spread abroad over the lands of the Muslims, may be readily surmised from what is known of the religious disputes of the fifth century and the character of the Nestorian controversy; what shape it afterwards took in the hands of the Arabian Encyclopædists we shall presently see. The other influence, the pantheism and mysticism, whose effect may be traced not only in the important development of Sufism, but in most of the Mohammadan heresies —in their mystical tendencies, their allegorical interpretations, and the leaning of some sects to the emanation theory—undoubtedly acquired its prime impulse from Indian teachers and writings, though the neo-Platonism of Alexandria probably had no inconsiderable share in developing it.

These two opposing movements of thought were working in a country whose trade gathered together an odd medley of faiths and opinions, where banished Greek philosophers, Nestorians and Christians of many other sects, Zoroastrians, infidels and heretics of all kinds, formed the heterogeneous population of the great cities. It is easy to understand the difficulties that Islām had to encounter when introduced into such a land. Like a rough country yokel among polished gentlemen, it blushed for its uncouthness, and undervalued the health and vigour which these same gentlemen, in their elegant decrepitude, held as signs of rusticity which no well-bred person could

tolerate; and it forthwith set about repairing its
deficiencies by the painful acquirement of accomplishments which were irreconcilable with its essential
character. In other words, the Mohammadan doctors
found themselves face to face with metaphysical
problems which had never troubled the head of their
Prophet; they began to perceive that the Korān
doctrine in its primitive simplicity was not merely
ineffectual among the cultivated people they had
conquered, but was positively ridiculous in their eyes;
and they determined to find in the Korān what was
not there—a metaphysical conception of life and the
universe. It took many a year of hard fighting before
the orthodox were thus induced to accept the sugges-
tions of their opponents. They clung tenaciously to
the old crude dogma which had worked such a revolution in the world, till rout after rout convinced them
that to hold its own among the cultured thinking class
Islām must adopt the weapons of its adversaries, defend
itself by the help of the long-hated dialectics of the
Greek students, and marshal its dogmas in a pseudo-
philosophical uniform.

We are not now concerned with this development
of Islāmic theology—which came to its ripeness in
the teaching of El-Ash'ary,* in which the more
thoughful part of the orthodox Mohammadan world
now reposes—except in so far as it affected the
progress of philosophical study. The bitter contro-
versies that divided the followers of the Prophet on

---

* *See* Chapter V.

such points as the eternity of the attributes of God, and the createdness or the uncreatedness of the Korān (to omit more decidedly theological questions), are important to us, partly as showing the influence of philosophy upon the Mohammadan doctors before the very first century of the Flight had expired, but especially in their effect of driving the condemned heretical sects more and more into the arms of philosophy. The theological disputes produced sects, and the numerically weaker, because the more intelligent, of these turned towards the philosophical doctrines their reasons approved, yet without absolutely leaving Islām; and these *rational Muslims*—we use the term with the same vague meaning as "rational Christianity" —of whom the most noted were the sect called Mo'tezilīs, or Separatists, habitually handled the weapons of dialectical training to worst their opponents, whose stolid orthodoxy, sustained by no familiarity with logic or metaphysics, proved no match for their nimbler wits.

Thus we find a body of metaphysical schoolmen growing up among the Mohammadan divines, and in the theological colleges of Islām. Doctors held forth on Greek philosophy, and applied its methods to the religion of Mohammad. The court and the capital and the large towns ran wild about Graecism for a while under the rule of the son of " the good Hārūn-er-Rashīd," the Persian-loving, speculative, sceptic El-Mamūn. In this movement there were all shades of rationalizers of the faith, from those who merely tried to systematize and reconcile the conflicting doctrines of the Korān, to those who virtually rejected the Korān altogether. There were moderate Muslim schoolmen, extreme Muslim schoolmen, and philosophers who were not Muslims at all—but these were few; and all alike owed their theories to Greek books. As early as the second 'Abbāsy Khalif's reign (760 A.D. *circ.*), the passion for translation from the Greek had begun with a rendering of Euclid; and later on El-Mamūn appointed official translators of Aristotle. Aristotle was the staple authority; but the works of the Alexandrian school, especially Porphyry's Isagoge, and Ptolemy's Almegist, held a high place in the general esteem. And soon a very considerable number of Greek writers were done into Arabic and devoured with avidity by a multitude of Mohammadan students.

It is astonishing how little we know of the details of this vehement study of Greek among the Arabs and Persians. It seems hardly credible that the vast number of works composed by the Arabian school of philosophy should have been almost wholly swept away by the overwhelming reaction to orthodoxy which succeeded the transitory enthusiasm for reason and culture. Yet even of the great names that shine out of the dry pages of the Eastern annalists, as lights in a dark world, we know very little at first-hand. We hear of the mathematical and astronomical (rather astrological) labours of El-Kindy, and his neo-Pythagorean view of the universe. Schmölders has published an introduction to Aristotle by El-Fārāby the ideal philosopher of the chroniclers; of the great

Avicenna (Ibn Sīnā) himself, what we know, except his medical canon, " El Kānūn," is chiefly derived from the account of a historian of Muslim sects, Esh-Shahrastāny. Of none of these voluminous writers do we possess much more than the titles of their works, or at most one or two special treatises out of a long series. What we know beyond this is gained from the notices of them by historians and other writers, not from their own works. The meagre section on Arabian philosophy in G. H. Lewes's " History " is a fair sample of the information to be had on the subject. Specialists can add some few details from rare and scattered manuscripts ; but a complete and comprehensive account of any of the great philosophers' opinions and methods, written by themselves or their disciples, is wanting. We only read a list of names, and are told by later writers that these men made great discoveries in mathematics, or astronomy, or medicine, or promulgated systems of philosophy. We want to know something more definite. We should like an *instauratio magna* of Arabian philosophy, or at least a comprehensive outline of what that philosophy was. Such an outline we have at last in the treatises Professor Dieterici has translated.

The Arabian chroniclers tell us how, in the latter part of the eighth century of the Christian era, a strange company used to meet together in one of the great cities of the Eastern Khalifate, for the interchange of ideas on literature, poetry, philosophy, and things in general. This debating society consisted of ten members : a Sunny, or orthodox believer in

Mohammadan tradition; a Shi'y, or upholder of the claims of the rival house of 'Aly, and consequently a despiser of all Sunnīs and all things and persons reverenced by Sunnīs; a Manichean, or dualist; a Muslim of the ultra-puritan sect; an erotic poet of extremely free notions, a materialist, a Jew, a Christian, a Parsy, and a Sabian. This motley group used to sit together in perfect enjoyment of each other's society, telling good stories, discoursing of letters, arguing on religion or philosophy or what you will, and all with perfect good-humour and tolerance of the most diverse opinions.

That debating club shows what a change of country and the admission of foreign ideas had made possible in a Muslim city. But it was a club of men who, we must believe, were not seriously moved to think at all. They belonged to various views, because in that intellectual epoch views were the fashion. But they were not stirred to search earnestly for the secrets of the world, they did not trouble themselves with the question, What is life? What is the meaning of the contrast between this luxurious Court of Baghdād, and the groaning, perishing multitude on whose death it lives? What will be the end of these things? And if they really thought seriously about a theory of life, doubtless that reprobate poet had it all his own way in the argument.

Two hundred years later a very different society met together in the city of El-Basra, famous in the history of Mohammadan theology for the doctors it has brought up, and so renowned for orthodoxy that it is said no day passes but God bestows a smile upon this holy town. There, towards the last quarter of the tenth century, a knot of earnest men began to meet together, at fixed seasons, in a house set apart for their meetings. They formed a sort of Masonic Lodge, and their proceedings were carefully concealed, and none but the initiated were permitted to be present at their debates. They called themselves "Brethren of Purity," and the name well indicates their objects. They were grieved at the state of the Mohammadan Empire at that time, where division was, instead of unity, princes tearing fragments from the territory of the acknowledged Vicegerent of their God, armies trampling the land under bloody foot, everywhere slaughter and rapine; no religion at the Court, no justice at the Kādy's, wrangling over split straws at the Mosque; on all sides misery, and tyranny, and crime;—no faith, no trust, no moral strength or purpose in the world. Against the reckless license and debauchery of the time these "Brethren of Purity" raised their protest. They met together to seek if there were any way in which they might aid their fellows; and if not, at least they would join in keeping themselves "unspotted from the world" they could not mend. They exercised the utmost caution in the election of members to their lodge. They had a great doctrine of friendship, by which each friend should supply some quality or virtue wanting in another, and thereby aid in the attainment of a wide truthfulness; for in numbers alone, they held, could truth be won; error was the result of individual, and therefore partial, knowledge. Every member of this Brotherhood must contribute in some manner to its completeness as an organ of truth. The admission of a vicious member might undo the whole society. The Brothers were classed in four grades, according to their moral worth and elevation of soul, the highest being composed of those who were weary of this body—which is but the egg-shell, meant to hatch the chick, and is useless when the chick, the soul, recognizes its separate existence— and were ready for the severing of soul from body and the home-journeying to God. This Home-Quest is the great idea of their theological teaching ; every member who is called must understand it, and believe in it with all his heart, and teach it to others, and live with his eyes towards it. It is in fact something very like the Nirvāna of Buddhism, to which in religion these Persian pantheists nearly approached. They have, too, the sweetness and gentleness of Buddhism, and in this they stand forth conspicuously from the pharisaism and hardness of dogmatic Islām. Their God is not the tyrant of the orthodox divines, but a supremely loving and wise Creator, who has breathed his life into all the universe for good and not for ill. And their virtues, equally, are not the virtues of Islām, not so much right-eousness and the due quittance of obligations, as mild-ness and gentleness towards all men, forgiveness, long-suffering, and compassion, the yielding up of self for others' sake. In this Brotherhood, self is forgotten ; all act by the help of each, all rely upon each for succour and advice, and if a Brother sees it will be good for another that he should sacrifice his life for him, he willingly gives it. No place is found in the Brotherhood for the vices of the outside world ; envy, hatred, pride, avarice, hypocrisy, and deceit, do not fit into their scheme, — "they only hinder the worship of truth."

This is only one side of the design of this Lodge of Pure Brethren—their campaign against immorality. They have also an intellectual side, and it is this which gives them their permanent importance. They were aware how easy it is for immorality and purposelessness of life to grow out of a general intellectual scepticism, such as prevailed among too many of their contemporaries. They knew that to enforce a high standard of action you must have a definite creed, a principle of life, whether theological or philosophical. Any theory of ethics must be shown to form a part of a wider theory of life to claim the adherence of men. No one system satisfied these Brethren. They were too well acquainted with other creeds, and too well trained in the logical use of thought, to accept the common orthodox Islām which had contented the desert Arabs. Yet all other creeds and systems equally appeared open to doubt or refutation. In this confusion they found their satisfaction in an eclectic theory. All these conflicting views, they said, must be only different ways of looking at the same thing. Truth must be one, and could not vary; these religions and philosophies were only portions of truth. God sent his spirit down upon all men; but, as a wise teacher can only instil into his pupil gradually and piecemeal the knowledge he would so gladly pour at one tide, so man could only receive truth partially and in fragments from his divine instructor. These fragments of truth were to be found in every system of faith and every method of philosophy; if men failed to detect them, the fault lay in their own imperfect intelligence—it was only the skill to read between the lines that was wanted to build up a harmonious whole out of the fragments of truth scattered about in sacred books and the writings of wise men and the mystic doctrines of saints.

The aim of the Brethren of Purity was, therefore, to construct such a whole out of these scattered parts. To effect this they ransacked every faith, every philosophy; " no science and no method is to be despised," they said ; no part of knowledge, no attempt to reach truth, was common or unclean to them ; they reverenced the germ of truth which they were convinced lay beneath all seeming falsehoods, and out of all these " guesses at truth," out of the miscellaneous collection of the then-known sciences, religions, and methods of thought, they endeavoured to build up a philosophy ; and they arranged their results in a definite and consistent order, in accordance with a well-conceived theory of emanation and evolution.

This theory and these results they set forth in fifty-one tracts, which they called " The Tracts of the Pure Brethren." The work only professes to be an epitome, an outline; its authors lay claim to no originality, they only summarize what others have thought and discovered. What they do lay claim to is system and completeness. The work does profess to contain a *systematized*, harmonious, co-ordinated view of the universe and life, its origin and destiny, formed out of many discordant, incoherent views; and it does claim to be a *complete* account of all things— to contain, in epitome, all that was known at the time it was written. It refers to more profound and special treatises for fuller information on the several sciences it touches upon, but it does claim to touch on all sciences, all departments of knowledge, and to set forth their leading results. In effect, it is, by its own showing, a *hand-encyclopædia of Arabian philosophy in the tenth century.*

It is not easy to exaggerate the importance of this encyclopædia. Its value lies in its completeness, in its systematizing of the results of Arabian study. We have complained of the fragmentary character of the remains of the chief Arabian philosophers: this encyclopædia meets the difficulty, and shows us their views as a whole. It was a favourable time for composing such a work. Most of the great names of Arabian science and philosophy had gone before—El-Kindy, El-Fārāby, Er-Rāzy, Thābit ibn Kurra and his son Sinān, and the rest, with Babek, the Sūfy metempsychosist—and the tide had already turned against the students, and orthodoxy had prohibited the sale of philosophical books.

There was no time to be lost if the labours of the philosophers were to be preserved; and so, just when Avicenna, the crown of Arabian philosophers and the embodier of all his predecessors, was coming into the world, the Brethren of Purity set about their task of gathering up the ideas of the age and putting them into their encyclopædia before orthodoxy could destroy them. Of that age of completeness, the age of Avicenna, this encyclopædia is the true mirror. Its defects are the defects of the age; the ideas it presents are the ideas of the age. It is a faithful portrait of the philosophy and science of the Arabs at the time when the enthusiasm for culture was coming to an end in the East, and only one great name was still to be added to the list of Arabian philosophers. And as we had no portrait of that philosophy that was at all perfect or complete, only a vignette or a profile or so, taken in a half-light, with the negatives destroyed, this full-length portrait of Arabian philosophy is of the highest value.

It has been said that this encyclopædia was not much thought of at the time of its appearance. If that were true it would not affect its real importance, and the fast-increasing power of the orthodox reaction would perfectly account for its unpopularity. But the facts that the work is quoted by one of the greatest of Arabian thinkers, El-Ghazzālī, that it was translated into Persian, and thought worthy of abridgments and epitomes, and, finally, that it was carried into Spain in time for Averroes to study it, seem to me to point to no slight popularity; and the record of a contemporary, credited by Barhebraeus (Abū-l-Faraj), confirms this view, and is interesting in giving us the opinions of the fellow-countrymen of the Brethren of Purity on their society and aims and writings. In the Chronicle of the Learned (*Tabakāt-el-Hukama*) of El-Kufty there is a report of a conversation which took place in 373 A.H. between Abū-Hayyān Et-Tawhidy and the Buweyhy Prince Samsām-ed-dawleh, who then sustained the dignity of Amīr-el-Umarā, or Prince of Princes, at the Khalif's court, and was virtually master of the Khalif himself.

The Tracts of the Brethren of Purity were just then making a sensation, and people were much exercised in their minds as to the authorship of these anonymous publications. Among others Samsām-ed-dawleh was desirous of knowing something more about their writers, and especially about the teaching of one Zeyd Ibn Rifā'a, who was reputed to be one of the writers in the encyclopædia, and, as we know now, was in truth its heart and soul. Abū-Hayyān was well acquainted with this Zeyd, and the Prince applied to him for information as to his friend's doctrine. And Abū-Hayyān answered : " He hath surpassing insight and clear understanding; he hath the command over verse and prose, excellently can he write—with logic and eloquence. His thoughts are of the destinies of mankind ; he listens to judgments, sifts opinions and beliefs, and is adroit every way, whether the establishment or the explanation of views be the matter in hand, or the bringing of the dispute to a close."

Then said the Prince : " What, then, is his system ?" I answered, says Ibn-Hayyān, " He stands in no definite relation with any one system. He knows how to form his school from all sides—in every question and in every divergence of opinion he displays his clearness in proving and his boldness in arguing.

"He lived long in El-Basra, and there associated with a number of people of different sciences and professions, among others Abū-Suleymān Mohammad El-Busty, known as El-Mukaddesy, Abū-l-Hasan 'Aly Ez-Zenjāny, Abū-Ahmad El-Mahrajāny, and El-Awfy. He mixed with them, and they formed a society of friends. They united in striving after holiness, purity, and uprightness, and set before themselves a doctrine whereby, they maintained, they should keep the road towards the attainment of the heavenly joy—for they held that religion was defiled by folly and entangled with error, and only by Greek philosophy could it be cleansed and purified; in which is both wisdom in belief and soundness in study. If one could but unite Greek philosophy with the religious law of Islâm, the perfection of faith, they thought, would be reached. With this design they wrote fifty tracts on all branches of philosophy, theoretical and practical, and furnished them with a table of contents, and entitled them 'The Tracts of the Brethren of Purity' (*Rasāïl Ikhwān es-safā*). They concealed their names and distributed the tracts among the booksellers' libraries, gave them, too, to the people, and stored them with pious phrases, religious parables, with self-evident propositions, and glossed methods."

The Prince said: "Hast thou seen these tracts?" and I answered: "I saw a number of them; they were diffuse, treated of everything, without bringing contentment or satisfying. There were extracts in

them, metaphors, entanglements, combinations. I
brought some of them to our sheykh, old Abū-Suleymān Mohammad Ibn Bahrām, the logician of Sijistān,
and laid them before him. He looked at them all
day, and went about with them for a long time, and
then gave them back to me. He said, ' They weary
without satisfying, deny without refuting, give without pleasing, weave without woof, comb out and curl
again. They believe what neither is nor can be.
They believe it is possible to class philosophy (to wit,
the doctrine of stars, and spheres, and measures, and
the Almegist) and the doctrine of the workings of
Nature, and music, and logic, in quality and quantity,
under the head of religion, and thus join faith and
reason. But that is a goal never yet reached, which
many, with keener spirit, more power, and conspicuous
judgment, have striven after before these without
attaining the desired end: rather did they succeed
in working mischief, grievous ill, and a sorry end.' "
And here the speakers plunge into a discussion as to
the possibility of a union between religion and philosophy, into which we will not follow them. The conversation proves that the work did create a sensation
on its first appearance, and shows how some scholars
regarded it.

Of the authorship of the fifty-one tracts, we have
seen that some doubt existed: the general opinion is
that Zeyd's writings were the nucleus of the collection, and that the four friends, mentioned by Abū-
Hayyān above, were his collaborators. Zeyd was the
leader in the crusade against the vices of the time.

His keen wit not seldom discomfited the hypocrites and abashed the scoffers. His career was one long struggle for a high moral standard and a noble purpose in life. He may well have given the impulse and direction to the Encyclopædists, and written some of the tracts himself. One thing, at least, is clear about the authors of the work: it is abundantly shown by internal evidence that they were learned in all the learning of the time, were well trained in the Arabian Greek school, and acquainted with the ancient literature of Persia and India. They knew, too, the Old and New Testaments well enough to correct the mistakes of the Korān; and their story of the Messiah is said to be "the worthiest record of the life of Jesus that can be met with in Arabic literature." In the critical faculty, indeed, they are singularly deficient, they admit false books of Aristotle side by side with true among their authorities; but that is a general deficiency in the oriental mind. In training and knowledge these men were well fitted for the work they undertook.

Dr. Friedrich Dieterici, Professor of Arabic at Berlin, has translated this Encyclopædia, chiefly from the Paris codex, but with collation of those of Gotha, Munich, Berlin, and Vienna. A printed text was published at Calcutta. For the last twenty years Professor Dieterici has been engaged on this translation, publishing a volume from time to time as each section of the work was completed. In 1858 appeared his rendering of the fable ("Mensch und Thier") appended to the twenty-first Tract of the Brotherhood of Purity; in 1861 their Natural Philosophy appeared in German; then in 1865 and 1868, respectively, their Propaedeutics and Logic; in 1871 and 1872 their Anthropology and Metaphysics. From those six "Quellenwerke," Dr. Dieterici composed his epitome of the whole in two more volumes, entitled "Makrokosmos" and "Mikrokosmos," in 1876 and 1879; and in the interval between these two, he published a popular lecture on the subject under the title of "Darwinismus im Xten und XIXten Jahrhundert," which included a somewhat superfluous attack upon the doctrine of evolution.

The publication of separate sections of the work at intervals, sometimes of several years, has been a great hindrance to its exciting the interest to which its real value entitles it. Though each part is important in itself, yet its importance lies chiefly in its relation to the whole work, as a part of an orderly exposition of Arabian philosophy. Moreover, Dr. Dieterici left several of the parts without any explanation of their origin; so that unless one had read the parable of "Mensch und Thier," the title of which is not a little obscure to any one unacquainted with the history of the Brotherhood of Purity, he would remain in perfect ignorance as to the authorship and aim of the work throughout the two or three hundred pages of the part. Now, however, that the whole Encyclopædia (with the exception of some of the theological tracts) is published, we need not criticise the way in which it gradually appeared. Of its merits as a translation it is impossible to judge without the original manuscripts. It does not pretend to be a literal rendering ; and the general sense of the Arabic doubtless presented few difficulties, except in philosophical and scientific terms, to Dr. Dieterici, who was studying Arabic in Egypt more than thirty years ago.

In technical matters, moreover, the translator has had the advantage of the assistance of several scientific men—as Professors and Drs. Bruhns, Förster, Karsten, Hanstein, Rammelsberg, and Ebrenberg.

Altogether, these twenty years of patient labour have resulted in a book which, whilst susceptible of much improvement, reflects the highest credit on Dr. Dieterici's industry and zeal, and is one of the most interesting additions to Oriental study that indefatigable Germany has produced for many years.

In the seventh Tract the Brethren put forward a scheme of knowledge, which will give an insight into their method, and is therefore subjoined. " The sciences," they say, "at which men toil, fall into primary studies, religious studies, and philosophical studies."

I. *Primary studies* are the educational sciences, intended to help men to a maintenance, and to direct them in their intercourse with others. They are nine in number: (*a*) writing and reading; (*b*) lexicography and grammar; (*c*) simple arithmetic; (*d*) poetry and music; (*e*) the doctrine of omens and forebodings; (*f*) that of magic, amulets, alchymy; (*g*) trades and handicrafts ; (*h*) selling and buying, commerce, agriculture, the breeding of cattle ; (*i*) biography.

II. *Religious studies* help the soul in its struggle towards the other world. They are five—revelation, explanation, tradition, law, and illumination.

III. PHILOSOPHICAL SCIENCES are of four sorts—propaedeutics, logic, physics, theology.

> A. PROPAEDEUTICS consist of arithmetic, geometry, astronomy, music.
>
> B. LOGIC is of two kinds : (*a*) analytica, the art of apprehending ; (*b*) rhetorica, or the art of those (sophists) who in theorizing and arguing would lead one into error.

1. The *Isagoge* aims at establishing a clear understanding of the six words employed in philosophical propositions : individual, species, genus, essential, enduring, and accidental properties—what each is in itself, what the six have in common, in what consists their difference, and how they bear upon the idea of the soul.

2. The *Categories* are to explain the meaning of the ten words, each of which denotes a *genus generum.* The first of these is substance ; the other nine, attributes. This tract shows what each of them is, how many species it contains. Further, it teaches the knowledge of the signs by which each is to be distinguished from the remainder ; and finally it points out how these all lead to the ideas which are contained in the notion of the soul.

3. The *Hermeneutics* lay down how to combine the

ten words, and the senses therefrom resulting, judgments and enunciations correct and false.

4. The *Analytica priora* explain the composition of premisses, and their various kinds, and the mode of forming out of them the syllogism, which binds together propositions and their conclusions.

5. The *Analytica posteriora* teaches how to form correct analogies and correct proofs.

C. PHYSICS are divided into seven sections:—

1. *The doctrine of the elements of bodies;* i.e. the knowledge of five things—matter, form, time, space, motion. Further, the values which result from a combination of one of these with another.

2. *The doctrine of heaven and earth;* i.e. the knowledge of the nature of the sphere-substances,—the stars, their number, the manner of their connection, the cause of their revolving; the question whether they are subject to development and decay, as is the case with the four elements beneath the moon-orbit; why the stars move and differ in rapidity and slowness; why the earth reposes in the midst of the universe; whether or not there is another world outside the universe; whether there is such a thing as a vacuum in nature; and the like.

3. The treatise on *development and decay* treats of the substance of the four elements—fire, air, water, earth—and shows how one of these changes into another by the influence of heavenly bodies, and thence spring new forms and things—mineral, plant, animal—which in turn decay and are changed back again into those elements.

4. The doctrine of *meteorology* shows how the air changes by the influence of the constellations. This happens by virtue of their motions and the falling of their rays upon these elements. . . . Proper to the air are colours, and alterations, such as light and darkness, heat and cold. The changes of wind, clouds, mist, rain, snow, hail, lightning, thunder-peals, falling stars, comets, rainbows, moon halos, and the like, arise over our heads as alterations and forms of air.

5. *Mineralogy* describes the substances which are condensed from the vapours pent up in the interior of the earth, and are formed from the moistures which are found in the air, in hollows and valleys, and in the sea-bottom. This is true of substances such as quicksilver, sulphur, alum, and salts, ammonium, gold, silver, copper, iron, lead and blacklead, stibium, beryl, hyacinth. Their qualities, uses, and disadvantages are mentioned.

6. *Botany* deals with everything that is sown or planted, or that springs up of itself on the surface of the earth, on the summits of mountains, in the depths of the sea, and on the banks of streams. These are trees, seeds, vegetables, herbs, grasses, and runners. The number of their species and genera are given, their habitats are stated, and how they drive their roots into the ground and lift up their branches in the air, how they spread over all the earth and reach out their boughs on all sides. Then is described the form of their boughs, which are long, short, thick, thin, straight or crooked; the shape of their leaves, which are broad or narrow, smooth or rough; their

flowers and blossoms, the formation of their fruit, kernels, and grains; their juice, their taste, their smell, their peculiarities, their uses and drawbacks, one after the other are spoken of.

7. *Zoology* has to do with all the other bodies, down to the vermin in animals, plants, fruit, grain, and the like; and it gives the number of genera and species and sub-species. It shows how the bodies spring from the womb, the egg, or putrefaction; how their limbs are put together and their bodies composed; their forms various and divisible into kinds. Further, their different sounds, their opposing natures and dispositions, as well as their proper occupations, are described. Moreover, the time of their rutting, the forming of their nests, their love in the bringing up of their young, are mentioned; how they take to their little offspring and care for them. Finally, their uses and disadvantages, their lairs, their masters and enemies, their accomplishments and the like, are dealt with. Such matters belong to natural science and medical and veterinary knowledge. Husbandry and breeding have to do with the taming of great and wild animals and birds. All arts and handicrafts are connected with Physics.

D. THEOLOGICAL SCIENCE is of five kinds :—

1. *The doctrine of the Creator.* It rests on the attribution of His oneness, and shows how He is the ground of all existing things, the Creator of all creatures. He holds existence within Himself, and bestows it. He is the essence of all excellence and goodness, He maintains order, gives duration, guides every-

thing. He knows the hidden. He is the first of all things as beginning, and the last as end. He makes all things known, is visible in His power, and embraces all secrets in His knowledge. He is hearing, knowing, kind, well-acquainted, and gentle with His servants.

2. *The doctrine of spiritual beings* treats of the simple, reasoning, knowing, acting, forms free from matter (as angels and God's purified servants), who, joined close to one another, form the spiritual spheres, which inclose the material spheres.

3. *The doctrine of souls* has to do with the souls and spirits which penetrate the spheres and natural bodies from the all-inclosing circle to the centre of the earth—showing how these set the spheres in their gyres and the stars in motion, nourish animals and plants, bury themselves in the bodies of animals, release themselves at death, and regulate the "Direction."

4. *The doctrine of "Directions."* They are of five kinds: the prophetic, the kingly, the popular, the household, and the individual.

5. The *doctrine of the Return* and the escape to another world, or the awakening of souls out of their dark bodies to the Return to the straight path. The aim of all science is to point out the path which prophets and philosophers trod. The beginning of all knowledge is the knowledge of self. Self-knowledge rests on four points: first, a man must know he is a compound being, composed of a sensuous body and a spiritual soul; secondly, he must know how and wherefore the soul and body are tied together; thirdly,

what the state of the soul was before it entered that body; fourthly, what the state of the soul will be when it is severed from the body by death.[*]

It will be noticed that while the Pure Brethren made use of the details of many philosophical systems, they arranged them after a manner peculiar to themselves. The salient feature in their metaphysics is the vivid distinctness with which they realised the relations of soul and matter in every form of existing things. According to their system, the whole universe is an emanation from God, but not a direct emanation. From *God* proceeds first a complete spiritual substance, containing within itself the forms of all things : this they named *Reason.* From *Reason* emanated an inferior substance, the *Universal* or *All-soul*, whence proceeded *primal matter*; when this becomes capable of receiving dimensions it is called *secondary matter*, and out of this were formed the spheres, the earth, and all existing phenomena. All material things become what they are by the influence of soul. For soul is a spiritual force of two kinds, and permeates all matter from the outer sphere to the centre of the earth. The two kinds of soul-force are its work-force, which forms and perfects all bodies, and its intellectual-force, which forms and perfects the inner being : both forces are sustained by a perpetual effusion from Reason.

The all-soul is one : but there is no created thing for which it has not a special force or *part-soul.* All

---

[*] "Makrokosmos," 124–130.

the efficient forces of the all-soul working on matter
are part-souls; whether it be the simple soul working
on simple bodies, like the spheres, stars, and elements;
or the specific soul working on specific bodies, animals,
plants, and minerals; or part-souls proper working
upon individual animals, plants, or minerals. The
all-soul rules the category, the simple soul the genus,
the specific soul the species, the part-soul the individual; and the all-soul nourishes the simple soul,
the simple the specific, and the specific the part-
soul.

This union of matter and soul, which forms the
universe, is, however, only temporary. Soul inhabits
matter only for the purpose of bringing itself towards
perfection. As the body is supported by food, so is
the soul nourished by wisdom and knowledge and
spiritual discipline. If the soul assimilate wisdom,
righteousness, and faith, it grows more beautiful and
approaches perfection. But so long as it is linked to
matter, the soul can never attain absolute perfection.
The body, or matter, is but the egg which enables
the chick, the soul, to prepare itself for a higher
existence. When the process of education is over,
and the soul has taken to itself all the elements of
wisdom and faith of which it is capable, then the
prison-house of matter is burst open, and the soul
flies forth to join the universal soul from which it
originally proceeded. The body is merely a city
which lies desolate when the inhabitants are departed.
The soul is the inhabitant of the body, and as this
waxes old the soul draws nearer its awakening and

at last reaches its goal in the general realm of spirit. This emancipation of the soul is the one end of life. To prepare for the great home-quest by spiritual exercises, study, self-denial, and purity of life, is the one object of man's existence; thus only can he attain rest and peace.

This doctrine of emanation and return, and of the temporary linking of soul to matter for a definite end, permeates every page of the Tracts of the Brotherhood, and is enforced by every variety of argument and much beauty of illustration. We can trace European analogies to it in the system of cosmogony and doctrine of worldly government of both the Dominicans and the Franciscans; but nowhere is it more nobly or more winningly expressed than in the teaching of the Brethren of Purity. The manner in which the relation of spirit to matter is viewed by them is most strikingly shown in the description of the awakening of the soul from the sleep of sloth and blindness to rise to the higher state; as we read we remember Milton's exquisite praise of purity:—

> So dear to Heaven is saintly chastity
> That when a soul is found sincerely so
> A thousand liveried angels lackey her,
> Driving far off each thing of sin and guilt;
> And in clear dream, and solemn vision,
> Tell her of things that no gross ear can hear,
> Till oft converse with heavenly habitants
> Begin to cast a beam on th' outward shape,
> The unpolluted temple of the mind,
> And turns it by degrees to the soul's essence,
> Till all be made immortal.

In their ideal of the higher life, indeed, the Brotherhood of Purity belong to Christianity rather than to Islām: but, in truth, their noble doctrine appeals to what is best in all philosophies and religions.

CHAPTER VII.

THE PERSIAN MIRACLE PLAY.

IT is the beginning of the Mohammadan year, the sacred month Moharram, when feasts and rejoicings and solemn services are held throughout the countries of Islām. In Cairo they are lighting up the streets where the few story-tellers that remain are reciting the old histories of Arab prowess and Bedawy love, and the Ghawāzy girls are distracting pious folk with their dances; and people are eating their 'Ashūrā cakes and giving alms for the sake of " our Lord Hoseyn "; and the crowd is heaving and struggling in the great mosque of the Hasaneyn, watching the dervishes and making the circuit of the sacred tomb where lies the trunkless head of the martyred Hoseyn. But we are in Persia, where they hold a different legend of this head, and have nothing to say to the pretensions of their Cairene rivals. Still, the Persians keep their Moharram after their own picturesque fashion. Long processions of banner-bearers and minstrels have been threading the streets between lines of weeping people, who groan and cast dust on their heads. There is a sound of lamentation ringing through the town, and every man is dressed in a sombre garb of mourning. There are no joyous revels, no feasts of delight; but the night is filled with the voices of praying men and the chant of funeral rites. As we push our way onward—at some risk of a mischief from the bands of savage fellows who parade the streets, bare-headed, stained with their own blood, brandishing clubs, and shouting, "O Hoseyn! O king of martyrs!"—we come to the great open court of a palace, whence issue dolorous cries, as though some horrid deed were a-doing within. We enter a square enclosure, tented over, and see a plain raised platform, whereon a few men and children stand gesticulating and reciting. Around are all the people of the place, crowded together, in dense lines from wall to platform, from the nobles in the shut-off boxes at the wall, to the street urchins crushed against the platform. Women are there, apart, seated each on a little bench. The men are all squatted cross-legged on the ground. A vast amphitheatre of faces, all bent eagerly on the group in the centre, and all showing the marks of grief and intense sympathy with what is doing there. Every now and then some one in the crowd lifts up his voice and groans aloud; then the rest take up the sound, and the whole place rings with cries of "*Ya Hasan! Ya Hoseyn! Ay Hoseyn shāh!*" till the groaning and the shouts fall away into silence as suddenly as they arose. At last there comes a pause: the group in the midst have relaxed their efforts, the people's paroxysms of grief are hushed; young men go round with water-skins to moisten the dried throats; and we can turn and ask what this strange thing may mean.

The answer to this question is very easy to discover. All the East knows it, and is ready to fight over it. This performance is the play of " Hasan and Hoseyn "; it is the dramatic representation of the tragedy which has divided the whole Muslim world from the beginning till now into the two great parties of Sunnīs and Shī'a, ever hostile and filled with bitter hate for each other; the tragedy of the suffering House of 'Aly, whence and in whose cause have come forward countless claimants to the Khalif's throne, rebels against the Khalif's law; whose power has seated dynasties in Egypt and in Spain; in favour of whose descendant even the 'Abbāsy Khalif essayed to alter the succession-line of the vicegerents of God. The sympathy which this oppressed House has evoked from subject races, and its pliant yielding to foreign ideas, made it the parent of the strangest and the most outrageous of the doctrines which have grown fungus-like upon the mighty trunk of Islām; the mysterious doctrines of the Ismā'īlians, the apostolic succession of the Imāms, the blind devotion of the credulous Berber, the horrors of the Karmathian the detestable Vehmgericht of the " Assassins," the reign of terror of the mad khalif of Egypt, and the wild apotheosis of the monster among the Druse dwellers of the Lebanon; all owe their origin to the schism of the House of 'Aly. The Shī'a have had a hand in most of the troubles of the East. Whereve they were found in subjection, there infidelity and sansculottism had a refuge. The hatred of the followers of 'Aly towards the upholders of his enemies has never slackened, neither has their love and reverence for the holy family one jot abated; and both find fuel in the moving scenes of the Passion Play of "Hasan and Hoseyn." They witness that play with an enthusiasm which strikes a Western beholder with amazement. The highest triumphs of the modern stage, when the actor's genius has thrown its whole power into the grandest productions of the old drama, and the artist, the historian, and the mechanician have combined to heighten the illusion by every contrivance of stage effect and minute accuracy of detail, awaken no fury of sympathy such as this simple ill-formed play produces with "properties" and accessories so rude that they would have been scoffed at even in that plain little Globe Theatre on the Surrey side, whose bareness Shakspere covered with his art as with a king's mantle. Only in the Passion Play which Ober-Ammergau has made famous can a parallel be found to this Oriental witchery; and even there, with far greater skill and preparation, and a more artistic setting, the audience seems cold and indifferent to the Saviour's griefs by contrast with the tear-stained faces of these heart-broken Easterns, who bewail with dust-defiled head, and heaving breast, smitten with passionate hands, the martyrdom of *their* redeemer. Where else in the whole world shall we see such passion of grief, such grandeur of selfless sympathy, as here, where the people forget the passing

14 *

of time and the change of place, and taking the rude platform for the real scene of the martyrdom, and the actors for those they represent, furiously stone the soldiers of Yezīd and drive them from the stage; and the murderer-actor so loses himself in his part, that he thinks he sees the real Hoseyn in the man before him, and actually beheads him before all eyes! Such things have been known in the playing of this wonderful drama; and so commonly, that it has become difficult to find actors who will take the unpopular parts, for fear of death or at least a serious bodily mischief; and Russian prisoners, Morier tells us, have been impressed to act the murderers, who as soon as the bloody deed was done, the martyrdom accomplished, fled from the theatre in mortal terror. Even the murderers cannot go through their parts without tears in their eyes—so deeply do the sufferings of their actor victims touch their compunctious hearts!

The story of these ancient wrongs, this tragedy of the early days of Islām, which is so real to millions in India and Persia, seems very far away and meaningless to us in England, who scarcely know the names of the martyrs, and can with difficulty separate the early history of the Arabs from our recollections of the "Thousand and One Nights." But this tragedy is no fiction, though it has furnished the basis for a thousand wild fancies of Mohammadan devotees for many centuries. Those of us who still read our Gibbon may remember the fine passages in which the greatest of England's historians relates the wrongs of the House of 'Aly. It is an affecting story, which moves us more in its simple outline than in the mythical dress with which adoring ages have wrapped it round, and whence modern writers have drawn their imaginary ideals of the martyrs' conduct and character. Little as Eastern history has entered into the ordinary circle of reading, we have most of us heard of the lion-hearted 'Aly, the Bayard of Islām, nephew of Mohammad and adopted by him as his own son,—the second convert to the new faith, and from first to last the staunchest friend and valiantest warrior that ever stood at the Prophet's right hand. It was the common report that 'Aly would succeed Mohammad as the leader of Islām, and when the Prophet died it was a surprise to the Muslims that he had not named 'Aly as the first Khalif. Without such express appointment the post was sure to be contested; and the jealousy of certain families and political parties, the seniority of other chief men, and the hatred of 'Āïsha, Mohammad's favourite wife, whom 'Aly with some reason had suspected of an intrigue, combined to exclude him from the supreme power, which had not been specially intrusted to him by the Prophet, and for which his near kinship with Mohammad constituted no claim. It is a mistake into which many writers, following Shī'y legends, have fallen, to compassionate 'Aly as the lawful Khalif deprived of his rights by usurpers. There were no rights in the case. However much a sentiment of reverence for the family of their prophet may have inclined the early Muslims to prefer them to other claimants, there was no doctrine of heredity established at the time of 'Aly. The election to the office of Khalif, or chief of the religion and the state, was vested in the whole body of the Faithful, and with certain restrictions was open to any candidate who might offer himself. The prime qualification was not near kinship to the Prophet, but the capacity to rule —the strong will, the wakeful energy, the prudence, the diplomatic skill, which could alone maintain order in the mixed and rebellious empire which Mohammad had united by his supreme influence, but which was now threatening to break up into its original divisions. The bold resolute 'Omar was undoubtedly the fitter man for this difficult position than the more shrinking and scrupulous 'Aly, and Mohammad's old friend Abū-Bekr had also, by his age and the respect in which he was held of all men, as well as by his wise, conciliating spirit, a valid title to the supreme voice. The people did well to prefer these men to 'Aly, who assuredly was not made of the stuff whereof conquering kings are fashioned. But when these were gone, and the feeble 'Othmān, the tool of the enemies of 'Aly, had met his death, there was no one so highly esteemed among the original supporters of Mohammad as his adopted son, and we may be sure that the fact of his being the husband of the Prophet's daughter Fātima, and the father of Hasan and Hoseyn, the favourites of their late grandfather, and now his sole male representatives, did not tell against 'Aly: and in 655 he became the fourth Khalif of Islām.

'Aly's reign was brief and troubled. He could not

enforce his authority in the distant provinces of the momently increasing empire ; and Mo'āwiya, the governor of Syria, and representative of a family which had always been at feud with that of Mohammad and 'Aly, openly refused to submit to his rule, and proclaimed himself Khalif in his room. Whilst still waging an unequal contest with this rival, 'Aly was assassinated in the mosque of Kūfa, not by his enemy's orders, but by the hand of the agent of a puritan sect, who deplored the divisions of Islām and thought to heal them by the removal of 'Aly and his opponents, Mo'āwiya and 'Amr, at the same time. Unfortunately they only succeeded in murdering 'Aly, and Mo'āwiya, who had made the Khalif's five years of reign a burden to him, survived to persecute 'Aly's sons and to establish his dynasty, which we call that of the "Ommiade" or Umawy Khalifs, firmly at Damascus.

The followers of 'Aly proclaimed his elder son, Hasan, Khalif; but this poor-spirited youth was content to sell his pretensions to the throne to his father's enemy for a handsome pension, upon which he lived at Medīna in the midst of his well-stocked harīm in luxurious retirement. On his death, his brother Hoseyn became the lawful Khalif in the eyes of the partisans of the House of 'Aly, who ignored the general admission of the authority of the "Ommiades," and sought to establish a principle of hereditary succession in the line of the Prophet's daughter, Fātima, 'Aly's wife. For a time Hoseyn remained quietly at Medīna, leading a life of devotion, and declining to push his claims.

But at length an opportunity for striking a blow at the rival House presented itself, and Hoseyn did not hesitate to avail himself of it. He was invited to join an insurrection which had broken out at Kūfa, the most mutinous and fickle of all the cities of the empire; and he set out with his family and friends, to the number of one hundred souls, and an escort of five hundred horsemen, to join the insurgents. As he drew nigh to Kūfa, he discovered that the rising had been suppressed by the "Ommiade" governor of the city, and that the country round him was hostile instead of loyal to him. And now there came out from Kūfa an army of 4,000 horse, who surrounded the little body of travellers, and cut them off alike from the city and the river. Hoseyn vainly besought his enemies to give him leave to return to the retirement he had always preferred at Medīna. His entreaties were disregarded, and, seeing death lay inevitably before him, he begged his little band of followers to secure their own safety in flight : but they were men of the true Arab mettle, and, staunch to the death, stood up to the overwhelming forces arrayed against their leader. A series of single combats, in which Hoseyn and his followers displayed heroic courage, ended in the death of the Imām and the men who were with him, and the enslaving of the women and children. How desperate was the fortitude, how terrible the anguish, of the "Family of the Tent" on this fatal field of Kerbelā, will be seen in analysing the drama which represents this tragical history.

Such is the bare outline of the misfortunes of

the House of 'Aly, so far as they are touched upon in the "Miracle Play of Hasan and Hoseyn." The later descendants of the afflicted line endured many injuries from the orthodox Khalifs of both the "Ommiade" and 'Abbāsy dynasties, and at times showed themselves worthy of their ancestry; but their story does not come within the scope of the play, which confines itself to the original events, with which nothing in the after history of the "Imāms," as 'Aly's successors were called, can compare. The bare incidents of this first and greatest epoch in the history of Shī'y misfortune, set plainly forth without the embellishment of religious fervour or political partisanship, do not seem to warrant the immense enthusiasm of the Persians. One may indeed fairly admire the many fine qualities of 'Aly, and deplore the butchering of his family; but to go further, and insist on the marvellous virtues of the whole household, and the indefeasible divine right of 'Aly and his descendants to the throne of Islām, is extravagance. The divine right resolves itself, as we have seen, into a popular vote; and even the virtues of the family do not bear very close inspection. The gentle 'Aly, of whom Mr. Matthew Arnold has invented a fine ideal, was certainly gentler than most of his contemporaries, but it was he who conducted the bloody capture of Khaybar; and his domestic qualities are placed in a singular light by the historians who mention his twenty-eight wives or their equivalents. His devotion to the Prophet, his uncompromising rectitude, his valour, and his indecision are the prominent characteristics of 'Aly : the rest is in the fond imagination of his biographers. As to Hasan, his son, the latest historian of Islām describes him as a voluptuary whom luxury reconciled to the loss of a crown, and in whose eyes women and wealth outweighed the ignominy of a purchased abdication. The story of his being poisoned by command of the Khalif Yezīd, son of the hated Mo'āwiya, appears to be a fable. Hasan died, like any common Muslim, in his bed, and was no martyr after all. The same authority brands Hoseyn as an adventurer who had laid himself open to the charge of perjury and high treason. It is possible to exaggerate as much on one side as the other, and Professor Dozy is perhaps as unfair to the House of 'Aly as Mr. Arnold is unduly partial. The truth seems to lie between—in the view which accords to 'Aly and his family all the merits of a worthy but persecuted line of pretenders to a throne they were ill qualified to fill, but which cannot grant them the aureoles of saints and martyrs.

Round this simple story of rival families, impotent claims, and cruel suppression, has grown up a wonderful crop of fables, by which the family of 'Aly, and especially Hoseyn, have been credited with qualities almost divine. Unable to believe that their Imām was conquered and killed against his will, the Shī'a have made the whole tragedy a predestined case of vicarious sacrifice. Hoseyn is foretold as a victim in the cause of Islām. "He shall die for the sake of my people," says Mohammad of his grandson, according to these legends, and the " Passion Play " is full of allusions to Hoseyn's redemptive work and voluntary sacrifice of his body for the sins of the Muslim world. Hoseyn himself knows, when only a child, the destiny that lies before him. "All the rational creatures," he says, "men and Jinn, who inhabit the present and future worlds, are sunk in sin, and have but one Hoseyn to save them"; and when 'Aly speaks mournfully of the woes that shall happen to his family, Hoseyn answers, "Father, there is no occasion to call these things trials, since all refer to the salvation of our sinful followers. Thou, Hasan, and I, together with my mother the virgin, will accept sufferings according to the best of our ability." Standing by the grave of Mohammad, before departing on the fatal journey to Kerbelā, Hoseyn says, "How can I forget thy people, since I am going to offer myself voluntarily for their sakes?" and Mohammad tells him he has taken off from his heart the burden of grief he had for the future state of mankind; and Hoseyn departs with this speech, which savours of Sūfism: "I have found behind this veil what my heart has sought after for years. Now I am made free. I have washed my hands of life. I have girded myself to do the will of God." And so throughout the journey and on the field of battle he and all those about him are continually referring to this voluntary expiation of the sins of his people; and he dies with this thought, and in meek compliance with the will of God, and will awake at the Resurrection with the intercessory power he has purchased with his blood.

Without the introduction of this important element

of self-sacrifice to idealise the character of Hoseyn, the unvarnished tale might not call forth the intense sympathy with which it is received among the Shī'a. When Hoseyn has been represented as a self-renouncing redeemer of men, and his sufferings voluntarily undergone out of love for mankind, the tragedy wears a new interest and gains a wider influence. The Persian sects have always shown a leaning towards asceticism and the renouncing of self—or what they fancied such—and this sacrifice of Hoseyn immediately appealed to their predisposition. But more than this; the story of a life surrendered for others' sake, the sad devotedness of Hoseyn, stir a feeling that exists in every heart—a certain admiration for self-denial which the most selfish men feel—a sort of worship for high ideals of conduct which has a corner in the most unromantic heart. It is the sorrowful resignedness, the willing yet tortured self-dedication of the martyr, that touches. One may see in it a Christian side to Islām. In the dry severity of the Arabian faith there is too little of the self-giving love which renounces all, even life itself, for the sake of others'; there is more of the stiff-necked pharisaical pride which holds up its righteous head on its assured way to the pleasures of Paradise. The death of Hoseyn, as idealised by after ages, fills up this want in Islām; it is the womanly as against the masculine, the Christian as opposed to the Jewish, element that this story supplies to the religion of Mohammad.

But this idealisation of the story of the "Family of the Tent" is not the cause but the effect of the widespread admiration of the Shī'a for the House of 'Aly, Men must have believed in the greatness and goodness of 'Aly and his sons, and their just title to the throne, before they came to idealise all the virtues they possessed or did not possess. There were many influences that made for the Shī'y cause, especially in Persia ; and once firmly planted there, it soon found the means of widening its boundaries and spreading over a great part of the Mohammadan empire. The Persians, as a down-trodden race, instinctively sympathised with the family that had suffered at the hands of the same oppressors as themselves. How quickly this sympathy was kindled, and how widely it was felt, may be judged from the fact that the famous Khalif El-Mamūn, the son of Harūn er-Rashīd, and the descendant of Khalifs of unimpeachable orthodoxy, himself recognised the title of the Imāms to reign on his throne, and went so far as to appoint (though the death of the Imām annulled the appointment) the then-living representative of the family of 'Aly, the Imām Er-Rizā, to whose splendid tomb in Khorasān the pious Persian still retires to die, as his successor on the throne of the Khalifs of Baghdād, and to inscribe the heretical name upon his coinage : and why?—because El-Mamūn was the representative of the Persians, by whose aid he had triumphed over his brother El-Amīn, and was bound to favour the sympathies of his supporters. And once the Persians had adopted the Shī'y cause, it forthwith gained in attractiveness by their development of its mystical side. There were many mysterious properties assigned to the members of the holy family, and the Persians, with their love of the supernatural, turned them to the utmost account, and elaborated a hundred quaint fancies and curious dogmas, which considerably aided the propagation of the Shī'y heresy, and especially met with an enthusiastic reception from the credulous Berbers, from whose fostering succour most of the great sectarian dynasties of Africa, Egypt, and Spain derived their first strength. The splendid organisation of the schismatics had no parallel in any of the other parties of Islām, and the Dā'īs, or missionaries, of the Shī'a spread the faith abroad in a propaganda which would not have discredited the Society of Jesus. Finally, the weakness of the orthodox 'Abbāsy rule and the unmanageable extent of the Khalif's dominions offered a favourable field for rebellion, and as it needed a religious excuse to rouse Muslims against their spiritual chiefs, the schism of 'Aly's house furnished a plausible colour to all treasonable agitators, and became an invaluable peg on which to hang an insurrection. The founders of all the great dynasties that pretended to a rival spiritual power claimed a descent, real or pretended, from 'Aly and the daughter of the Prophet.

From these and like causes Shī'ism found favour in a large part of the kingdoms of Islām; and though in Africa it has lost most of its hold, Persia and a part of India remain devoted to the House of 'Aly. Instead of journeying to Mekka, the Persian pilgrims to the Meshhed 'Aly, the supposed tomb of 'Aly, in the desert near Kūfa, and to the Meshhed Hoseyn, "the holy, blissful martyr for to seke" in his tomb amid the beautiful gold-roofed mosques and minarets and the green gardens of Kerbelā. " In the fourth century a tomb, a temple, a city arose near the ruins of Kūfa. Many thousands of the Shī'a repose in holy ground at the foot of the vicar of God; and the desert is vivified by the numerous and annual visits of the Persians, who esteem their devotion not less meritorious than the pilgrimage to Mekka." The rich pay vast sums for the privilege of being buried there, and the earth of the vicinity is sold to pilgrims at a great price, by reason of the virtue it is said to possess. No person, past or present, receives such honour and reverence in Persia as the family of 'Aly. It is possible to curse freely anything in that country or in the world outside without annoyance or hindrance—save the holy Imāms and the wife of the man you are addressing.

Every year, as the month of Moharram comes round, this devotion displays itself in a grand festival, lasting ten days, in which the history and sufferings of the holy family are commemorated, concluding with the agonising climax of the martyrdom of Hoseyn. The whole town—every town throughout the country —goes into mourning during these days, and the streets are filled with grief-stricken faces. No one seems to sleep, and the night is noisy with funeral wakes, and the solemn voices of the Seyyids Rūza-khāns, and services are going on perpetually at the theatres, where also twice a day the melancholy drama is performed which shows the vast multitudes who resort thither the tragical history of the martyrs of

Kerbelā. The theatre (*tekya*) is a plain inclosure, built or boarded off in the court of a mosque or palace, or any other open space, or permanently attached to a rich man's house. It is sheltered from the sun and the rain by an enormous awning, stretched on masts, hung with panther and tiger skins, shields and swords, and countless lamps. In the centre is a brick platform, surrounded with a scaffolding of black poles, from which hang coloured lamps to light up the evening performances. At the back of the platform is placed the *tābūt*, or model of the martyrs' tombs, which forms a very important part of the " properties," and in the houses of the rich, instead of the common lath and plaster and tinsel, this is made of gold and silver, or ivory and ebony, elaborately inlaid.

These *tābūts* are not only found in the theatres, but are placed all over the city; rich and poor erect them; bonfires are kept constantly blazing before them, and groups of frantic men and women dance round them, and leap through the flames, to the music of castanets and the yells of wild Berbers, who beat themselves with chains and prick their flesh with needles, in remorse for the sin of one of their race, who is reported by tradition to have mocked at the sufferings of the holy martyrs. Even the poorest keep some sort of illumination alight during this great festival, if it be only a nightlight in a jar sunk in the earth.

In front of the *tābūt*, in the theatre, are placed the " properties " of the play—Hoseyn's banner, sword and spear, and the like, and the tank which is to represent the river Euphrates ; and in front is a movable pulpit. Simple as are these preparations, the theatre is often a spectacle of Oriental magnificence of the most splendid and profuse order. The performances and the decorations are generally the gift of some noble or rich man, who has a mind for popularity in this world and the next, and has no dislike to making an opportunity for the display of his jewellery and treasures, which are sometimes exhibited to the value of millions of pounds. All religious people are aware that to give a *ta'zīya*, or performance of the miracle-play, is to collect bricks for one's eternal mansion in the skies : and the costlier the bricks, the better for the soul. A specially gorgeous chamber in the wall is often prepared to assist in the representation of scenes which are meant to depict splendour, such as that where the Khalif's court at Damascus is introduced; and in this chamber royal jewels of untold value sparkle, and the richest stuffs and embroideries of the country are used to decorate it. Round the walls of the theatre are beautifully ornamented side-boxes (or the windows of the over-looking houses may serve) which are quickly filled by their wealthy decorators,—else anyone might enter them, for the play is open free to all the world, except Sunnīs. The whole theatre is bathed in a dazzling light, from the thousand wax candles that surround the *tābūt*, and the lamps and lustres and chandeliers of coloured glass that hang in all directions from the awning and light up the beautiful porcelain vases and the paintings and the hundred treasures of art and antiquity that are spread recklessly around. We might believe that the golden prime of the good Harūn er-Rashīd was come back to the world that had long mourned its departure, and that we were again walking in the magic world of Afrīts and bottled Jinn, and lamps, and rings, and one-eyed "Calendars," which Ja'far and his master, with black Mesrūr, invaded in their nocturnal rambles.

These theatres with their decorations are costly gifts to the people. Their preparation and embellishment, together with the pay* and entertainment of the actors, who are always royally entreated, and the constant distribution of largesses, sometimes reach no trifling total, and seven millions of francs have been expended on a single theatre during the ten days. Hardly anything can be used twice—the decorations are given to the poor at the end of the performance, except those portions which are solemnly buried on the last day. Yet so little is the cost taken into account, that a large town, like Teheran, will erect a number of *tekyas*, on every available open space; and theatres have been built so large as to gather within them twenty thousand persons.

The audience—except the blazing mass of jewellery and gorgeous apparel in the side-boxes occupied by

---

* The pay of a *jeune premier* with a good voice has been known to reach 300 tomans, or nearly £150, for the ten days of the performance: but it must be remembered that the actors generally perform half a dozen *ta'zīyehs* in one day in large towns, the same troop going from one *tekya* to another from five o'clock in the morning to late in the evening. The men of Isfahan are preferred for the leading parts on account of their graceful dialect and their exceptional elocutionary powers.

the rich and noble—are seated cross-legged on the floor, squeezing close up to the platform, so that the actors mount to it over them. And before that eager multitude, heated with the crowding and the excitement of the time—in the midst of that glare of light and flash of jewels and mingled glory of Eastern colour—on that plain platform, with no scenery, no accessories, a heap of straw for the plain of Kerbelā, and a copper basin for "the great river, the river Euphrates " — without backgrounds or footlights, without a trace of mystery or illusion—a body of earnest men, and children filled with a solemn child's awe of unknown mysteries, aided by a prompter and chorus, will act, in the chanting manner of the East, the story of the martyrs, the Passion Play of " Hasan and Hoseyn," till the whole multitude, actors and audience, will forget where they are and who they are, and will sway and groan and weep and shout as though the things they saw were no acting, but the real sufferings of their martyred saints.

This Drama, played in this rude fashion, yet with the skill which comes of real enthusiasm added to careful training, is a potent means of keeping alive the zeal of the Shī'a. It touches the people in their tenderest sympathies. It reminds the Persians of their own oppression under a foreign yoke, in recalling the persecution, by the same oppressors, of the martyr whose cause they identified with their own. Hoseyn was their kinsman, not only by the bond of suffering, but by the tie of marriage; for he had wedded the daughter of the last Sassanian King Yezdegird, whom

Sa'd and his Arabs vanquished on the field of Kādisīa. It reminds them of tragedies in their own history, before Shī'ism became the ruling faith, when the hateful Sunnīs were trampling them under bloody feet. It brings to their mind cruelties which were but the legitimate continuation of the murderous work at Kerbelā. It fires them with fierce indignation against their oppressors. The softening influence of the self-sacrifice of Hoseyn, as depicted in the play, whilst it draws tears from their eyes, calls forth no answering gentleness and long-suffering in their own lives. They see not the example, but the victim to be avenged; and so real and earnest is their hate, that it fares ill with any Sunny whom they may meet in this period of excitement. The festival of Moharram is an anxious time for the Government of India.

Travellers in Persia and Indian residents have often written of this play. At the beginning of this century Morier published accounts of his two journeys through Persia, and described, though briefly and without specimens, this drama; and a native of the Deccan, Ja'far Sherīf, in his " Qanoon-e-Islām, or the Customs of the Moosulmans of India," translated in 1832 by Dr. Herklots—a work which seems to have escaped the observation of later writers—devotes considerable space to a minute description of the play and the rites of Moharram. The Comte de Gobineau, in his "Trois Ans en Asie," and more fully in his "Religions et Philosophies en Asie," has accorded it very detailed and interesting notices, which Mr.

Matthew Arnold has popularised for English readers in an essay which appeared in the "Cornhill Magazine," and was afterwards incorporated in the new edition of "Essays in Criticism." Professor Dozy, in his "Essai sur l'Histoire de l'Islamisme," has devoted much space to a graphic description of the Moharram festival and the play. The best account, however, is to be found in Chodźko's beautiful little volume, the "Théâtre Persan," in which not only is the performance and the setting of the play described, but five scenes are translated at length. But no complete version or translation of this remarkable drama had appeared in any language until Sir Lewis Pelly brought out his handsome volumes. It would perhaps be more accurate to speak of the plays rather than play; for on no two occasions is the performance precisely the same; the treatment of the subject, the number of scenes, and the choice of them, vary in every instance, and the words are subject to the extemporaneous modifications of the actor as well as the changes which the anonymous playwrights, following the progress of the art of developing legends, are compelled from time to time to introduce. The scenes extracted from Count Gobineau by Mr. Arnold do not tally with the corresponding scenes in Sir Lewis Pelly's edition; and the former mentions scenes which are absolutely wanting in the latter. Chodźko, again, differs from Sir Lewis Pelly, and his manuscript of thirty-three scenes contained incidents altogether missing here. But practically the scenes are very much the same in all accounts; the difference is chiefly of words, and the absence of certain portions may be accounted for by Sir Lewis Pelly's admission that out of fifty-two scenes he omitted fifteen, with the design, as he says, of " drawing the line somewhere even in harrowing up the feelings " : a more obvious reason is surely the shortening of an apparently endless book.　The differences between the several versions are so immaterial, and the general aim and character of the play are so constant in all, that those who read Sir Lewis Pelly's " Miracle Play of Hasan and Hosain," may be sure they have a fair example of the drama that exercises so powerful an influence on innumerable audiences in Persia and among our Indian fellow-countrymen.

In the performance of the play there is a sort of equivalent to an overture, which varies in every case. A prologue is recited by a dervish or mulla, or in their absence by the ordinary choragus of the actors. It is thus briefly described by Sir George Birdwood,* but longer addresses are recorded by Count Gobineau and Mr. Arnold :—

The thronging visitors at first cover the whole area of the inclosure, laughing and talking like a crowd at a fair.　But in the midst of the hubbub a signal is given, it may be by the muffled beating of a drum, in slow time, the measured beats becoming fainter and more faint, until step by step the people fall back into their places, and are at length hushed in a silence which is most expressive in its dramatic effect.　Then a mulla enters the pulpit, and intones a sort of "argument" or prelude to the play.　He begins in some such form as this: " O ye

---

* In the Introduction to Sir Lewis Pelly's " Miracle Play of Hasan and Hosain."

Faithful, give ear! and open your hearts to the wrongs and sufferings of his Highness the Imām 'Alī, the vicegerent of the Prophet, and let your eyes flow with tears, as a river, for the woes that befel their Highnesses the beloved Imāms Hasan and Hoseyn, the foremost of the bright youths of Paradise."

For a while he proceeds amid the deep silence of the eager audience, but as he goes on, they will be observed to be swaying to and fro, and all together ; at first almost imperceptibly, but gradually with a motion that becomes more and more marked. Suddenly a stifled sob is heard, or a cry, followed by more and more sobbing and crying, and rapidly the swaying to and fro becomes a violent agitation of the whole assembly, which rises in a mass, everyone smiting his breast with open hand, and raising the wild, rhythmical wail of *Ya Ali! Ay Hasan! Ay Hoseyn! Ay Hasan! Ay Hoseyn! Hoseyn Shāh!* As the wailing gathers force, and threatens to become ungovernable, a chorus of mourners which has formed almost without observation on the arena, begins chanting, in regular Gregorian music, a metrical version of the story, which calls back the audience from themselves, and imperceptibly at last soothes and quiets them again. At the same time the celebrants come forward, and take up the "properties" before the *tābūt*, and one represents Hoseyn, another El-'Abbās, his brother and standard-bearer, another El-Hurr, and another Shemmar, all going through their parts (which it seems to be the duty of the chorus every now and then more fully to explain), not after the manner of actors, but of earnest men, absorbed in some high sacrament, without consciousness of themselves or of their audience.

The ten days' performances (*ta'zīyas*) ought to represent severally the events of each of the ten days of the original history; but it is doubtful whether this is ever strictly carried out in India. It is certain that the arrangement of the play, like the form and decoration of the theatre, and the manner of the performance, varies greatly in different parts of the East. The first day should properly describe the departure of Hoseyn, against the entreaties of his friends, on the fatal journey to Kūfa; but it is usual to act various preliminary scenes before arriving at this point. A certain amount of suspense increases the excitement of the audience; and accordingly the actors go through some incident taken from the Old Testament or from Eastern history, or from the legends of 'Aly or of Hoseyn's youth, before they enter upon the main theme. Thus, Sir Lewis Pelly's edition presents eleven scenes (and others have probably been omitted) before that describing the departure of Hoseyn from Medīna, though it must not be inferred that all these scenes were acted at a single Moharram. The prompter or manager would probably select two or three, and then proceed to the great subject of the drama.

The first scene in Sir Lewis Pelly's version represents the familiar picture of Joseph thrown into the well by his brethren. His sufferings and Jacob's anguish at the loss of his son are expatiated upon only in order to enhance the impression of the still greater sufferings of the martyrs at Kerbelā presently to be set forth, and Jacob is made to admit the triviality of his woes in comparison with Hoseyn's to the angel Gabriel, who is sent to console the bereaved patriarch.

Gabriel (to Jacob). Peace be unto thee, thou wise prophet: the incomparable God, sending thee salutation, says: "What thinkest thou, O afflicted one? Is thy Joseph more precious than Mohammad's dear grandson, before whose eyes all his companions were first slain, and his own body being riddled by arrows, he was afterwards most cruelly put to death, and his corpse thrown on the ground?"

Jacob. Oh, may a thousand ones like me and my Joseph be a ransom for Hoseyn! May a thousand Josephs be the dust of his feet! May the curse of God rest on Yezīd and his party, who cruelly murdered that Imām! Come, O Gabriel! show me the plain of Kerbelā, for God's sake!

Gabriel. O Jacob, may Gabriel be a ransom for thee! May I perish for thy name, thou manifest messenger of God! Come and peep through my finger. Behold thence the land of Kerbelā.

Jacob. Declare unto me, O messenger of the glorious Lord, part of the sad transaction of Kerbelā, for thy speech has greatly grieved me; it has rendered my eyes like the river Jeyhūn.

Gabriel. Alas! the tyranny of the cruel spheres! Who can hear the sad things done in Kerbelā! Injustice and oppression, hatred and enmity, shall attain to their perfection in that plain of trial as regards the descendants of God's Prophet. One shall hear no cry from that holy family but for bread and water. Their sad voices shall reach the very throne of the Majesty on high. Their tears shall saturate all that field of battle. The children of that King of religion shall subsist on the tears alone of their own eyes.

And so the scene ends. Throughout all the early part of the play, before the actual journey of Hoseyn begins, the one object is to foreshadow the great sacrifice by examples of lesser sufferings. Everyone knows already, or is told by Mohammad or by Hoseyn, the approaching tragedy of Kerbelā; and the pains of all are alleviated by the contemplation of the greater sufferings of the days to come. Everything leads up to the crowning act of Hoseyn's life. The child of Ibrāhīm, the warrior 'Aly, the Imām Hasan, all are anxious to sacrifice their lives for the sins of the people of Islām; but it is only to point out the way to Hoseyn's greater surrender of his life for the souls of sinners, by which he alone obtained the high power of intercession with God in the Last Day.

Throughout these earlier scenes, Hoseyn is the principal character, overshadowing in his splendour even the brightness of Mohammad himself. In the second scene, when Mohammad has to choose between the death of his own child Ibrāhīm and 'Aly's child Hoseyn, he sacrifices his own fatherly love to the happiness of the family of 'Aly, and permits Azrāīl, the Angel of Death, to draw out the soul of Ibrāhīm. Gabriel then proposes to Mohammad that Hoseyn shall be made a propitiation for the sins of "his beloved people, his true family, his broken-winged birds," the people of Islām ; and on the Prophet's consent Gabriel promises that on the Day of Judgment God will forgive all the sins of the people "for the Imām's meritorious blood's sake" : and Azrāīl, struck with Hoseyn's appearance, recalls a sentence from the Preserved Tablet, the great Book of God, that "he who loves Hoseyn and mourns for him is passed from death unto life." It is one of the most dramatic scenes in the play. The terror of the child at the approach of the Angel of Death, the soothing of Hoseyn, and the grief of Mohammad, are finely expressed.

In the third scene, Mohammad is enlightened by Gabriel as to the distribution of the various classes of sinners in the seven hells, and finds to his dismay that even Muslims may be damned : he is led to the graveyard, where he hears the cries of a disobedient son who is condemned to perpetual torture because his mother will not forgive him. His agonies in the flames are vividly described. All the bystanders are filled with compassion, and one after another the sacred family endeavour to induce the mother to forgive her son and deliver him from hell; but she continues obdurate until Hoseyn softens her heart with a description of the pains he is destined to suffer at Kerbelā, and Gabriel threatens her with untold punishment if she does not yield to the entreaties of the holy Imām; and at last she consents to release her son from his agony. And so all the scenes bear upon the goodness and the influence of Hoseyn, and his knowledge and willing acceptance of the coming death at Kerbelā, which shall be the redemption of the sinners among the Muslims whose damnation had so deeply moved the soul of Mohammad. In the fourth scene, 'Aly shows himself ready to sacrifice his life for the sake of his erring fellow-creatures;—it is only a finger-post to the plain of Kerbelā. In the fifth scene, the death of Mohammad, from whose dying moments the (historical) presence of 'Āïsha is studiously omitted, serves to admit the (supposed) declaration of 'Aly's appointment as the first Khalif, and Mohammad's consignment of the turban, Moses' rod, Solomon's signet, and the like to this favoured disciple. The sixth directs the indignation of the Shī'a against the usurping Abū-Bekr, and the cruel 'Omar, whose endeavour to force 'Aly to recognise the former is detailed in all its fictitious violence. The death of Fātima in the seventh scene is the occasion for the display of the sacred relics of the Shī'a—the tooth which Mohammad lost at the battle of Ohud, the ring which will refresh the lips of 'Aly

Akbar at Kerbelā, and the torn shirt which Hoseyn will put on when he goes to his death. Distinctions of time are boldly disregarded in the whole of this curious drama; everyone speaks of the history of the "Family of the Tent" at Kerbelā and all that will happen to them, as though they were accomplished facts. The death of 'Aly and the poisoning of his successor the Imām Hasan, when the hated dowager, 'Āïsha, is introduced, in order to receive the full brunt of Shī'y indignation, on her refusal to allow Hasan to be interred in the sepulchre of Mohammad, bring the introductory scenes almost to a close. Two more, describing the execution by the governor of Kūfa of the envoy whom Hoseyn had sent, in order to test the loyalty of the city, and the murder of the envoy's sons, in violation of the laws of hospitality—the children's deaths are told in an affectingly simple manner—lead us to the main theme, the journey and fighting and death of the Imām Hoseyn (scenes xii–xxiii. in Sir Lewis Pelly's edition).

On the first day of the sixty-first year of the Flight, or in October 680 A.D., in spite of the warnings of his friends and the presentiments of his own heart, or, as the Shī'a say, in order to accomplish his known fate and work his redemptive mission, Hoseyn left Medīna for Kūfa. When Zeyneb, his sister, asks Hoseyn why all this slaughter must take place at Kerbelā, he answers, "The helpless people of the Prophet of God have no rock of salvation to fly to for a refuge except Hoseyn. They have no advocate with God on the Day of Judgment except Hoseyn.

The way of salvation is shut up against them on account of their manifold sins ; and, except Hoseyn, none can make a proper atonement or propitiation for transgression. Who could save the people of God from the wrath to come, seeing the empire of faith has no other king but Hoseyn ? " And so he goes like a lamb to the slaughter. Letters from Kūfa arrive, saying how the Euphrates is as restless as quicksilver in its longing for him, and the land of Kerbelā has worn out its eyes looking for his coming. The country of Kūfa is as a tulip-field, but without the rose of the face of Hoseyn it seems but thorns to its inhabitants. As Hoseyn knew beforehand how deceptive were these promises of support, and was aware he should die in that same tulip-field, the introduction of these despatches was needless. But it is noticeable that in the attempt to adhere to a certain amount of historical truth, and yet to retain the favourite traditions and fancies of the Shī'a, consistency is wholly lost sight of. The audience are too deeply moved to notice the fault, and in such a work as this it would be absurd to expect anything different.

When Hoseyn draws nigh to Kūfa, he meets with a reconnoitring party of the army that has been collected to meet him, and by the advice of the captain, El-Hurr by name, turns off the main road and arrives at Kerbelā. Here, encircled by enemies, forbidden either to advance or to retreat, the little band meets death bravely in a series of single combats. El-Hurr, who had deserted to the party of the

Imām, is the first to fall, then others go out and fight and are slain, and next 'Aly Akbar, the eldest son of Hoseyn, who is determined to be the first of his family to die for the Imām.

The death of Kāsim, son of Hasan, immediately after his marriage with Fātima, a daughter of his uncle Hoseyn, is one of the more striking of these preliminary encounters, and forms the subject of a special ceremony in the Moharram festival. On the seventh day this scene is acted, and the acting is not confined to the performance in the theatre. A wedding procession winds through the streets by night. The wedding presents come first, surrounded by armed men; richly dressed servants carry salvers with fruit and flowers and sweetmeats. The bridal litter follows, gorgeously embellished with silver and lighted up by a crowd of torch-bearers. Musicians close the rear, and a multitude of spectators. They come to the theatre, and with joyous shouts make the tour of the inclosure, finally placing the wedding gifts by the model of the Tombs. Hardly are the gifts deposited, when another procession appears. A long line of mourners, bearing the bier of the martyred bridegroom, surrounded by wailing people, who lead in their midst the horse of the martyr, on which are hung his turban, sword, and arrows, solemnly traverses the theatre, just as the joyous bridal party had traversed it before, and takes up its station, like the other, by the Tombs. And then the play goes on. No more powerful or effective contrast could be imagined. The thought of the bridegroom tearing.

himself from his bride's caresses and rushing to meet death for his saintly uncle on the wedding-day moves intense sympathy in the spectators. The peculiar improbability of a marriage in a beleaguered family hourly expecting death, the reluctance of everybody to this strange union, which the Imām abruptly declares must be arranged in accordance with some forgotten wish of his brother Hasan, are all unnoticed; the one thought is the heroic devotion of the bridegroom.

Scene after scene, we find nothing but accounts of single combats between the relations of Hoseyn and the enemy. They are all very much alike. They begin with general lamentations of the whole of the "Family of the Tent." Then one of them resolves to go out and fight. A heart-breaking farewell is gone through, and he departs. After abusing the enemy in melodious verse, to which the foes reply in common prose, he falls on them and produces a panic of fear. Exhausted with his exertions he returns to the tents and begs Hoseyn to give him water, for he is dying of thirst; or else he comes back to see his best-loved brother and sister once more; or perhaps he never returns. A second onslaught ends his life, and he dies with the profession of faith on his lips. The death of 'Abbās, the brother and standard-bearer of Hoseyn, is something of an exception to this common model. The sufferings of the Imām's little daughter Sukeyna impel 'Abbās to appeal to the enemy for leave to get water from the Euphrates, which lay beyond them. He urges that however treasonable Hoseyn's acts may be in the eyes of the enemy, his children at least are guiltless; and they are dying of thirst. But leave is refused, and 'Abbās returns in shame to the camp. Hoseyn consoles him in his failure, and they both resolve to go out and fight. "It is high time," Hoseyn says, "both of us should swim in our own blood"; and having wrapped themselves in winding sheets, which was the gloomy custom with these martyrs, the two take a lengthy farewell of their sisters, and ride towards the enemy.

Hoseyn (addressing 'Abbās). Dear brother, gird thy loins, for our time is very short; turn to the field of battle and make ready for war. If this army, God forbid, should separate us the one from the other, we should never be able to see each other's faces any more.

'Abbās. I shall never separate myself from thee so long as I live; and if I die for thy sake, how fortunate would I then be! Should the enemy, however (God forbid!), make a separation between thee and me,—should they be able to remove me far away from thee,—where am I to see thy dear face, beloved brother, and how am I to be acquainted with thy circumstances in the field?

Hoseyn. If thou be separated from me by accident, go out of the field at once in the direction of the camp, and seek me there; and if I miss thee in the field, I shall try to find thee there; if I fail to discover thee, I will draw out my sword against this wicked enemy, and ask, " Where is my brother?"

'Abbās. When I am removed from thee, lay a sword on these villains, destroy the whole of them; then probably thou wilt find me. I hope, O king of religion, that in passing through the lines, thou wilt be kind enough to sit at my head and lament loudly over me.

So they ride on till they come near the enemy, whom they harangue in the following duet:—

Hoseyn (to the enemy). O ye who are devoid of all reputation and honour—

'Abbās. Ye who have given the name of faith to infidelity—

Hoseyn. Ye who were destined to ill at your incarnation—

'Abbās. Are ye companions of God? Nay, rather ye are at enmity with his Prophet?

Hoseyn. Yezīd the tyrant is from the seed of adultery.

'Abbās. And how can one born of an adulteress deserve the Khalifat or be fit to rule?

Hoseyn. Can he be an ornament or adornment of the throne?

'Abbās. 'Aly alone and his holy children can be such as Hoseyn.

Hoseyn. O people, I am the child of the Prophet.

'Abbās. Hoseyn is lord, and I am his servant.

Hoseyn. I am the true follower of the Prophet's religion.

'Abbās. I am the heir of Haydar's high office.

Hoseyn. O ye people, far removed from morality, I am Hoseyn.

'Abbās. And I am entitled the moon of Beny Hāshim.

Hoseyn. I do not care an atom whether I am killed.

'Abbās. Martyrdom is the heritage of my forefathers.

Hoseyn. I shall shed so much blood in the plain of enmity—

'Abbās. That the Creator of the world will say "Bravo!"

Hoseyn. O ye inhabitants of Kūfa, what are our faults?

'Abbās. Why should a stop be put to our proceedings?

Hoseyn. Do ye not know, O wicked people—

'Abbās. That of the family of the Prophet, small and great—

Hoseyn. One faints from weakness, and instantly falls to the ground—

'Abbās. Another cries out, "Thirst! Thirst!"

Hoseyn. Have ye compassion on our souls?

'Abbās. Give ye some water for our children.

Hoseyn. For the sake of Yezīd, who is born of adulterer's seed—

'Abbās. How can it be lawful to be cruel to the family of God's Prophet?

Hoseyn. If ye will not intercept us in our way—

'Abbās. We will go to Turkey or Europe.

Hoseyn. But if ye will not let us escape with our lives—

'Abbās. We shall lay hold of the cutting sword.

Hoseyn. What will ye say to my mother [Fātima, daughter of the Prophet] in the Day of Judgment?

'Abbās. My judge shall be your adversary on that day.

'Omar ibn Sa'd, the general of the enemy, in reply, orders his soldiers to fall upon the brothers :—

Ibn Sa'd. O ye soldiers of the army, ye ill-starred Syrian troops, ye brave men of the field of battle and lion-like heroes, the famous 'Abbās, the standard-bearer of the thirsty army, the defender of the oppressed! verily 'Abbās has come to the field for water; overthrow him with a volley of arrows; slay him with spears and daggers.

They engage; the two brothers become separated :—

'Abbās (at the waters of the Euphrates). It is not right to drink water while Hoseyn, the king of religion, is parched with thirst; thou art a good servant indeed; do not, then, be so faithless.

So he returns to the fight. The army itself reproaches its general for attacking the sons of 'Aly—Hoseyn upbraids them—and a rout takes place.

The Army (to Ibn Sa'd). O prince of the world, the reins are gone from our hand. Mercy! mercy! Deliver us from 'Abbās, the fierce lion, and save us from the King of the Age himself! Help thy army, for they are all undone; the world is darkened. Alas! alas!

Ibn Sa'd rallies the scattered troops, and 'Abbās is severely wounded. Not seeing Hoseyn, he drags himself back to the camp, according to their agreement before the battle, and asks his sister Kulsūm if she has seen Hoseyn.

Kulsūm. He came, dear brother, but he seemed to have lost himself; he had received many arrows in different parts of the body. He fell from time to time on the centre of the army, every now and then saying, "Where is my brother?"

Hoseyn, who has been desperately seeking for his brother over the plain, now comes back, and learns from Kulsūm that 'Abbās, not having found him at the camp, had gone back once more to the battle. Hoseyn again follows him, and rushes among the enemy. Shemmar tells him he has cut off the hands of 'Abbās and made him brotherless.

'Abbās. My right hand, O God, has fallen off from my body; enable my other hand to reach the skirt of Hoseyn.

Hoseyn (still seeking for him). O land of Kerbelā, where is 'Abbās the brave? O land of Kerbelā, where is the nightingale of my rose-garden?

'Abbās. O hope of loving souls, come and save thy brother, who is wallowing in his own blood.

Hoseyn (at the head of 'Abbās). O brother, brother! Now my back is broken, now my hope is lost.

'Abbās. O Hoseyn, art thou pleased with thy servant? Art thou satisfied with his past deeds?

Hoseyn. Oh, may I be a sacrifice for thee and these thy wounds! I am satisfied with thee, may God be pleased with thee too!

'Abbās. Now I go, with an earnest desire, to meet the messenger of God, saying, *I testify that there is no God but the true God.*

The death of 'Abbās is followed by a similar martyrdom of a certain Hāshim, who volunteered in the Imām's cause. At this moment, when the enemy are pursuing Hoseyn very close, the angels obtain leave to come to his assistance; but their aid is rejected by the martyr. He shows the angels' envoy the corpses of his dearest friends lying around him, and he says, though the crown were put on his head and the universe were subservient to him, and the Great Alexander himself were to obey his orders, and two worlds were under his control, and though Solomon were to consent to be his doorkeeper—"Verily, after the death of these youths, to reign would be torture. The crown of the King would feel like a pan of fire on my head." So

16 *

he goes on fighting. Yet so wonderful is his courage, so nimble his skill, so heavy his shock, that he still carries slaughter among the enemy, and death has not yet claimed him. (The story is here strangely interrupted by a legend of a Sultan of India threatened by a lion. Hoseyn leaves his fighting, is transported to India, addresses the Sultan at some length, the lion roaring at the two meanwhile, and then proceeds to draw tears of remorse from the penitent animal, whom he then takes back with him to Kerbelā, and shows him the bodies of the martyrs, who begin to talk in a piteous manner.) There is little now left of the fated family. The men are all dead save Hoseyn. The women gather together to carry his armour and standard. The Imām himself puts on the old torn shirt we have heard of before, and prepares for the last fight. A dervish from Kābul mysteriously appears, and throws himself upon the spears of the enemy. The king of the Jinn comes and offers the help of troops of his genii. But Hoseyn is not tempted: " What can I do with the empire of the world, or its glories, after my dear ones have all died and gone?" and he goes to meet his foes for the last time. He staggers back, wearied and hopeless, and lays his head in the dust. The enemy approach and stone him; one draws nigh to slay him. His grandfather, the great prophet Mohammad, appears to him to console him, and tells him how all this sacrifice of life tends to the happiness of the world. And Hoseyn answers: " Seeing thy rest consists in my being troubled in this way, I would offer my soul, not once or twice, but a thousand times, for the salvation of thy people." And his dead mother Fātima comes and weeps over him. Then "the accursed Shemmar" stands over him with the gleaming dagger; and Hoseyn dies with these words :—

Hoseyn. O Lord, for the merit of me, the dear child of thy Prophet; O Lord, for the sad groaning of my miserable sister; O Lord, for the sake of young 'Abbās rolling in his blood, even that young brother of mine that was equal to my soul, I pray thee, in the Day of Judgment, forgive, O merciful Lord, the sins of my grandfather's people, and grant me, bountifully, the key of the treasure of intercession. (*Dies.*)

There are fourteen scenes more before the play is over, but with them we shall not concern ourselves. They describe the fate of the survivors of Kerbelā, the women and children, the cruelty of their captors, various conversions of Christians by the miraculous intervention of the departed Imām, and the deaths of Zeyneb and other holy personages. The last scene represents the Resurrection. The patriarchs and prophets of the Jews arise from their sleep one after the other, and implore mercy for themselves, but show no anxiety about their flocks or the rest of the world. Mohammad is the first to inquire about the fate of his people, and to intercede for them. His intercession, and Hasan's, proving of no avail, Hoseyn comes forward at the head of the martyrs of Kerbelā, and, in the name of their woful sufferings, prays God to have mercy on mankind. The sight of this mangled group—Hoseyn bristling with arrows, 'Aly Akbar headless, Kāsim bleeding all over, 'Abbās lopped of his hands, the rope of Zeyneb, the chain of Zeyn-el-

Ā'bidīn, the little 'Aly Asghar with his gashed throat —prevails over the stern decrees of the Deity, and Gabriel delivers the key of Paradise to Mohammad, who in turn by Gabriel's orders delivers it to Hoseyn, with these words :—

Mohammad. Permission has proceeded from the Judge, the gracious Creator, that I should give to thy hand this key of intercession. *Go thou and deliver from the flames everyone who has in his lifetime shed but a single tear for thee, everyone who has in any way helped thee, everyone who has performed a pilgrimage to thy shrine or mourned for thee, and everyone who has written tragic verses for thee. Bear each and all with thee to Paradise.*

Hoseyn. O my friends, be ye relieved from grief, and come along with me to the mansions of the blest. Sorrow has passed away, it is now time for joy and rest; trouble has gone by, it is the hour to be at rest and tranquillity.

The Sinners (entering Paradise). God be praised! by Hoseyn's grace we are made happy, and by his favour we are delivered from destruction. By Hoseyn's lovingkindness is our path decked with roses and flowers. We were thorns and thistles, but are now made cedars owing to his merciful intercession.

And so the Play ends.—*El-Hamdu li-llāh!*

The people who have been assisting at the festival of Moharram, being dismissed with the comforting promise of Mohammad respecting all who mourn or write tragic verses for Hoseyn, now devote themselves to the great ceremony of the last day—the burial of the *tābūt*—the model of the Tombs of Kerbelā. For centuries the great towns of Persia have set apart a plain outside the walls for this very purpose. It represents the plain of Kerbelā, and thither a mighty procession marches. Hoseyn died on the battle-field, and he must be buried as a warrior. Flags float, shots are fired, shields clashed. First come the sacred banners, then musicians chanting sad airs, next the sword-bearer, and then Hoseyn's horse, before whom walks a servant bearing the symbol of the Sun, and over whom the royal parasol is carried; Hoseyn's coat-of-mail and turban, and bow and arrows, hang from the saddle. Two censer-bearers usher on the *mulla* who will recite the funeral oration. At last come the sacred things—the funeral monuments, the litter of the bride of Kāsim, and the wedding gifts. Servants mounted on elephants distribute alms on the road, and muskets are discharged all the way to the burial-ground. A vast multitude surrounds the procession, clad in mourning, barefoot, with dust on the head, and raising continually the cry of *Hasan* and *Hoseyn*. When they are come to the place, they bury the model of the Tombs with its fruits and its flowers, and the perfumes and the presents, in the vault prepared for their reception, and take themselves to their homes. And Moharram is over.

Sir George Birdwood gives a vivid description of the ceremonies of the last day at Bombay, where the tombs are carried, not to a sepulchre, but to the sea, into which indeed the very Euphrates by whose bank Hoseyn died pours its waters. " On the 10th of Moharram every house in which a *tābūt* is kept, or in which one is put up for the occasion, sends forth its cavalcade, or company, to join the general funeral procession, which in the native Mohammadan states sometimes assumes the character of a solemn military pomp. First go the musicians, with pipes and cymbals, high horns, and deafening drums, followed by the arms and banners of Hasan and Hoseyn, and the ensigns and crests, in gold, and silver, or other metals, of 'Aly and Fātima, and these by a chorus of men chanting a funeral dirge, followed in turn by Hoseyn's horse. Next come men bearing censers of burning myrrh and frankincense, and aloes wood and gum benjamin, before the *tābūt* or model of the tombs of Hasan and Hoseyn, which is raised aloft on poles, or borne on an elephant. Models of the sepulchre of 'Aly also, and of Mohammad at Medīna, and representations of the Seraph-beast Burāk, on which Mohammad is said to have performed his journey from Jerusalem to heaven, are also carried along with the *tābūt*. There may be one or two hundred of these separate funeral companies, or cavalcades, in the general procession, which is further swollen by crowds of fakīrs and clowns, or 'Moharram fakīrs,' got up for the occasion in marvellously fantastic masquerade, figuring—one as 'Jack Priest'; another, 'King Tatterdemalion'; and others, 'King Clout,' 'King Ragamuffin,' 'King Doubledumb,' and a hundred others of the following of the 'Lord of Misrule' or 'Abbot of Unreason' of our Catholic forefathers. An immense concourse of people, representatives of every country and costume of Central and Southern Asia, runs along with the procession. In Bombay, after gathering its contingent from every Shī'y household as it winds its way through the tortuous streets of the native town, the living stream at length emerges on the esplanade on the side opposite Back Bay—the whole esplanade ('the Plain of Kerbelā' for the day) from Bombay harbour to Back Bay lying almost flush with the sea. The confused uproar of its advance can be heard a mile away, and long before the procession takes definite shape through the clouds of dust and incense which move before it. It moves headlong onward in an endless line of flashing swords, blazoned suns, and waving banners, state umbrellas, thrones, and canopies, and towering above all the *tábúts*, framed of the most elegant shapes of Saracenic architecture, glittering in silver and green and gold, and rocking backwards and forwards in high air, like great ships upon the rolling sea, with the rapid movement of the hurrying crowd, beating drums, chanting hymns, and shrieking, ' *Yā 'Aly, Ay Hasan, Ay Hoseyn, Hoseyn Shāh !* drowned, drowned, in blood, in blood; all three, fallen prostrate, dead! *Ya 'Aly, Ay Hasan, Ay Hoseyn, Hoseyn Shāh !*' until the whole welkin seems to ring and pulsate with the terrific wail. Ever and anon a band of naked men, drunk with opium or hemp, and painted like tigers or leopards, makes a rush through the ranks of the procession, leaping furiously, and brandishing their swords and spears and clubs in the air. The route, however, is strictly defined by a line of native policemen, and before these representatives of British law and order, the infuriated zealots will suddenly bring themselves in full charge to a halt, wheel round, and retreat back into the body of the procession, howling and shrieking like a flight of baffled fiends.

" So, for a mile in length, the route advances, against the rays of the now declining sun, until the sea is reached, when it spreads out along the beach in a line at right angles to the 'Sacred Way' by which it has come across the esplanade. Nothing can be more picturesque than the arrival and break-up of the procession in Back Bay. The temporary *tābūts* are taken out into the Bay as far as they can be carried, and abandoned to the waves, into which all the temporary adornments of the permanent *tābūts* are also thrown. This operation has a wonderfully cooling effect on the mob. Their frantic clamours suddenly cease. In fact, the mourners of Hasan and Hoseyn, having buried their *tābūts* in the sea, seize the opportunity to have a good bath; and a little after the sun has finally dropped below the western horizon, the whole of the vast multitude is seen in the vivid moonlight to be slowly and peacefully re-gathering itself across the wide esplanade into its homes again, and the saturnalia into which the last act of the Mystery of Hasan and Hoseyn has degene-rated in India is closed for another year."

It is a wonderful thing, this enthusiasm of Mohar-ram, and the most wonderful thing in it is the powerful effect of the Miracle Play. The more we read it, the more we are astounded at its influence. Making every allowance for the difference between East and West, for the absurd diction of the transla-tion, for the absence even of such surroundings as the play has on its simple stage, especially for the melody of the Persian language, in which the play is chanted,—it is still the most intolerably tedious and dreary composition we have ever struggled through.

One gets desperately weary of the perpetual wailing of women and men, the constant introduction of the merits of the inextinguishable Hoseyn, the continual single combats, and the weeping over their uniform ends, the endless recapitulation of the several injuries of the individual members of the morbid " Family of the Tent," the conversations with all the dead bodies. One would be thankful when each member is killed, but that he is as offensive dead as living. Any change would be grateful, but none comes. It is one long recital of woes, and one long river of tears. There is no attempt to individualise characters. They are all alike and talk alike. The only trace of originality we can find is in the child Sukeyna, who is perpetually screaming, and defying all her aunt Zeyneb's attempts at consolation. Before reading the play one needs to be converted to the particular form of the Mohammadan religion which it immortalises. Plotless, characterless, full of iteration, of a length unbearable, the play must be judged by other than literary standards. It is in its associations, in its thousand references to the fiery memories of religious persecution, that its strength lies. That its associations should be powerful enough to overcome its dramatic defects constitutes its claim to our reverence. But that such a play should be a sacred thing in the East, and produce the frenzy of enthusiasm it does produce as surely as the month of Moharram comes round, is a new wonder added to the many strange things in the history of Islām.

CHAPTER VIII.

SABIANS AND CHRISTIANS OF ST. JOHN.

AMONG the various problems that have vexed the souls
of learned men, few have provoked greater controversy,
or given rise to more fanciful and conflicting theories,
than that connected with the name of Sabian. What
the Pelasgians and Etruscans have been to classical
commentators, the Letters of Junius and the personality of the Man in the Iron Mask to students of
modern mysteries, the origin, character, and *habitat*
of the Sabian religion have proved to Oriental writers
and their European followers. To write the history
of the numerous significations which have been
attached to the word Sabian is to chronicle the
errors of the learned world in its Oriental depart-
ment; whilst to denominate anything as " Sabian "
is even less definite than to call it " Turanian."
Omne ignotum pro Turanio has been the maxim of
philologists; and to cast every unknown or problematical creed into the general rubbish-hole of " the
Sabian religion " has been the principle of Orientalists.
The conquered subjects of the Khalifate recognised
this principle, and when they wished to escape the

financial penalties of heathendom, and could not persuade their Muslim lords that they were Jews or Christians, they would boldly style themselves "Sabians," in the full conviction that the Mohammadans knew no more about that religion than that the Prophet of the Arabs had specially excluded it from the general outlawry of idolatry. The problem is one of comparatively modern growth. The ancients knew no such sect as the Sabian; Greek and Latin historians, the early Armenian annalists, the Syrian Fathers, make no mention of such a creed. The *Sabœans* of Arabia Felix are the only people of similar name referred to by the classical writers; but these, though their name has given rise to frequent confusions among scholars of all ages, have absolutely nothing in common with the genuine Sabians. The Sabæans are simply the people of Saba in the Yemen, the traditional descendants of Sheba, the rulers of that wonderful but little known Cushite kingdom in Southern Arabia which is now known by the name of Himyerite: as Philostorgius puts it, τοὺς πάλαι μὴν Σαβαίους νῦν δὲ Ὀμερίτας καλουμένους.* In language, religion, race, and history, these Sabæans are totally distinct from the Sabians of the Korān and of the mediæval antiquaries.

The Mohammadan writers are the first to mention the Sabians, and it is not till the study of Arabic and the Jewish redactors of Arabic works became the fashion in Europe that we have any discussion of this mysterious people. Maimonides' " Moreh han Nebu-

---

* Hist. Eccl. iii. 4.

kim," in the fifteenth century, was the beginning of
the fray; and since the discovery of his passage on
the Sabians no scholar-knight thought his spurs won
till he had broken a lance *de Zabiis.* Casaubon lighted
on the place, and forthwith wrote urgently to Joseph
Scaliger, " Doce me, obsecro, quæ hæc gens fuerit ";
to whom Scaliger, omniscient as ever, " Scito esse
Chaldæos, Arab. Tzabin; dicti a vento Apeliote:
quasi dicas Orientales." He has not the least doubt
about it, and Casaubon receives the decision meekly.
Our own John Selden walked in the same way, and in
his work on the Syrian gods, " De Diis Syriis," identified the Sabians with the ancient Chaldeans, curiously
citing Eutychius to prove that Zoroaster was the
founder of the Sabian religion. Salmasius came to a
similar conclusion, and laid it down that the Sabians
were a sect of the Chaldees. Stanley, in his " History
of Philosophy " (1655), devotes a remarkable chapter
to the Sabians, in which he collects a fine cluster of
myths, cites the passage in the Book of Job wherein
it is related how " the Sabeans fell upon " the
patriarch's oxen and asses, " and took them away;
yea, they have slain the servants with the edge of
the sword "; and ends by placing the Sabians (*i.e.*
Sabæans) in Arabia, adding the definition " Arabes,
hoc est Sabæi," which, if over comprehensive, is sufficiently correct as regards the Sabæans, but entirely
false if taken to describe the Sabians. Pococke in-
geniously, but erroneously, derives the name from a
word meaning " army," and defines the Sabians as
worshippers of the heavenly host; and Bochart and

Golius follow him in his etymology. So the theories went on. Everybody had a conjecture to offer about the Sabians, but nobody really had the necessary data on which to ground an opinion. The only point on which all agreed was that the essential characteristic of the Sabian religion was the worship of the stars; and this idea has generally been the prevailing notion in Eastern and Western minds when they thought of the Sabian creed. Meanwhile, travellers in the East were bringing back accounts of a peculiar people, called Sabians, who dwelt in the fens of Lower Mesopotamia, and had a religion of their own which could not be explained altogether by the old conception of star-worship, and whose reverence for St. John Baptist gained for them, among Europeans, the name of " Christians of St. John." Ignatius a Jesu published at Rome, in 1652, his " Narratio " of the origin, ritual, and errors of the Christians of St. John; and for a long time after this the history of the controversy is only a " narratio " of the errors of Ignatius a Jesu. Further complications were introduced by the discovery of many references in Oriental writers to a sect also called Sabian, dwelling at Harran. The problem now seemed involved beyond hope of extrication. To distinguish or to unite the Sabeans of Job and Philostorgius, the Sabians of Babylonia, and the Sabians of Harran, was beyond the skill of the scholars of the day. They tried to identify the Sabians of Babylonia with those of Harran, and had to invent for that purpose a new Harran in Mesopotamia, instead of the ancient Carrhæ; but a junction between these and the Arabian Sabæans was not to be effected.

The wonderful growth of Oriental studies in the present century could not fail to clear up much of this obscurity. It was easy to separate the Sabians from the Sabæans, when it was discovered that the two words began with different letters, and went on with different letters, and had, in fact, nothing in common. It did not require much scholarship to do this; but as the writings of the vast body of intelligent, observant, studious men who composed that enormous Arabic literature which is slowly being unfolded to our view, became better known and understood, it became apparent (1) that there was a distinction between the two sects called Sabian, that of Harran and that of Babylonia; and (2) that the solution of the difficulty, at least as far as the Babylonian division was concerned, would have to be sought elsewhere than in the Mohammadan literature. The Muslim writers maintain a difference between the two kinds of Sabians, and give considerable details about those of Harran; but of the Babylonian Sabians they tell us next to nothing. Now, interesting as the sectarians of Harran seemed to be, with their bizarre combination of Greek philosophy and the old heathen religion of Syria, the geographical position of the more eastern sect, as well as its greater mystery, gave it an even superior charm. Who could these Sabian " Christians of St. John " be? Living in the swamps of Lower Babylonia, on the site of the old Chaldean empire, could they be a relic of the Wise Men of the East? Might we not find among

them the religion which the Assyrians borrowed from
the Babylonians, with its triads of gods and its planet-
worship?   Would their divinities have Accad names?
Might we not even find the people now " weeping for
Tammuz," as they did in the days of Ezekiel (viii. 14),
and in older days, long before the Greeks set up their
answering Adonis ?

However delightful such speculations might be, a
little serious study soon proved their futility. The
publication of one of the sacred books of the Babylonian Sabians, under the title of the " Book of
Adam," or Codex Nazaræus, by Norberg, at the
beginning of this century, provided scholars with
something approaching to a definite ground on which
to build with more security than before. Although
by no means a scientific edition, containing mistakes
which led to corresponding errors in those who worked
from Norberg's premises, the Codex Nazaræus was a
genuine Sabian authority, and dispelled a good many
of the mists which surrounded the character of this
people and their religion. But the first really scientific
work on the subject did not appear till 1856, when
Chwolsohn in his " Ssabier und Ssabismus " conclusively demonstrated who were and who were not
Sabians, showed the fallacies and confusions of the
earlier hypotheses, and, touching lightly on the Babylonian Sabians, gave a very comprehensive account of
the Harranian sect. This elaborate and thoroughly
scientific work cleared the ground for ever of all the
undergrowth of fancies and myths which had sprung
up round the name of Sabian; and though among

the advanced German school of Orientalists it is now the fashion to adopt a somewhat patronising tone towards the "careful and painstaking" Chwolsohn, and to dispute his conclusions about the Babylonian sect, his researches into the antiquities and religion of Harran have a worth that can never be depreciated, and his labours in this direction will not have to be done again.

The disappointing thing in Chwolsohn's book is the slight notice he takes of the Babylonian sect, which he admits to have been the true Sabians, as understood by the early Mohammadan writers, but to whom he nevertheless devotes only one short chapter, whilst the rest of his bulky volumes is entirely concerned with the Sabians of Harran, who only took the name of Sabian in A.D. 830, under the reign of the Khalif Mamūn, in order to escape the penalties of heathenism, and to enrol themselves among the recognised sects of the Korān. Mohammad had said in the fifth Sūra, "Verily, everyone who believes, and the Jews and the Christians and the Sabians, who believe in God and the Last Day, and do what is right, on them shall come no fear, neither shall they grieve." The people of Harran could not pretend to be Christians or Jews, but the other sect mentioned with these in this sentence of amnesty, the Sabian, was so vague, and the Mohammadans knew so little who they were, that the Harranians adopted the name, and thereby avoided the obloquy and oppression which was the lot of those whom the Korān treated as heathen. This sect, therefore, was only adoptively Sabian, and it is to these adoptive Sabians, and not to the true Sabians of Babylonia, whom the Mohammadan writers had long before recognised as the people referred to in the Korān, that Chwolsohn devoted his main attention. However much we may regret that he did not investigate the other part of the subject more closely, it is impossible not to feel grateful for the completeness and accuracy of his researches into Harranian religion. Though not true Sabians, the Harran adopters of the name are well worthy of study. Their religion is one of the most curious religious phases that Syria, the land of changing creeds, has produced. It was the old heathenism of the country, mixed with many foreign elements. " Eclecticism prevailed at that period, and it was not only Greeks and Romans that found the influence of foreign, chiefly Eastern, metaphysical speculation irresistible." We find at Harran Biblical legends, Jewish ceremonial laws, Greek gods, such as Helios, Ares, and Kronos —probably translations of native divinities—and finally something of Aristotle and a good deal of the neo-Platonism of Porphyry. It was the symbolical veneration of the planets, which formed a part of this græcised Syrian heathenism, that gave rise to the common idea that Sabian means star-worshipper. After the people of Harran adopted the name Sabian, the Mohammadan writers began to use the word as synonymous with star-worshipper, and finally called all and any idolaters Sabians. The process is very similar to that by which Hellēn came to mean Pagan ; and Harran itself was called Hellenopolis, the city of paganism.

17 *

The explanation of the true Sabian religion, as preserved in the remnant of a religious sect in Babylonia, was reserved for another hand. Whilst Chwolsohn was clearing up the obscurities surrounding the name of Sabian, and explaining the characteristics of the adoptive Sabians of Harran, Petermann was travelling in Mesopotamia, studying the true Sabians (or Mandæans, as they call themselves) *in situ*, learning their language, and taking down their traditions and doctrines from Priest Yahya, the most learned man of the sect. The results of these researches appeared in his "Travels" in 1860, and seven years later he published the text of the great scripture of the Sabians, which Norberg had imperfectly edited before, whilst Dr. Euting performed the same service for another of their sacred books. Petermann's writings still form the highest authority on the true Sabian religion, and the publication of accurate editions of the Sabian scriptures enabled other scholars to investigate the mythology and legends in detail, and finally gave Professor Theodor Nöldeke the means of making an exhaustive study of the Sabian language, and to collect the most important results of his investigations in his "Mandäische Grammatik." The linguistic importance of the sect would alone make them worthy of careful study. They speak an Aramaic dialect closely allied to Syriac and Chaldee, but much freer from foreign influences than either. Whilst Syriac shows in many ways the effect of Greek influence, and Chaldee is obviously deeply affected by its greater Hebrew kinswoman ; Mandæan, the dialect of the Sabians of Babylonia, is comparatively untouched, for the importation of some Persian words does not affect the language in any fundamental manner. Hence no one who wishes to understand the character and history of the Aramaic branch of the Semitic family of languages, especially in its syntactic relations, can afford to neglect the Mandæan dialect, which is, in fact, the legitimate descendant of the tongue of the ancient Shemites of Babylonia.

Finally, the French Vice-Consul at Mōsil, M. Siouffi, published in 1880 the results of his conversations with a Sabian youth who had been converted to the Catholic faith by the energies of the Carmelite mission at Baghdad. As far as ceremonies and customs go, M. Siouffi's book is interesting and useful; but as soon as he ventures upon theological ground he is not to be trusted. Both the knowledge and the honesty of the young convert Adam are questionable ; he certainly seems to have endeavoured to deceive M. Siouffi on more points than one—a feat, however, not very difficult of accomplishment, inasmuch as the enquiring mind of the Vice-Consul was wholly unread in the subject, and he knew absolutely nothing of the discoveries of Petermann and Chwolsohn. The extracts from various superseded authorities at the end of the volume show the extent of the author's ignorance, whilst the invention of a sole supreme god, Alaha (probably an improvement on Hayya), shows the imaginative faculty of the Sabian convert and his desire to convince M. Siouffi of the monotheistic character of his former religion, at the expense of veracity. The spelling of the names of the divinities and the translations of formulas show that M. Siouffi knows next to nothing of the Mandæan language. Indeed, had he really studied it to any purpose, he could hardly have failed to hear of Norberg, Petermann, Euting, and Nöldeke, and to have read the Sabian scriptures in the European texts.

One word must, however, be said in favour of M. Siouffi's account of the Mandæan religion, as explained to him by the convert Adam. It has been assumed that, because this account differs widely from that set forth in the Mandæan scriptures, it is therefore wholly inaccurate. Admitting M. Siouffi's ignorance and his teacher's possible dishonesty, these are scarcely sufficient to account for the origin of all the traditions and beliefs described in the " Etudes sur la religion des Soubbas." We cannot help thinking that the religion set forth in the pages of this work has some existence in fact, and is not merely the result of an ingenious fabricator and a too confiding and ill-informed pupil. The Mandæan religion, as found in the scriptures of the sect, is too complicated and too profound for the mass of believers ; moreover, even in this form, it shows a remarkable process of degradation from its original conception. Very few of the modern Mandæans know the contents of their sacred books, and it is quite possible that an exoteric doctrine grew up beside the priestly religion, and that some of M. Siouffi's traditions really represent the vulgar religion, as opposed to the scriptural. Among a people filled with the legends of such a land as Babylonia, with neighbours on all sides of every imaginable difference of mythological tradition, it seems impossible that the form of Gnosticism which the Mandæan scriptures represent should have remained long unmixed with the many and diverse beliefs of the soil. The doctrine of the sacred books is itself an amalgamation of several mutually inconsistent creeds, and there is no reason why the process of corruption and adulteration should have come to an end when the Mandæan scriptures were finally redacted. On the contrary, there is every probability that the common people clung to the local traditions, though the priests rejected most of them, and that they continued to mix the teaching of their spiritual guides with the mass of legendary myths they had inherited from their forefathers. In that case, Petermann's account of the Mandæan creed would be the esoteric, the priestly, view; whilst the basis of M. Siouffi's probably garbled description of the religion of the Subba would represent the popular belief of the ignorant and superstitious Mandæans of to-day. At present it is only possible to suggest this theory as one that deserves to be tested: nothing but a further examination, on the spot, of modern Mandæan beliefs can settle the question whether M. Siouffi is merely the dupe of a cunning deacon, or the expositor of the vulgar conception of their religion by the Christians of St. John.

There is, however, no doubt that the true source

of a right understanding of the historical Sabian religion, as taught and practised by its priests, is to be derived only from the sacred books and the explanation thereof given to Petermann by his instructor, the Mandæan priest Yahya. We shall have occasion to relate some of M. Siouffi's traditions of the common folk at a later page; but the first thing necessary is to comprehend what is meant by Sabism or Mandaism as thus authoritatively expounded. To avoid confusion it is necessary to premise that *Mandæans* (equivalent to οἱ λογικοί or "Gnostics") is the proper name of this sect, and the only one used among members of it. *Sābi*, or Sabian (plural *Subba*), is the name given to it by Mohammadans, and is derived from a Syrian word meaning "a washer," and was applied first by the Syrians to the Mandæans on account of their frequent baptisms. We shall use the terms Mandæan and Sabian indifferently.

The principal scripture of the Mandæans is the Sidra Rabba, or "Great Book," also called the Ginza, or "Treasure" (and incorrectly, by Norberg, the Book of Adam, Liber Adami), which contains the whole doctrine of the sect in a hundred separate unconnected sections. It is divided into two parts, called respectively "the right" and "the left." The "right," which occupies about two-thirds of the whole work, contains the dogmatic teaching of the religion, legends, moral doctrine, polemics against heresy, and the like. It is wholly wanting in order and method, frequently self-contradictory, always confused. Much of it is as yet incomprehensible to the most accomplished scholar; and in reading it we feel that we are in the presence of a strange medley of creeds, imperfectly understood even by its professed expositors. The second part, the "left," deals with the future state of the soul, and is apparently designed for liturgic use. This chief scripture must have been composed about 700 A.D., but portions of it are earlier. It is evidently the work of many writers and different ages. It has undoubtedly preserved its present form (as edited by Petermann) for many centuries. Another important book is the anthology of hymns and formulas edited by Dr. Euting, under the title of " Qolasta." Besides these, the Mandæans have two or three collections of prayers, a book on Astrology, and another containing the Legends of St. John Baptist. The " Divan," attributed to them by Ignatius a Jesu, is unknown by that name in the present day; it was probably the Sidra Rabba.

The result of an examination of these authorities is to reveal to us one of the strangest religions that the world has seen. The sect variously known by the names of Sabians, Mandæans, Nazarenes, and Christians of St. John, presents the most curious combination of wholly diverse creeds that can well be conceived. As the descendants of the ancient Semitic population of Chaldea, and the inheritors of the Babylonian language, it is natural that we should find among the Mandæans some trace of the early religion of the country. The mythology, indeed, cannot be connected to any great extent with that of ancient Babylonia, so far as we know it at present, but the astrological and magical leanings of the people, the names still given to the planets, and the preference for certain sacred numbers, *e.g.* 360 and the epoch of 480,000 years, point distinctly to their Chaldean and Nabathean ancestry. It is even asserted by a Mohammadan historian of the tenth century that in his time the Mandæans kept the feast of Thammuz, the Babylonian prototype of Adonis, and it is likely that many other of their beliefs and practices may be traced to their Babylonian descent. Next to the Chaldean must be placed the Parsy element, which was introduced by the problematical Parthian founder of the sect, and which is shown in the occurrence of Mithra and Rauso and Razista of the Zend Avesta among the Mandæan objects of veneration. But the most considerable element in Mandæan religion is derived from those peculiar Gnostic sects which sprang from the dying struggles of paganism. We shall not here concern ourselves with the founding or the history of the sect; for nothing certain is known of either. Chwolsohn's ingenious and learned reasoning is now pronounced by the highest Mandæan authority to be mistaken; otherwise we might follow him in identifying the Sabians with the Elkesaites or Elchasaites of Pseud-origines, Theodoret, and Epiphanius—the Mughtasila or " Washers " of the Fihrist—founded at the end of the first century of the Christian era by a holy man named El-Hasaih or El-Chasai, 'Ηλχασαί, 'Ηλξαί, who came from Parthia and taught Parsy ideas and doctrines to the Babylonians. The sect of the Elkesaïtes

is now pronounced to be distinct from that of the
Mandæans, and Professor Nöldeke is even inclined to
identify the former and not the Mandæans with the
Sabians of the Korān, in spite of the general agreement of Mohammadan writers to the contrary effect.
The influence of some sect like the Elkesaïtes is seen
in the Mandæan adoption of the custom of frequent
baptisms and ablutions, as well as in other customs,
whilst the name Nazarene or Nasorene, so often
applied to the Babylonian Sabians, is the common
appellation of the Judæo-Christian sects, and must
have been derived from them; and the few Jewish
legends which are found in the Sidra Rabba must
have come from the same source.

The origin of the Mandæans is to be found in the
convulsions of religious belief which succeeded the
first spread of Christianity. It is one of those bizarre
creeds which rose up on the ruins of the great pagan
religions. Those who have tried to follow the history
of Gnosticism, who have wandered through the mazes
of the systems which sprang from the dying throes of
Hellenism, and have dived into the writings of the
Alexandrian and Syrian schools, have read the Her-
metic books, and endeavoured to trace the workings
of gnostic and cabalistic doctrines among the Judæo-
Christian sects, will understand what a tangle of
dogma is found in the Mandæan creed, when we say
that it is at bottom a corrupt gnosticism, half understood, and utterly confused. The name Mandæan,
which is the only one used among the sectaries, means
" gnostic "; and the fundamental notions of gnos-

ticism can be traced, in spite of infinite confusions and the presence of foreign conceptions of every description, in the theology of the Christians of St. John. To show how far this theology is purely gnostic, how far Jewish and cabalistic, how far taken from Parsy or even Buddhist sources, and how far, finally, local, the relic of the Chaldean land-religion, is an impossible task. The sacred books are so much confused, and their accounts vary so hopelessly in different places; the names of the divinities or æons are so frequently confounded, the same being employed in different places for two or more distinct emanations or manifestations, or different names being used for the same, that it is beyond the power of scholarship as yet to separate the various elements in the Mandæan religion and ascribe each to its proper source. Even the learned Dr. Nöldeke writes, in a pathetic conclusion to a review of Petermann's and Euting's editions of the Mandæan scriptures : "I have busied myself with the Mandæans for years; I have read the two newly-edited books carefully through twice, and parts of them much oftener; . . . I have endeavoured by a study of the gnostic and other systems to gain an insight into this literature : and yet I have not so far arrived at any adequate understanding." But though there is an infinite amount of uncertainty and obscurity about much of this strange creed, or collection of creeds, the main outline has been tolerably clearly drawn by Petermann from his priestly teacher; and we cannot do better than recapitulate his account.

At the beginning of all things there were two

existences, which may be looked upon as the male and female principles. There was the primæval matter, the *hyle* which, like the Orphic egg of the world, held all things in its womb. And beside this was the intellectual creative principle, *Mana Rabba*, the Lord of Glory, who was throned in the æther of the shining world, through which flowed the great Jordan, the river of the water of life, whence all things and plants that dwell in the shining world derive the spark of life. Mana called into being *Hayya Kadmaya*, " First Life," and, having thus far advanced the creation, retired into the profoundest obscurity, where he is visible only to certain of the highest emanations, and to the souls of the holiest among the Mandæans, whose greatest privilege it is to be permitted to see once after death the glorious Mana from whom they all originally issued. Hayya Kadmaya is regarded as the creating working god—not, however, the Demiurgus of the gnostics—and to him belong the deepest veneration and worship. He, and not Mana Rabba, who is above all mortal reverence, is addressed first in the prayers, and every book begins with his name. It is easy to see that this working god might readily be confounded with Mana, the original creative principle, and as a matter of fact the scriptures abound in such confusion. The same attributes are often given to Hayya Kadmaya as to Mana. Like the latter, he is described as throned in the shining æther world, where runs great Jordan, and where dwell countless angels (Uthre) in perpetual bliss.

From Hayya Kadmaya proceeded *Hayya Tinyana*,

or "Second Life," and *Manda d'hayya.* These two are the Cain and Abel of the Mandæans. The former wishes to raise himself above Hayya Kadmaya, and he is punished by being expelled from the world of the shining æther and put into the lower world of light. Manda d'hayya, on the other hand, is the ideal of purity and goodness. He is called Father, King of Angels, Lord of Worlds, Beloved Son, Good Shepherd, High Priest, Word of Life, Teacher and Saviour of Mankind, the conqueror of hell, and the chainer of the devil; he dwells with the Father (Mana or Hayya), and is the Christ of the Mandæan religion. They call themselves after his name. Manda d'hayya, who is also called *Adam Kadmaya,* reveals himself through his three sons, Abel, Seth, and Enos, or in Mandæan *Hibil* (or *Hibil-Ziva*), *Shithil,* and *Anush.* Just as Hayya was confused with Mana, so Hibil-Ziva frequently receives the same attributes as his father Manda d'hayya, and is treated with equal reverence.

The first emanation from the ejected Cain, or "Second Life," was *Abāthur,* or the Father of Angels. He sits at the confines of the world of light, at the great door which leads up from the lower regions, and with scales in hand he weighs the deeds of the dead, and sends the souls back to purgatory, or on into paradise, according to the weight of their actions. At first there was nothing under Abāthur but a void, and then a stagnant black water; but as he looked down his form was reflected in the water, and thence sprang *Petahil,* or Gabriel, the Demiurgus of the creed. Petahil received a command from his father to form the common world and bring mankind into being, and assisted by evil spirits, as some say, or by his own unaided powers, he created the world and made Adam and Eve, but he could not give them souls. So Hibil-Ziva and his brethren were given a portion of Mana Rabba's spirit, and they poured it into mankind, so that they worshipped Hayya Kadmaya instead of Petahil. Abāthur was enraged with his son for the manner in which he had arranged the creation, and he expelled him from his place, and sent him down into the Mattarāthas or hells, where he must dwell till the judgment-day, when Hibil-Ziva will bring him up and baptise him and make him king of angels. There are four purgatories, each ruled by its kings, but the true hell is beneath them all, and its government is distributed among three old men, Shdum, Giv, and Krun the deepest of all. Some slimy water refreshes the inhabitants of purgatory, but in hell even this fails, and in Krun's kingdom there is only dust and emptiness, and a fire that does not lighten, but consumes.

The progress of the soul after death is very minutely described in the Mandæan books. It repairs first to the Turquoise mountain, traverses the superior world, till it arrives at the great encircling ocean, over which a Charon, after certain delays varying in length according to the sinfulness of the soul, will convey it to the entrance to the Mattarāthas, in each of which horrible tortures await it if it has sinned overmuch. At the gate of each purgatory it is asked its name, and has to answer that it was baptised in

the name of Hayya Kadmaya and Manda d'hayya, and
has given alms, before it can be let through. It has
to pass by terrible monsters, even Ur, who eats 3,000
souls daily, but providentially sleeps when a good
Mandæan passes. Then it goes on to Petahil's Mat-
tarãtha and to Abãthur, who admits it to the world of
light, where it wanders, in delight, and may peradven-
ture attain to the vision of Mana Rabba.

Hibil-Ziva, having completed Petahil's work, invaded
hell and laid bare its hidden things, and carried off
Ruha, daughter of Kin, queen 'of hell, to the upper
worlds, where she gave birth to *Ur* (or " Fire ") the
most terrible of all demons, who dared even to attack
the world of light. Him Hibil-Ziva cast into the
black water and chained there, and enclosed with iron
and golden walls. From this unnatural son Ruha
bare three litters of seven and twelve and five sons.
The first became the seven planets, placed in the seven
heavens, the sun being in .the fourth or middle
heaven ; the second birth furnished the twelve signs
of the zodiac ; the third, five stars, including Sirius,
baneful to mankind, and the authors of all hurt and
mischief. Heaven is of most transparent water, in
which the stars and planets float in boats. It is so
clear that we can see straight to the Pole Star, which
is at the apex of heaven, before the door of Abãthur
—and the Pole Star is the Kibla to which the face
must be turned in prayer. The earth is a disk, three
parts surrounded by water, but bounded on the fourth
side by the lofty mountain of blue turquoise. It is
only the reflection of this turquoise mountain that

makes the sky look blue. Beyond the mountain is another and superior world, dwelt in by Pharaoh and his Egyptians, who are great Sabian heroes, and by the holiest saints of the Mandæan faith. A vast sea girdles both worlds.

The Mandæans, in common with many ancient peoples, believe in world-cycles. There have already, they say, been several cycles ; the present race will be destroyed about 5,000 years hence by a mighty storm, when a new couple from the better world beyond the turquoise mountain will repeople the earth and their progeny will endure for 50,000 years, after which Ur will destroy all the lower world, and the world of light will alone remain.

Man consists of three parts, body, soul ($\psi\nu\chi\acute{\eta}$), and spirit ($\nu o\hat{\nu}s$). The soul (*ruha*) is merely the animal nature, the evil tendency, and hence the same name is given to Ruha, the mother of Ur, from whom all mischievous arts and magic are believed to have sprung, and only one good gift, the gift of bearing children, which she gave to women. The spiritual or higher soul is the $\nu o\hat{\nu}s$, which was implanted by Hibil-Ziva, as has been related, and is in constant warfare with the natural soul. So far are the Mandæans from acknowledging any affinity with orthodox Christianity, from which they derived their conception of Manda d'hayya, that they regard the Messiah as the son of Ruha, the arch-witch, whom they identify by an obvious etymological process with the Holy Ghost, and hence give Christ the character of a magician, and place Him among the planets as the trickster Mercury.　They do not recognise any of the prophets or books of the Old Testament any more than the Gospels ; all were false prophets, they hold, except John the Baptist, who is their sole law-giver and teacher, and of whom they relate marvellous legends.

The tradition of St. John the Baptist and the subsequent history of the Mandæans, as given by M. Siouffi, may form a curious if not perfectly accurate supplement to the account of this peculiar religion which has just been given on the authority of Petermann.　The legend is obviously corrupt, but it is none the less likely to be commonly accepted by the Mandæan populace.　The sect, it must be remembered, does not by any means admit its late origin, but, on the contrary, claims for itself the remotest antiquity, and regards its foundation as coeval with the creation of man.　From time to time, however, it has suffered reverses at the hands of unbelievers, its bishops and priests have become extinct, and the diminished people have adopted the faith of the infidels among whom they dwelt.　It was at such a time, when the Sabians had joined themselves to their Jewish neighbours, and deserted the true religion, that Yahya, whom they identify with John the Baptist, but who might equally well have been any other John, was sent to recall the people to their ancient faith.　As there were no more true believers, it followed that no soul went to paradise, and the inhabitants of that blessed region, tired of their own unvaried company, and desirous of some fresh additions to their society, made their plaint to the authorities, and demanded the resuscitation of the true religion and the consequent arrival of new souls. So Manda d'hayya sent a bowl of magical water to a woman among the Judaised Mandæans, whose name was Inoshwey—the Elizabeth, in short, of the Sabian tradition. Now Inoshwey and her husband, Abu Sawa, were both well stricken in years, and had no children. Nevertheless, no sooner had she drunk of the magic water, than Inoshwey conceived, and in due time, specified as nine months, nine days, nine hours, and nine minutes, bore a child. The Jews suspected that some ill would befall them at the hand of this miraculous infant, and had instructed their women who attended Inoshwey to kill the boy as soon as he was born; but their designs were frustrated by an angelic messenger, who caught the child up to paradise, where he was brought up and instructed in all the mysteries of the Sabian faith. When John was perfected in wisdom and had attained to manhood, Anush carried him back to the earth. The two were met by a maidservant of Inoshwey, who recognised the family likeness of the youth, and ran to her mistress and told her she had seen a young man as beautiful as the full moon. The mother was so transported with joy at the return of her son that she hastened to meet him without first putting on her veil. Her husband, deeply offended by this sin against the customs of the people, had a mind to divorce her, but, being warned by an angel, he changed his mind, and embraced his son on the banks of Jordan. Anush, having restored John to his family, called upon the sun and the moon to protect him, and returned to paradise. Meanwhile John went back to the parental roof, and forthwith began his mission by baptising his father and mother, after which he gave proofs of his divine authority by performing various miracles, as healing the sick, giving sight to the blind, and restoring strength and soundness to the halt and maimed, so that many of the Jews believed in him and became Sabians. Then John appointed bishops and priests over his people, and baptised Christ, and, having ordered all things, gave himself up to unceasing prayer night and day. His first prayer was to be preserved from the blandishments of women, for he was fair to look upon, and feared to become a prey to their love. And as their prophet would not marry, the whole people in like manner renounced marriage, so that the number of souls that went to paradise became much diminished. Then the dwellers in heaven sent a message to John, and said, "The end of all your austerity will be the destruction of the Sabian race. You will prevent our paradise from being peopled. Be less severe on yourself in praying, and take a wife to whom to devote a portion of your time." So John married, and the Sabians took wives again. And it came to pass, after four-and-forty years, that Manda d'hayya came and took John over the sea, and through the Mattaráthas, to the abode of blessedness, and his people knew him no more.

After the passing of John, the Sabians were greatly persecuted by the Jews, who were fearful lest all their people should turn Sabians. A daughter of Eleazar, the chief rabbi, had joined the religion of John, and the Jews in revenge massacred the greater number of the Sabians, and the remnant, after having destroyed Jerusalem by divine aid, migrated to another land. It was at this time (continues the tradition, in defiance of chronology) that Moses attacked them, and fought in single combat with the Sabian champion, Ferrokh Malka (King Pharaoh), who drove the false prophet into the sea. But the waters opened behind Moses and let him escape, whilst the Sabians pursuing were all drowned, except Ferrokh Malka and thirty followers, who fled to Shuster. Here, being deprived of their clergy, a new teacher was sent them, named Abu-l-Faras Adam, who performed miracles and taught them the law, and ordained bishops and priests; and then returned to the invisible world beyond the turquoise mountain. After this the Sabians were greatly persecuted by the Muslims, and were scattered abroad. To centuries of oppression were added the horrors of the plague, which in 1831 (they say, with a curious leap in the chronology) carried off all the clergy, so that for ten years the Sabians had to do without marriage. At this time they went back to Shuster. Some established themselves at Suk-esh-Shuyukh on the Euphrates. They chose fresh priests and bishops, and the order has been unbroken ever since. Misfortunes have reduced them to four thousand souls; but their books say they have still many evil things to endure, that they will yet again be deprived of their priests, and their numbers will be diminished even more.

Such is the popular tradition of Mandæan history, according to the convert Adam, which must be taken for what it is worth. Much more valuable are the accounts preserved by M. Siouffi on the manners and customs of this strange people. The most characteristic of their religious observances is the frequent habit of baptism, in which we cannot but see a relic of some aboriginal Babylonian river-worship, though the sacerdotal adoption of the practice was doubtless due to the various Judæo-Christian sects which enforced the importance of baptism; from sects such as the Hemerobaptists and the Elkesaites, whom many scholars indeed identify with the Mandæans, the doctrine of purification by water might have been easily derived; but there must, we imagine, have been some substratum of ancient Euphrates-worship among the faiths of the Chaldean soil, which brought about so complete and rigorous an adoption of the custom of baptism in running water. A good Sabian ought to be baptised soon after birth, directly after marriage, on every Sunday, before the great feast-days, on returning from a journey, after a funeral; when one has been bitten by a dog or serpent, or has killed a bird, or eaten food prepared by unbelievers, or bled at the nose. In any of these circumstances, and many others which it is impossible to describe, at all hours of the day and night, and in every variety of weather, the Sabians hurry to the river and plunge in. The poor fellows turn quite blue in cold weather; and it is worse still for the women, who must go before daybreak, in the chill of the morning, to avoid being seen.   These lustrations are variously termed baptisms or ablutions according to the presence or absence of a priest, and other differences ; but practically the two are very much the same thing, as in ablution the performer keeps his face to the pole-star and plunges three times, repeating the formula of invoking the names of Hayya and Manda d'hayya, just as in baptism.   No one who is not baptised is a Mandæan ; and the souls of children who die before baptism go straight to the monster Ur, who devours them.   It is forbidden even to kiss an unbaptised child.   In christening, a child is given more names than one.   For sacred matters he uses his mother's name, for worldly affairs his father's, whilst he has also a general appellation among his fellow-citizens. Prayer is a very important and exacting duty among the Mandæans.   They had originally three obligatory prayers, one before sunrise, the second at noon, and the third at sunset ; and each of these ought to last two hours or more ; but, finding these devotions incompatible with business, they suppressed the noon prayer.   Four or five hours' prayer a day still remains for laymen, and the bishops and priests have even longer orisons to make.   All prayers are addressed in the first place to Hayya, and then to Manda d'hayya, Hibil-Ziva, Anush, Yaver-Ziva, and a host of other divine emanations, including John, and the Persian Sâm, who has often been confused with Shem the son of Noah.   The substance of the prayers is little more than an invocation to the gods to protect the worshipper from all ills that may befall him, from evil spirits and jinn, and the imprecations of women. The Mandæans believe that women have a peculiar vein or nerve which was put into them by the devil, which renders them powerful for mischief, and makes their good vows of none effect, whilst giving extraordinary potency to their malisons. Hence, when a Mandæan sees an angry woman, he puts his fingers in his ears and flies with all possible speed from the spot, lest he should fall a victim to her curse. A believer must never pass a river without invoking peace upon it. Fasting proper forms no part of the Sabian religion, but the people are enjoined to abstain from flesh meat on thirty-two special days of the year. Besides Sundays, they have five great feasts in the year. The first is Naurōz, or new year's day, which is believed to be also observed in paradise; it includes new year's eve and the first six days of the new year. Among the many ceremonies and prohibitions of this feast, it is curious to note that it is not allowed to draw any water while Naurōz lasts : all that will be needed is drawn the day before, and the people take the same occasion to be baptised. They pass the night before new year's day without sleeping. On the day itself they remain at home, to be secure against possible defilement; for to touch as much as a blade of grass would render fresh baptism necessary, and total abstinence from food for twenty-four hours. On this day the priests consult their astrological books, to see what will befall in the new year, and whether it will be fat or lean. Next day everybody calls on the priests and pays them the customary fees. No beast or bird may be killed during the feast, nor is it permissible even to milk the kine. The next feast is on the 18th of Taurus (the Mandæan months are named after the zodiacal signs), and lasts five days. It is held in commemoration of Hibil-Ziva's return from his conquest of hell; and the new life of the earth in spring is deemed the fittest time for such a festival. The third feast-day is a month later, and is in honour of the Sabian hero Ferrokh or Pharaoh. The fourth is on the first of Capricorn; and the last is the greatest of all, *Pancha*, which is held on the five additional days that make up the year, when the twelve months, of thirty days each, are over.

The priestly office is regarded with the highest veneration among the Mandæans, and is in nowise underpaid. On the other hand, it is no sinecure. The priest is constantly called upon to baptise, to hear confessions, and administer a species of eucharist, to marry people, visit the dying, kill the meat for the community, draw horoscopes for children, and write amulets for the sick, foretell future events, and, in fact, do everything that has to be done outside the ordinary routine of work. The office of public sacrificer is not the lightest part of the priest's duty. No meat can be eaten by a Mandæan which has not been properly killed by either a priest or a duly authorised deputy; and the supply of meat to the community involves considerable energy on the part of the sacred butchers. The custom is very analogous to the Mohammadan law of food. The priests themselves have special rules as to eating. They must take their meals in solitude, apart from their family. If a layman touches the viands, or a fowl passes by them, they become unfit for a priest's palate. They must fetch their water themselves from the well, and must not mix it with the water drunk by the other inmates of their house. Every priest is compelled to marry, and may marry a second time on his wife's death. Women may take orders; virgins can become deacons; but to be made a priest a woman must first marry a priest. There are three orders in the clergy. Any boy of pure descent (*i.e.* without divorce or illegitimacy in his family), who is free from physical defects, may become a deacon (*shganda*). The apprenticeship, according to M. Siouffi, lasts twelve years, from the age of seven to nineteen; and then, after a year of diaconate, the deacon may become priest (*tarmida*). From the ranks of the priests, in general synod, is chosen the bishop (*ganzibra*), whose first duties are two months' separation from his wife, three baptisms on three successive Sundays in the river, the public reading and explanation of the principal Mandæan scriptures, and the visiting of the death-bed of a holy Sabian, whom he must charge with a message to Abāthur. The last condition sometimes involves the scouring of the country for a dying man, before the bishop can assume his functions; and very unseemly rejoicings take place when the dear departing one is discovered. There used once to be a still higher grade, that of *Rēsh-amma*, or " head of the people," who enjoyed temporal as well as spiritual authority; but the last who held this office is related to have been the prophet Abu-l-Faras Adam already referred to. The dress of the clergy, when engaged in sacred rites, is of pure white—a white stole and white turban, a gold ring on the little finger of the right hand, with the inscription " The Name of Yaver-Ziva," an olive staff in the left hand, the feet bare. The dress of the lay folk ought strictly to be white like the priests', but, as a matter of fact, they dress very much like the ordinary Muslim Fellahīn, in blue or brown and white striped blouses, with a coloured cloth on the head. The men wear their hair long, but that of the women is cropped close. They are very fond of turquoise ornaments—doubtless they remind them of the blue mountain which lies on the road to paradise.

Their churches are curious little edifices, constructed of the rudest materials, and built just big enough for two men to move in them. There are no altars, no ornaments. The door faces south, so that on entering the pole-star is before you. Hard by there is always running water. They are only for the use of the priests, who prepare there the eucharist cakes (which after consecration turn into the veritable manna of heaven), and perform the various ceremonies peculiar to their order. The consecration of a church is a singular ceremony. It requires four priests and a deacon, and lasts the whole of the five days of the feast of Pancha. After mutually baptising each other, the priests and the deacon enter the church, carrying with them a hand-mill, some charcoal, a dove, and some corn and sesame. The deacon grinds the corn in the hand-mill, while the priests light a charcoal fire and extract the oil of the sesame. They then make a cake, kill the dove, and drop four drops of oil and four of blood on the cake, saying a certain number of prayers the while. Finally they pray aloud, and the people outside the church respond, the priests touch hands solemnly, and retire to their own houses, after carefully closing the church door. For four days similar rites are performed, and at the end of the fifth day they bury the remains of the dove under the floor, put the cakes away in a vase, and the church is regarded as consecrated for one year, after which the ceremony must be repeated. The lay people do not take part in the services in church; indeed they know extremely little about their religion beyond its common external observances. Petermann says they are expected to learn by heart one hundred and eighty rules of conduct, but most of them do not accomplish this, and are quite satisfied with the knowledge of the formulas of baptism; and the priests themselves often know little more; yet the value of their instruction is so highly estimated that M. Siouffi says a priest who has the charge of fifty or sixty souls draws a yearly income of a thousand francs.

A weighty part of the priest's duty is the exorcism of devils. The Mandæans believe in a variety of evil spirits, and attribute all the accidents and misfortunes of life to their influence. When a man is possessed by a devil, the priest is immediately summoned, and if the fiend is of a gentle and compliant disposition he will probably depart at the bare sight of the holy man;

but if he prove obstinate, a solemn ceremony must be performed and the name of the Giver of life invoked. It is usual upon this for the devil to demand time in order to effect a convenient retreat; and when the time granted has elapsed, the priest returns to see if the evil spirit has departed. Should he be a dilatory devil, another exorcism is performed on the ensuing Sunday, with much burning of incense, saying of prayers, and application of amulets. It is a rare thing for this second effort to prove unsuccessful; but should the fiend by some extraordinary perversity remain still in the man, the whole body of priests come and exorcise him *en masse*. No devil was ever known to resist this final resource, except one peculiar and terrible species, which is born of the union of human beings and demons, and can never be expelled. M. Siouffi's instructor has seen and assisted in many exorcisms, he says, and entertains no doubt whatever as to their efficacy. He also records a curious superstition about these spirits, who are supposed to live on food snatched from the tables of talkative people. Adam says it has often been noticed that the meat ran short after some one had spoken. Hence the Mandæans eat their meals in complete silence.

Another responsible duty of the priest is that of interpreting the stars. The Mandæans have enough of the old Chaldean spirit to prefer divine to natural assistance, and always value the priest's amulet more than the doctor's prescription. No newly-born child is considered properly cared for till his horoscope is drawn; and no affair of the slightest consequence is undertaken without first consulting the stars through the priests. Before setting out on a journey, or building a house, the priest is referred to, and the most propitious time is selected; and the stars are even consulted as to the lines of the foundations and the position of the doors. Sick people and childless wives resort to the priest for amulets inscribed with sacred formulas, and pay high sums for them.

The Mandæans in no sense worship the heavenly bodies; though they fear the five stars that Ruha bare at the last birth, and ascribe powerful influences to the planets, who are believed to cause wars, inspire men with discoveries, and make the thunder and lightning. In spite of their veneration for the science, the Mandæans know nothing of astronomy, and hold the most superstitious and ignorant notions about the phenomena of the sky. A halo round the sun or moon is believed to be a ring of stars summoned in council to arrange administrative details. Shooting stars are messengers from the moon to the planets. Eclipses are the result of the seizure of the sun or moon by the guardian angels who are appointed to watch their proceedings. If either of these luminaries conceives a malicious design against the world, its guardian immediately squeezes it until it abandons its wicked intention: and this squeezing produces the eclipse.

A bishop has the special duty of superintending the *Massakhta*, which is a sort of mass, generally said for the souls of the dead, but which anyone may say for his own soul before death, and thus escape many penalties in the other worlds. It involves seven days'

unceasing prayer, and a variety of initiatory ceremonies; after which the performer is considered dead
to the world, and is the object of intense reverence:
when his soul is weighed in Abāthur's balance it is
found to be as heavy as Shithil's own.

The " whole duty of man," as conceived by the
Mandæans, has been summarised by M. Siouffi, and
will serve as a fit conclusion to the sketch we have
given of the tenets and customs of the " Christians of
St. John." A year after birth—if possible earlier—
the Sabian must be baptised. At seven years he
enters a school, kept by a deacon, where he learns (or
ought to learn) to read the sacred books and to say
the prescribed prayers. On leaving school he must
be apprenticed to a trade—generally he becomes a
goldsmith, carpenter, or ship-builder. In a foreign
country, or a strange house, he must eat no food which
he has not dressed himself. He must be baptised every
Sunday. He must pay the debts of others, labour
for the freeing of those who are in captivity, be
generous, hospitable, kind-hearted, never complaining.
He must be humble, and rise if even a beggar salutes
him; chaste and modest; his dress unassuming. He
must never be angry or return blow for blow, but
must rather seek reconciliation with his enemy. In
society he must always seek to take the lowest place,
his voice must be always subdued. He must never
cut his beard, and he must always be in a state of
legal purity. He must not forswear himself, nor steal,
nor lie. He must keep the Sundays and feast and fast
days, must honour his parents, and kiss his mother's

brow and his father's hand each day; he must not covet another man's goods, and in the presence of women he must avert his eyes. He must always be agreeable and respectful to his wife, and devote himself assiduously to the bringing up of his children. His alms must be given in secret, and his prayers earnest and regular. To be quite perfect, he should copy the sacred books and perform the Great Mass.

Although the modern " Christians of St. John " do not always attain to the standard of excellence thus held before them, they are a very well-meaning, inoffensive people. They hate orthodox Christianity, and only tolerate Islām " upon compulsion "; but they manage to live fairly peaceably with their Mohammadan neighbours. They work steadily at the trades they adopt, and are famous for their skill as jewellers. And if they are ignorant of the fundamental doctrines of their religion, at least they are indefatigable in carrying out its ceremonious law in the wholesome matter of baptism, and are cleanly if they are not godly. Their diminishing numbers, and the secrecy in which they preserve the mysteries of their faith, render a further enquiry into their tenets and customs very desirable. There is so much that is conflicting and obscure in our present information as to the Mandæan religion, that a visit to the people by some qualified scholar could not fail to throw fresh light on the peculiar creed of the Babylonian Sabians or Christians of St. John.

London: Printed by W. H. Allen & Co., 13, Waterloo Place, S.W.

CATALOGUE OF
ORIENTAL COINS IN THE BRITISH MUSEUM.

In Eight Volumes.

(*Published by order of the Trustees.*)

www.ingramcontent.com/pod-product-compliance
Lightning Source LLC
Chambersburg PA
CBHW020944120726
47905CB00008B/2669